# Praise for *The Painted Word*

"If *The Painted Word* were a club act, I'd sit there drinking in Cousineau's revelations, tales and mythologies until they kicked me out of the joint. Reading this brew of etymology, history, lore, and pop connections, with lambent illustrations by Gregg Chadwick, is just as intoxicating. A Cousineau riff on a (passionately selected) word is like Mark Twain meets Coleridge meets Casey Stengel meets—well, everyone who's fun and informative, whether the riff is on *autologophagist* (someone who eats his/her words) or *jack*, which, believe me, the world-traveled Cousineau knows when it comes to language."

—Arthur Plotnik, author of
*The Elements of Expression: Putting Thoughts into Words*

"Phil Cousineau takes us on an insightful journey to discover the essence of ideas that form our thoughts and feelings. It's a masterful detective story that crosses continents and centuries to uncover the meaning behind the core elements of our own culture. He reveals how everyday words developed from mythic metaphors, and how many fantastic concepts sprang from hilariously mundane things. Words are how our minds make pictures. The book paints a fascinating landscape of how the history of these tools of thought helps us make sense of the world we live in, and ourselves."

—Jeff Hoke, author of *The Museum of Lost Wonder*

# THE
# PAINTED
# WORD

## A TREASURE CHEST
## OF REMARKABLE WORDS
## AND THEIR ORIGINS

## BOOKS BY PHIL COUSINEAU

*The Hero's Journey: Joseph Campbell on his Life and Work*, 1990
*Deadlines: A Rhapsody on a Theme of Famous Last Words*, 1991
*The Soul of the World: A Modern Book of Hours* (with Eric Lawton), 1993
*Riders on the Storm: My Life with Jim Morrison and The Doors*
(by John Densmore with Phil Cousineau), 1993
*Soul: An Archaeology: Readings from Socrates to Ray Charles*, 1994
*Prayers at 3 a.m.: Poems, Songs, Chants for the Middle of the Night*, 1995
*UFOs: A Mythic Manual for the Millennium*, 1995
*Design Outlaws: On the Frontier of the 21st Century* (with Chris Zelov), 1996
*Soul Moments: Marvelous Stories of Synchronicity*, 1997
*The Art of Pilgrimage: The Seeker's Guide to Making Travel Sacred*, 1998
*Riddle Me This: A World Treasury of Folk and Literary Puzzles*, 1999
*The Soul Aflame: A Modern Book of Hours* (with Eric Lawton), 2000
*The Book of Roads: Travel Stories from Michigan to Marrakesh*, 2000
*Once and Future Myths: The Power of Ancient Stories in Modern Times*, 2001
*The Way Things Are: Conversations with Huston Smith on the Spiritual Life*, 2003
*The Olympic Odyssey: Rekindling the Spirit of the Great Games*, 2004
*The Blue Museum: Poems*, 2004
*A Seat at the Table: The Struggle for American Indian Religious Freedom*, 2005
*Angkor Wat: The Marvelous Enigma* (photographs), 2006
*Night Train: New Poems*, 2007
*The Jaguar People: An Amazonian Chronicle* (photographs), 2007
*Stoking the Creative Fires: 9 Ways to Rekindle Passion and Imagination*, 2008
*Fungoes and Fastballs: Great Moments in Baseball Haiku*, 2008
*The Meaning of Tea* (with Scott Chamberlin Hoyt), 2009
*City 21: The Search for the Second Enlightenment* (with Chris Zelov), 2009
*The Oldest Story in the World: A Mosaic of Meditations on Storytelling*, 2010
*The Song of the Open Road* (photographs), 2010
*Wordcatcher: An Odyssey into the World of Weird and Wonderful Words*, 2010
*Beyond Forgiveness: Reflections on Atonement*, 2011
*The Art of Travel Journal*, 2011
*Around the World in Eighty Faces* (photographs), 2011
*And Live Rejoicing: Chapters from a Charmed Life*
(by Huston Smith with Phil Cousineau), 2012
*Shadowcatcher* (photographs), 2012
*The Soul's High Adventure: Clews to the Mythic Vision*
*of Joseph Campbell* (forthcoming)
*How Baseball Saved Civilization* (forthcoming)

# THE
# PAINTED
# WORD

## A TREASURE CHEST
## OF REMARKABLE WORDS
## AND THEIR ORIGINS

by **PHIL COUSINEAU**
Artwork by **GREGG CHADWICK**

VIVA
EDITIONS

Published in the United States by Viva Editions, an imprint of
Cleis Press, Inc., 2246 Sixth Street, Berkeley, California 94710.

Printed in the United States.
Cover design: Scott Idleman/Blink
Text design: Frank Wiedemann
First Edition.
10 9 8 7 6 5 4 3 2 1

Trade paper ISBN: 978-1-936740-17-8
E-book ISBN: 978-1-936740-25-3


Library of Congress Cataloging-in-Publication Data

Cousineau, Phil.
 The painted word : a treasure chest of remarkable words and their origins /
Phil Cousineau ; Artwork by Gregg Chadwick.
     p. cm.
 ISBN 978-1-936740-17-8 (pbk. : alk. paper)
1.  English language--Etymology.  2.  English language--History.  I. Chad-
wick, Gregg, ill. II. Title.
 PE1574.C68 2012
 422.03--dc23

                              2012019770

The Wound Dresser - Walt Whitman - Washington DC, 1865

*This book is dedicated to*
*my poet-painter pals*
*from our colorful days working for*
*Painter's Palette in San Francisco:*
*Antler, Jeff Poniewaz, James Jensen,*
*and the late Ted Cresswell*

"Painting is silent poetry, and poetry is painting with the gift of speech."

—Suetonius, 2nd century

"The pleasantest of all diversions is to sit alone under the lamp, a book spread out before you, and to make friends with people of a distant past you have never known."

—Kenko, *Essays in Idleness*, 1330

"Words are the best telescopes ... Words mark inner discoveries of consciousness."

—Owen Barfield

"With word and tint I did not stint, I gave her reams of poems to say…"

—from *Raglan Road*, Patrick Kavangh
via Van Morrison

# ACKNOWLEDGMENTS

According to the World Word Forum, as of 2009 there are now over one million words in the English language. But the **beauty**[1] of words isn't how many of them you can get through, but how many of them get through to you. This book of words is possible because of the vast number of friends and colleagues, past authors, and future friends whose words have gotten through to me. For all our years of colorful collaboration I find it *wishworthy*, desirable, to acknowledge Gregg Chadwick, friend, colleague, artist supreme, fellow **flâneur,** who generously offered to prop up his *easel* and stock another *atelier* full of his marvelous oil-on-linen paintings. Our teamwork embodies the English proverb "All arts are brothers; each gives light to

---

1    All bold and italicized words—for example, *atelier*—are *headwords* defined, described, and derived later in this book. All bold and underlined words—for example, **beauty**—can be found by riffling the pages of *Wordcatcher*.

the other." His work is a constant reminder to me of the truth behind Horace's saying "A picture is a poem without words." Four other kindred spirits I would like to thank are Antler, Jeff Poniewaz, James Jensen, and the late Ted Cresswell, my house-painting partners at Painter's Palette, in San Francisco, with whom I shared the scaffold and stage, fighting the rage for beige for seven colorful years. While in the exhibition hall of gratitude, I send a *fillip*, or finger snap, to all those informants who contributed their favorite painted words to this gallery. They include the **peripatetic** Pico Iyer for his suggestion of the Japanese beauty *monogashi*, the *aesthetic* James Norwood Pratt for his insights into the Civil War–era *absquatulate*, R. B. Morris for his onstage riff on *biscuit,* the zetetic Mort Rosenblum for his insights into the theobromic history of *chocolate*, Douglas George-Kanentiio (Mohawk-Iroquois) for his brilliant summation of the deeply nuanced *tomahawk*, and the sympathetic Rosario Maria Theresa (ChiChing) Herlihy for her nuanced comments about the depths of the Tagalog *utang na loob*. Finally, *sláinte* to North Beach's piquant pintman Myles O'Reilly, who tapped his bottomless keg of knowledge about such bardic Irish words as **skedaddle** and shenanigan, and the doughty Dara Malloy for his help translating some ancient Gaelic for this book. For years of literary inspiration, thanks to such bibliophile friends as Alberto Manguel, Willis Barnstone, the late sociologist Theodore Roszak, Alexander and Jane Eliot, art critics and word magicians. Special thanks to the late Frank McCourt, the Irish raconteur who told me that when he first read Shakespeare it was like tasting jewels, and everlasting gratitude to the late James Hillman, who plumbed untold depths in both the soul and the history of words.

Finally, *To-dah-hey*, It's good!, as my Pawnee friend Walter Echo-Hawk says, to my editor Brenda Knight at Viva Editions, for her ardent belief in bibliomancy and her unstinting support for a sequel to *Wordcatcher*, to my publisher Felice Newman for her faith in another word book, Mark Rhynsburger for his patient and punctilious copyediting, Frédérique Delacoste for her painterly guidance with the cover and design, and Kara Wuest, Kat Sanborn, Nancy L. Fish, and Cat Snell, who have all helped with the exhibition of these painted words.

An especially warm thank-you to my agent Amy Rennert, whose spirited support made sure this book got down the river of words, so a raft of hearty thanks. Thanks as well to two of my greatest allies in the world of books, Karen West and Elaine Petrocelli of the Book Passage bookstore in Corte Madera, California, for without logophiles like you books like this would have no chance. *Grazie* to the proprietors of Caffè Trieste, in North Beach, one of the most word-loving places in the world. Finally, to my family, Jo and Jack, a hug of thanks for your unwavering encouragement for me to keep on keepin' on with this logoloco, word-crazed life of mine.

# A PARABLE
## IN LIEU OF A PREFACE

There is an ancient legend which tells us that when a man first achieved a notable deed he wished to explain to his tribe what he had done. As soon as he began to speak, however, he was smitten with dumbness, he lacked words, and sat down. Then there arose—according to the story—a masterless man, one who had no special virtues, but was affected—that is the phrase—with the magic of the necessary words. He saw, he told, he described the merits of the notable deed in such a fashion, we are assured, that the words became alive and walked up and down in the hearts of all his hearers.

There upon, the tribes seeing that the words were certainly alive, and fearing lest the man with the words would hand them down untrue tales about them to their children, they took and killed him.

But later they saw that the magic was in the words, not the man.

—Rudyard Kipling

# INTRODUCTION

The itch to make dark marks on white paper is shared
by writers and artists.

—John Updike, *The Writer's Brush*

Nineteen-seventy-six was a time that the journalist Herbert
Mitgang describes as being between "the friendly typewriter
age" and our "chilling electronic era." That year he interviewed
the author E. B. White for the *New Yorker* magazine and brazenly
asked him, "Do words still count in this country?" Taking a sip
from his martini, White told him, "Television has taken a big
bite out of the written word. But words still count to me."

Words still count.

Everyone who loves reading books, dictionary-diving,
singing songs, solving crossword puzzles, cracking riddles,
deconstructing scientific papers, limerick-slinging, and joke-
jousting, as well as good **conversation**, poems read by fire-
light, baseball on late-night radio, crackling movie dialogue, or

soaring oratory—everyone who **thrills** to words—can feel reassured by the elegant stylist's **cool** certitude.

Words still count.

But do they still count thirty-five years further on down the road, in a world where the one-eyed blast of television has morphed into the hydra-headed, ravenous creature of the digital age—which boasts a far bigger bite?

No worries, as my Irish friends say. Words count for the same reasons they have always counted. They are still our best hope for weighing our thoughts, learning to think for ourselves, finding our voice, and most poignantly, reaching across the abyss of silence that often stretches out all around us.

But chances are words count more the more colorful they are.

Of course, that doesn't mean we need to make our conversation coruscate with unnecessary sparkle, but to daub our *manuscripts* with word *color* that honors whatever we're talking or writing about. By *naming* the *cerulean* sky, *incarnadine* skin tones, or *lapis lazuli* tile work, we move closer to the soul of the thing. What this means is that we can breathe new life to the old meaning of **eloquence**, the practice of letting language flow clearly, easily, persuasively. If we express ourselves with our own natural poetry, we will see how "eloquence is a painting of thoughts," as philosopher Blaise Pascal said. We might come to see the eloquence of **color** as the **synesthesia** of words, as expressed by George Eliot in *Middlemarch*: "It is **strange** how deeply colors seem to penetrate one, like scent."

## The Boy Who Made Lists

As the sequel to *Wordcatcher*, which appeared in 2010, *The Painted Word* is another collection of **strange** and marvelous, rare and recently coined, curious and sometimes hilarious words. Not unlike *Wordcatcher*, this **volume** reflects my unswerving belief in the need to unroll the scroll of language, from spindle to spindle, so we can to learn to say what we really mean, and mean what we really say. Not out of what the **proteanly** talented David Foster Wallace called "snootitude," his nose-in-the-air description of "extreme usage *fanatics*." But out of a desire be alert to what **travel** writer Tim Cahill calls the "callouses" that grow over our words if we use the same ones over and over again.

My own pilgrimage into the land of words began when I was a boy growing up just outside Detroit, in what must have been one of the last homes in America where books were read aloud. When our old black-and-white Philco television broke down, it often took years for my father to fix it, and *strange* to say, we rarely missed it, because my parents insisted there were always books to read, movies to see, museums to visit, parks to romp around in. The thread that tied together these diverse activities was the presence of the family **dictionary** always nearby, whether next to my father's reading chair or in the backseat of the old Ford Galaxy station wagon.

"Look it up," my father used to say. Unfailingly, if he caught us stumbling over a word we didn't know, he ordered us to march over to the dictionary and look it up *and* down, inside and out, until we knew the mystery word's meaning, origin, even pronunciation. That's when my manic list making began. Ever since, I've been one of those incorrigible collectors of names, making languid lists out of the constellations in the night sky, baseball *averages*, trees, and cars. Sometimes out of the fear of being feckless; other times out of an almost medieval belief in the **glamour**—the enchantment—of transforming chaos into order.

You name it, and I named it.

When I read in art historian Kenneth Clark's book *Looking at Pictures*, "All artists have an obsessive central experience round which their work takes shape," a shiver runs down my spine. All of my work revolves on the *carousel* of words that I've been riding since I was a towheaded kid running across the living room to the old *Random House Dictionary*.

Since then I've called time-out whenever I encountered an intriguing word in order to scribble it down, whether in twenty-nine-cent spiral notebooks while climbing in the Pyrenees, on index cards while perched on painter's scaffolding in San Francisco, or on shooting **schedule** sheets while making documentary films in Iceland. If it's true that a writer is someone who loves to hang around words, he or she needs to flex the old vocabulary, like a piano player playing scales, or a ballplayer loosening up his arm. How else can you keep your mind limber?

## Chasing the Light

My father was a believer in the Holy Grail of etymology, the theory first proposed way back in 1596, in *The Table Alphabetical*, by Edmund Cooke, that the purpose of a dictionary was to convey "the true meaning ... and understanding of any hard

English words." In contrast, my *fascination* has focused on their *stories* that I like to dig up with the fervor of a spelunker exploring the catacombs far below the surface of a slumbering city. Chasing words like this has always struck me as being closely aligned with the compulsion photographers feel in "chasing the light," or detectives who thrive on running down clues.

Fortunately, my *fanatic* passion for words has been augmented in recent years by a series of creativity workshops with fellow writers, musicians, psychologists, and artists, notably my friend and colleague the *iridescently* talented painter Gregg Chadwick. As a writer who is avidly interested in painting, I feel as if I'm working with my mirror image, since he is a painter who is wildly enthusiastic about writing. That selfsame spirit of illuminating the parallels between words and images imbues *The Painted Word*. This book is a reverie on the open secret that the arts don't have to be separated at birth, like Siamese twins, nor do they need to compete with each other, like wrestlers sizing each other up on the mat. Instead, they can move together like Matisse's cavorting dancers in his painting *Joy*, or glide arm in arm across the dance floor like Fred Astaire and Ginger Rogers.

Not as two but one.

Words and *color*, meaning and light.

### The Philexicon

For this book I needed to update my *philexicon* (to coin a word from the Greek *philo,* **love**, and *lexicon*, **dictionary**), my collection of lovable words—or should I say words I've come to love? I've riffled the pages of scores of old dictionaries and ransacked my father's old army trunks, which now contain hundreds of my journals and notebooks. More than once during my restocking I've thought of the startling line in J. M. Barrie's *Peter Pan*, where Captain Hook is described: "The man isn't wholly evil; he has a **thesaurus** in his cabin." Recently, I felt even more vindicated about my ardent belief in the beauty of word books when I heard the ***deadpan*** comedian Stephen Wright say on late-night television, "I was reading the dictionary. I thought it was a poem about everything." Neither Dr. Johnson, nor Pablo Neruda, nor Mary Oliver could have said it better. In other words (and there are always other words), libraries, collections, and lists do not alone make for exciting books about words, but finding the poetry lurking in them just might. Out of a million or so English words (at last count), only a relatively few appear here. Selections need to be made; standards set; **wisdom** winnowed. For me, it's the old standby, the *frisson*, the shiver down the spine that Vladimir Nabokov described as the recognition of a deep truth. If a word provides that telltale shiver in me, I'm confident other people will feel the excitement as well.

Contrary to erroneous belief, the words needn't be ***sesquipedalian***, although it can be ***fun*** to learn a few "foot-and-a-half-long" ones. A *cruciverbalist* is someone who loves to do crossword puzzles; *lexicograpbolotary* is the worship of dictionaries; *xenolexica*, distrust or confusion over unusual words. They will do nicely. And they needn't be newly minted words, although a smattering of neologisms can't hurt, whether it's James Joyce's daring description of the night sky in this line from *Ulysses*: "The heaventree of stars hung with nightblue fruit," or recent coinages like *smirt*, a **smirky** combination of *smoke* and **flirt**, to describe what happens on the sidewalk outside a nonsmoking pub or restaurant.

What the entries here have to be are "lost beauties," as Charles Mackay affectionately called them. For him, they were archaic words worthy of revival, which are to language what *chiaroscuro* is to art, shadow-strewn with mystery, such as **oubliette**, a forgotten place, **hwyl**, a sudden outburst of **eloquence**, or **skirl**, to shriek like a bagpipe. But for the purposes of this book they are all "lost beauties," in the sense that their original meaning has been mislaid or misunderstood. They also possess the sublime quality that Italian painters call *luce di sotto*, the light below, as evident in early Flemish painting when scarlet was glazed over a gold ground to give the illusion of a living flame. For instance, if we gaze deeply at the deceptively simple word **opportunity**, we have a chance to see hidden **beauty** shining from below, which is the Roman god *Portunus*, patron of harbors. Seen in this light every new circumstance is like sailing into a **strange** and distant port, which may offer a haven, if we choose to take refuge.

Together, old and new words can be prismatic in the way they refract or disperse or **color** whatever is viewed through them. That's why we marvel at them. Not because they brandish our erudition, but because they celebrate the choices that await us when we dip our brush onto our brilliant palette of language.

To untangle the knot of interlocking meanings of these painted words, each entry begins with a *headword* that is drawn out with my own brief definition rendered in *italics*, then filled in with a tint of etymology and a brushstroke of quotes showing how the word is used, and ends with some touch-up by way of *companion words* that offer a few variations. The words themselves range from the commonplace, such as **biscuit**, a twice-baked cake for Roman soldiers, to loanwords, like **chaparral**, from the Basque shepherds who came to the American West; words from the myths, such as **hector**; metamorphosis words, such as **silly**, which evolved from "holy" to "goofy" in a mere thousand years; and words well worthy of revival, such as **carrytale**, a wandering storyteller. Whether old fangled or new fangled, they all possess that ineffable quality that Victoria Finlay refers to in her scintillating history of *color* as the "**numinous** in the luminous."

All this in the spirit of our word history, which brings us to one of the most challenging questions that I had to field while on book tour for *Wordcatcher,* from an intrepid high school student in Davis, California. "All very interesting, sir," she said firmly, "but you never told us where the word *dictionary* comes from."

As Detroit's Bob Seger sang, "I wish I didn't know now what I didn't know then." Only because I feel bad for not having the story on the tip of my tongue so she too could be inspired by the possibility of a lifelong friendship with dictionaries. For **dictionary** is one of those words you figure has always been lingering around the library of life, partly because we know that word lists date back to over 3,000 BC, to the ancient clay tablets of Sumer. But the English word itself, describing a list of word descriptions and definitions, is a thornier issue since it doesn't appear for another 4,200 years. Around 1225, a twenty-five-year-old English grammarian by the name of Joannes de Garlandia (John E. Garland) was teaching Latin at the University of Paris and looking for a way to help his students learn their vocabulary. In the 13th century, university rules mandated that not just all classes, but all **conversation** between students and teachers be carried out in the old Roman language. To help his students, Garland devised a mobile *aide-mémoire* based on walks he led though medieval Paris. While guiding them through the labyrinthine lanes of the teeming city he named the various things that they encountered along the way.

Uncannily, his innovation was both an echo of the **peripatetic** or walking schools of ancient Greece and a precursor of **flânerie** in modern Paris, the art of strolling in search of serendipitous encounters. Garland daringly began his dictionary by naming the parts of the human body, then moved out into the city, where he named the various and sundry shops, stalls, trades, and tradesmen, then sauntered out into the countryside where he named the animals of the forests. Finally, he came home to his own garden to contemplate what used to be called "the signature of all things," which is the secret strength of all dictionaries.

Out of these learned but entertaining strolls came the *Dictionarius,* a word Garland conjured up out of his prodigious knowledge of Latin, from *diction*, words, and the suffix *-arius*, to do with or pertaining to; hence a concise name for a book simply about words. In the introduction to her 1981 **translation** of Garland's pilgrimage of words, the medieval scholar Barbara Blatt Rubin tells that he wrote "in a delightfully discursive manner" for his students and future readers. Garland's own description was that the book simply consisted of things "which I have noted down as I wandered through the city of Paris ... the most necessary words which every student needs to keep ... in order to obtain an easier command of speech."

*The most necessary words.* An apt phrase for the kind of book many of us have found necessary ever since, meaning we can't seem to live without one. *Necessary words* is also a way to describe what follows in this book. The story is included here as a tribute to the prodigiously clever inventor of the *Dictionarius*, and also because it is a **metaphor** for the profoundly human need to name the world around us, as colorfully and clearly as possible. Garland described his effort as a presentation to his students of "the names of things." Nearly eight hundred years later our passion for naming is still the pounding heart of word books. The Garland story is a parable that reminds us that if we name the things of the world we can rest assured that words count when they endure. I am unregenerate enough to favor the named over the unnamed, the acknowledged over the ignored, the word over the silence. And in that spirit I trust that this little book will be a pleasant *divertissement*, an amusement, but even more, a source of joy and delight.

### The Endurance

Finally, a parable about the relationship between words and memory. In the early 19th century the German adventurer and scientist Alexander Humboldt set out across the **Amazon** rainforest in search of a remote tribe. He endured a treacherous journey to reach their village, where he was startled to learn that the tribe he had been looking for had recently been wiped out in a skirmish with a neighboring tribe. Undeterred, he sought the **rival** tribe, and to his surprise they were so **happy** to see him they led him to meet the sole survivor of the village. But what they presented to him wasn't human. Instead, he came face-to-face with a brilliantly colored parrot the warriors had captured from the village they had just destroyed. The bird was ablaze with **fury**, screeching in an unknown language. The warriors stared at the explorer. Surely, they thought, he could translate what the bird was saying. But the intrepid adventurer and scientist just gawked in wonder at the squawking bird, hearing words no one would ever again understand.

For me, this chromatic story is not only a painful parable about the tenuousness of words, but an illustration of the universal longing for **translation**, which means literally the "crossing over" of words from language to language, and the universal longing for words to endure. Sublimely, the story threads together the words of a lost South American tribe with those of a European explorer, words that were tied together when printed in Germany, and which I read nearly two hundred years later in Humboldt's famous **travel** journals, and which you are reading now, in the gallery of your mind.

Phil Cousineau
San Francisco—Donegal, Ireland, 2012

# A

## ABBEY-LUBBER

*A holy, lazy fool.* A medieval term for someone in perfectly good health who grew "idle and fat" off the charity of religious houses, whether of monks or parishioners. Figuratively, it has come to mean someone who pretends to be ascetic or holier-than-thou or who's just goofing off, or one who one uses the parish larder to live large. Picture, if you will, a cross between Friar Tuck and Orson Welles. In the irreplaceable *Dictionary of Phrase and Fable* (1898) E. Cobham Brewer cites *The Burynge of Paules Church* (1663): "It came into common proverbe to call him an *Abbay-lubber*, that was idle, wel fed, a long, **lewd**, lither loiterer, that might worke and would not." Companion words include *lollygagger, dawdler, goldbricker.*

## ABERRATION

*Strange* behavior, actions that stray from the norm, an unorth-
*odox path*. One of the surprisingly wide range of words
related to **travel**, as revealed by its Latin roots in *aberrare*,
to wander from a given path or to deviate from the *normal*.
Figuratively, *aberration* means breaking the rules by leading
an *uncouth* life, which originally referred to someone who
took an unknown path, as into Dante's dark wood, where
the paths diverged, or Galahad's forest, "where there is no
way or path." Companion words and phrases include *err,
errata, erroneous,* and *errant,* as in *knight errant,* and *deviate,* to
turn out of the way. Albert Schweitzer writes: "The time
will come when public opinion will no longer tolerate
amusements based on the mistreatment and killing of
animals. The time will come, but when? When we reach
the point that hunting, the pleasure in killing animals for
*sport*, will be regarded as a mental *aberration*?" More ironically, French philosopher Anatole France writes, "Of all
the sexual *aberrations*, chastity is the strangest."

## ABOMINATION

*Something so ominous it causes disgust. The Concise Oxford
Dictionary* provides a handy definition: "Loathing; odious
or degrading habit or act." This detestable word harks back
to Roman times, the Latin *abominabilis*, and the white-
knuckled phrase, *"Abominor!"*—in plain English, "I pray
that the omen be averted!" or "Omen away!" From *ab,*

away, *omen*, good or evil or portent. An *abomination* is the monster that's unleashed, an *Abominable* Snowman or Frankenstein, of our own mysterious creation. Matt Groening, the ingenious creator of *The Simpsons*, uses the word in a way that will be hilarious to some, odious to others: "I pledge impertinence to the flag waving of the unindicted co-conspirators of America, and to the republicans for which I can't stand, one *abomination*, underhanded fraud, indefensible, with Liberty and Justice—forget it." J. T. Tiptree Jr. writes mordantly, "*Abomination*, that's what they are; afterwords, introductions, all the dribble around the story." Companion words include *abominate*, to desecrate; *baleful*, portending evil; and *croaker*, someone in the habit of foretelling bad events, after the **strange** caws of a raven.

## ABSQUATULATE

*To flee, abscond, or boogie.* This facetious frontier **slang** combines the notion of speculating with squatting or camping. An example of America's "barbaric brilliancy" in language, as H. L. Mencken **sneered**. My informant, the tea maven, James Norwood Pratt, tells me that when he was growing up in North Carolina *absquatulate* meant to "absent one's family and self abruptly to take up 'squatting' elsewhere." According to dictionary.com, it reflects a humorous 19th-century linguistic trend in the United States to combine words that sound funny together. Coined around 1833, the word was first recorded in William B. Bernard's play *The Kentuckian*, uttered by the Western **character** Nimrod Wildfire who described "a frontiersman preparing to *absquatulate* and head for the wilderness." A disputatious story, but the truth can still be "rooted out" from the Latin *ab*, away, and *abscond*, and *at, to echo perambulate*, and *squattle*, a mock derivation of *squat*. Language maven William Safire quoted Senator Orrin Hatch warning Congress about early withdrawal from Iraq, in 2007: "Mr. President, *absquatulation* is not a policy!"

## ACHIEVE

*To accomplish, earn, complete.* A great catch of a word, a splendiferous *achievement* of the English language, a glorious example of vivid folk observation resulting in a kind of "catchword." Its roots date back to the Latin *ad caput venire*, to come to a head or a good result, to complete or finish something. By the 14th century, *achieve* was absorbed into French as *achever*, to accomplish something, which infers using your head and deciding to finish what you started. The original meaning remains when we say someone is an *overachiever*, going above and beyond expectations, or "playing over his head," as sudden stardom in sports is seen. Regarded in this way, *achievement* is a many-headed beast of a word. Abraham Lincoln wrote: "That some *achieve* great success, is proof to all that others can achieve it as well." On the flip side is Woody Allen's nebbish observation: "I don't want to *achieve* immortality

through my work. I want to *achieve* it through not dying."
Companion words include *mischief* and *bonchief*, a bad result
and a good result, respectively, and an "oddyssey" of a
word, *strange-achieved,* knowledge or experience learned
in foreign (*estrange*) lands, which sounds like a tantalizing
**travel** book title. *Mischieve* was a popular word in the 14th
century to describe a malicious deed or a selfish accom-
plishment, and if revived could readily fill an unfortunate
gap in our language.

Achieve: *Abraham Lincoln*

## AESTHETICS

*The study of the perception of* **beauty** *and good taste.* According to the venerable *Oxford Dictionary of English*, *aesthetics* is a nuanced appreciation of the beautiful. *Aesthetics* is also a branch of philosophy, a critical study of art that goes out on a limb to study the way people judge the beautiful, art, and good taste. Depth psychologist James Hillman elucidated an aspect of the word that takes my breath away: "The activity of perception or sensation in Greek is *aesthesis*," he writes in *A Blue Fire*, "which means at root 'taking in' as in breathing in the beauty of the world, which is a far cry from the dryasdust notion, perpetrated by the likes of John Donne, that what is *aesthetic* is merely physical sensation." Digging deeper into the loam of the word we find *aesthetikos*, sensitive, perceptive, from *aisthanesthai*, to perceive, to feel through the senses and the mind. By extrapolation, if it doesn't take your breath away, it ain't art. Deep and abiding beauty takes your breath away. This "in-search," as Hillman calls it, culminated in the French *esthetique*, the study of art itself, which in turn inspired Immanuel Kant, who regarded *aesthetics* as "the science which treats of the conditions of sensuous perception." The French polymath André Malraux wrote in *Museum without Walls*, "From *aesthetic* stems the idea of **beauty**, not so much that only beautiful things should be painted but only such things that would be beautiful if they existed." Companion words include *aesthete*, "a professed appreciator of the beautiful," according to the OED, and *beauty sleep*, the sleep taken before midnight, presumably because it amounts to the most refreshing rest of all, the one that allows us to appear young, attractive, even breathtaking.

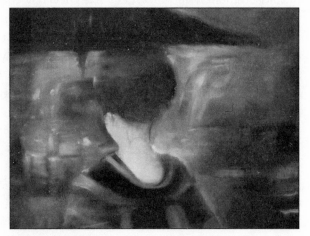

Aesthetics: *Red in Rain*

## ALLURE

*To attract, captivate, lure, in a mysteriously **fascinating** way; to powerfully charm, tempt, attract.* Curiously, this is one of many hunting terms that have gone through what linguists call "sense evolution," while maintaining strong metaphorical power. It derives from the 14th-century word Old French *aleurer*, to attract, captivate, and more exotically, to train a falcon to hunt. The roots are à, to, and *loirre*, falconer's lure. The archaic sense is that of a passage, walkway, or

gallery along a castle parapet, which reverts to the Middle
English *alour, alure,* gait, course, gallery, from *aler,* to go.
By the magical power of metaphorical extension, English
novelist Anthony Trollope writes, "She knew how to *allure*
by denying, and to make the gift rich by delaying it." If
your lover purrs to you, "You *animal*," you know that you
have proved to be *alluring*, in the original sense of the word.
H. L. Mencken wrote, "The *allurement* that women hold
out to men is precisely the *allurement* that Cape Hatteras
holds out to sailors: they are enormously dangerous and
hence enormously ***fascinating*.*"

## ALOOF

*Away, apart; standoffish, shy, or superior.* A word that drifted
into English from Holland, where English itself was born
around the 11th century, according to Melvyn Bragg. From
the Dutch *a-loef,* luff, to steer into the wind to avoid danger
and away from the shore. Figuratively, *aloof* proved to be a
strong **metaphor** for the desire of many sailors and land-
lubbers alike to steer away from people; it drifted out to sea
in its current meaning, as the *American Heritage Dictionary*
defines it: "being without a community of feeling, distant,
indifferent." The *New York Times,* in 1990, wrote of film
star Greta Garbo that her "*aloofness* frustrated the press,
which published thousands of photographs of her franti-
cally clutching a drooping hat over her face as she shopped
or raced for a train, ship or plane." Sir Arthur Conan Doyle

sniffed in his historical novel *Sir Nigel*, "To his pure and knightly soul not Edith alone, but every woman, sat high and *aloof*, enthroned and exalted, with a thousand mystic excellences …" My informant on Inishmore, the Celtic monk Dara Malloy, tells me that the local phrase for staying *aloof* is *Fan amach ón duine*, which he translates as "Give that person a wide berth." Companion words include *apart, chilly, cold fish*, which is what you get if you stay too long in your drifting boat and don't come ashore.

## ALPHABET

*A standard set of letters used in a language.* The Concise Oxford Dictionary adds in succinct fashion that this is the "*first rudiments*" of language. Scholars have determined that about fifty-six different *alphabets* are still in use around the world. The most common is ours, the Latin one, that derives from the clever decision to use *alpha* and *beta*, the first two letters of the Greek alphabet, which had already come from the first two letters of the Phoenician alphabet, meaning *ox* and *house*, respectively. The symmetry of the word gave some order to the chaos of Roman letters, resulting in the dulcet Latin *alphabetum*, from the Greek *alphabetos*. According to Robert Cawdrey, in his 1604 *First English Dictionary*, an *abecedarie* is handily defined as "the order of the letters, or hee that vseth them." The Greek historian Herodotus credited the Phoenician prince Cadmus with inventing both the *alphabet* and books, which the Greeks wrote as *phoinikeia grammata*, "Phoenician letters," and customized for themselves. Herodotus even described encountering the Cadmean alphabet on an engraved tripod in the temple of Apollo at Thebes, with an inscription that read: "Amphitryon dedicated me from the spoils from the battle of Teleboae," which, if true, reveals the origins of the *alphabet* in an account of war reporting. To this day I open up books from my father's library and find book marks from the Little Professor Bookstore in Dearborn, Michigan, which featured this quote from an 1818 letter by Thomas Carlyle: "May blessings be upon the head of Cadmus, the Phoenicians, or whoever it was that invented books." Companion words include *abecedarian*, arranged alphabetically, also a **pupil** studying the *alphabet*; and the nostalgic *alphabet soup*, a tomato soup with kernels of letter-shaped pasta floating within. The digital publishing world refers to a person who is interested in testing software development as a *beta*, and pre-alpha, alpha, and beta often read other's work before it is posted or published, an especially popular practice in "*fan* fiction." The **deadpan** comic Stephen Wright asks, "Why is the *alphabet* in that order? Is it because of that song?"

## AMBROSIA

*Food of the gods; anything delightful to taste or smell; bee-bread.* The Greek *ambrosios* meant "of the immortals," from *a*, not, *mbrotos*, mortal: not mortal. Those who ate it were rendered immortal by virtue of sharing the food of the gods on Mount Olympus. ***Fascinatingly***, the word reaches back even further, to Proto-Indo-European, the earliest roots of English: *\*mer* (the asterisk denotes the clever work of linguists to reconstruct a word's roots on the basis of other material), to die, a reflection of the timeless thought about mortality and immortality. Pliny and Dioscorides both described certain herbs that were used in various foods for mortals since the 1680s (originally in fruit drinks); used figuratively for "anything delightful" by 1731. In Homer's *Iliad*, Zeus orders Aphrodite to "anoint the body of Hector with *ambrosia*." Companion words include *ambrosia*, the marshmallow-like dessert, *ambrosial*, divinely fragrant or delicious, and by extension, *nectar*, a drink that helps you *overcome death*. The actor James Earl Jones (the voice of Darth Vader in the "immortal" *Star Wars*) said, "In the wintertime, in the snow country, citrus fruit was so rare, and if you got one, it was better than *ambrosia*." The Sanskrit *amrita* refers to the "immortal" drink of ancient Hindus.

### AMOK (MALAY)

*Jumbled; confused; running about in frenzied thirst for blood.* The OED simply defines it as coming from the Malay word *amuk,* attacking ferociously, as if in a trance. The first known reference comes in *The Book of Duarte Barbosa: An*

*Account of the Countries Bordering on the Indian Ocean and Their Inhabitants,* published in 1516: "There are some of them [the Javanese] who ... go out into the streets, and kill as many persons as they meet ... These are called *Amuco*." Later the word entered the various European languages as well as English, always referring to a kind of a violent frenzy. In an NPR interview, Claire O'Neill, author of *Autochromes: The First Flash of Color*, recounts, "There's a legend that when the Lumière brothers—pioneers of motion pictures—showed their film of an approaching train in 1896, the audience ran *amok* in terror." Companion words include **berserk**, deranged, furious, wildly out of control.

### ANALEMMA

*The path of the sun plotted on a globe or photograph.* This unusual word is what I like to think of as a *whatchamacallit*. Have you ever wondered what that curious figure-eight-like drawing on the surface of a globe is called, or if there is even a name for the similar figure-eight pattern of a rising and setting sun as captured by time-lapse photography? Well, now you know it—one word that covers both phenomena. The Greek *analemma* was a sundial set on a pedestal, from *ana*, up, and *lambanein*, to take, which provides a vivid word-picture of a device propped up on a stone in order to take or catch sunlight. When caught it cast a shadow in order to tell time. If watched over the course of the day that shadow moves in a beautiful pattern, which depicts the sun's declination for each day of the year. That pattern came to be drawn on the portion of common globes that showed the Tropics. If you look it up, as Casey Stengel advised sports reporters who never believed his references, what you will find is this marvelous mouthful: "orthographic projection of the sphere on the plane of the meridian," the eye being supposed at an infinite distance, and in the east or west point of the horizon. Let's call an *analemma* a beautiful and orderly curve that represents the *mean* position on the celestial sphere. *Analemma* is commonly applied nowadays to the figure traced in the sky when the position of the Sun is plotted at the same time each day over a calendar year from a particular location on Earth. Companion words include *lemma*, a word stem, or deepest reach of a root word, such as ***throw*** from *thrown*, or **catch** from caught.

### APOCRYPHAL

*Of doubtful authenticity; sham; wrongly attributed; esoteric.* In ancient Greek *kryptien* meant "to hide," coming into Latin as *apocrypha (scripta),* hidden or secret writings (implying that something is not sanctioned), from the earlier Greek *apokryphos*, from *apo*, away, *kryptein*, hide. Hidden away, obscure, referring to writings or books of "unknown or unofficial and unapproved authorship," especially those included in the Septuagint and Vulgate books of the Bible.

Two examples of probable *apocryphal statements*, the first by Mark Twain, the most popular thing he never said: "The coldest winter I ever spent was a summer in San Francisco." Equally erroneous but similarly irresistible is the alleged eureka moment of the French monk Pierre (Dom) Pérignon, moments after imbibing his newly blended champagne: "Come quickly, I am drinking the stars!" It's enough to make you wonder if the writers of the early *Superman* comics were reading the Greek myths—in the original—when they conjured up *kryptonite*, the "hidden or secret" stone that was Superman's Achilles Heel. Companion words include *apocalypse*, literally the "lifting of the veil" from the Greek *apo*, away, and *kalypsis*, veil, away with the veil, as in the revelation or disclosure of a secret.

## ARABESQUE

*Arabian-like, featuring swirling architectural flourishes reminiscent of Arabic calligraphy.* According to Owen Barfield, its origins may date back to the Crusaders, who along with ideas and architecture brought to Europe other marvel-filled Orientalisms such as *damask* (from Damascus), *tangerine* (from Tangiers), ***azure, orange,*** and *saffron.* By the 1610s, it described Moorish ornamental design, from Italian *arabesco*, which derived from *Arabo,* Arab, with reference to Moorish architecture. As a ballet posture, first attested in 1830. Yet the word has great figurative meaning as well.

The rapscallion philosopher Alan Watts wrote: "How is it possible that a being with such sensitive jewels as the eyes, such enchanted musical instruments as the ears, and such fabulous *arabesques* of nerves can experience itself as anything but a god?" In a 1990 interview with Katy Butler, Rumi scholar Coleman Barks said, "In the Persian, Rumi is full of rhyming. You can have six internal rhymes in a single line. To the medieval mind, these *arabesques*, and all the repetitions, were a sign of devotion—it's like Arab architecture." Companion words include *arabesque,* a musical ornament, dating to 1864, and one of its most luminous illustrations, Debussy's *Arabesques*.

## ARGUS-EYED

*Extraordinarily vigilant, alert, awake.* According to Ovid, the hundred-eyed guardian Argus, also called Panoptes, or "All-eyes," was commanded by Hera to guard the nymph Io, after she caught her husband Zeus *in flagrante delicto* with her. Outraged, Hera humiliated Io by turning her into a cow, which prompted the outraged Zeus to command Hermes to slay Argus. The story goes that after Argus's death, Hera transferred his hundred eyes to the **iridescent** tail of the peacock. Around the late 14th century, the Greek word *argos*, "the bright one," shining, bright, came into Latin as *argus*. It is used in the figurative sense to mean "a very vigilant person." Essayist Joseph Addison wrote, "A beautiful eye makes silence eloquent, a kind eye makes contradiction an assent, an enraged eye makes beauty deformed. This little member gives life to every other part about us; and I believe the story of *Argus* implies no more than that the eye is in every part; that is to say, every other part would be mutilated were not its force represented more by the eye than even by itself." Companion words include *Argus*, of the eponymous ship built for Jason and his **Argonauts**, and the variant *Argos*, the dog of Odysseus, who waited faithfully for him to return for lo those twenty years, then died of a broken heart when the king of Ithaka arrived home. *Argosy,* a fleet of ships or a rich supply, is a *false friend*, unconnected with Argus, actually originating in the Italian phrase *nave Ragusea*, a ship of Ragusa, an ancient port town on the Adriatic which we now call Dubrovnik, Croatia.

Argus Eyed

**ART**

*A creative work; the way we **color** our world.* As the Detroit
preacher sang out, "Do ye feel it, do ye feel the mystery?"
As poetic as it sounds, *art* is a sticky wicket of a word. Our
use of it dates to the early 13th-century, but it refers to
a phenomenon that dates back at least 41,000 years, the
age of the recently discovered prehistoric rock art caves
at Le Chauvet, in France. Coincidentally, our word first
appeared in Old French as *art*, from Latin *artem*, work of
art, which originally referred to a practical skill or the
outcome of learning or practice, as well as a business craft.
Word mavens speculate that this short (three-letter) word
has an epically long history that reaches all the way back
to the Sanskrit *rtih*, manner, mode, and then into Greek
*arti*, just, *artios* and *artizein*, to prepare. From ancient times,
*art* referred to skill in scholarship and learning, notably in
what used to be called the seven sciences, or liberal arts.
Later, during the Renaissance, *art* was used to contrast
human works with works of nature. The sense of being
*artful*, cunning or tricky, was recorded in 1600, a dim
reflection of the ineffable talents of *artists*. By the 1610s *art*
had taken on the meaning it maintains to this day: great
skill in creative arts, such as painting, sculpture, music,
literature—but also works that are deeply imbued with a
transcendent dimension. Citations are as boundless as the
archives at the Louvre. It was none other than Leonardo da
Vinci who said, "Art is never finished, only abandoned."
The poet Gwendolyn Brooks focused on the personal: "Art

hurts. Art urges voyages—and it is easier to stay at home."
Choreographer Agnes Martin commented: "When I think
of art I think of **beauty**. Beauty is the mystery of life. It
is not in the eye, it is in the mind. In our minds there is
awareness of perfection." Companion words and phrases
include *Ars longa, vita brevis,* art is long, life is short, which
is taken from a longer aphorism about the immortality of
great art by the Ancient Greek physician Hippocrates.

## ASPERSION

*Hint, insinuate, refer to; slander.* The most common use of
the word is with the verb *cast,* as in "to cast *aspersions,*"
which first appeared in Henry Fielding, in 1749, and has its
origins in the casting or sprinkling of water, from *asperge,* to
sprinkle on. Picture a priest swinging the smoking censer at
Mass—he is casting his *asperges* in the cast metal ceremonial
container of holy water or incense. In the *Devil's Dictionary,*
Ambrose Bierce defines a common word in an uncommon
way: "BAPTISM, n. A sacred rite of such efficacy that he
who finds himself in heaven without having undergone
it will be unhappy forever. It is performed with water in
two ways—immersion, or plunging, and by *aspersion,* or
sprinkling. But whether the plan of immersion is better
than *aspersion* let those immersed and those *aspersed* decide
by the Authorized Version." More recently, in *Charlie
Wilson's War,* Gus Avrakotos (Philip Seymour Hoffman),
a case officer and division chief for the CIA responsible for

arming Afghanistan's mujahideen, says: "Well, … Harold Holt is a tool. He's a cake-eater, he's a clown, he's a bad station chief, and I don't like to cast *aspersions* on a guy, but he's going to get us all killed." Companion words include *asperities*, hardships to be endured.

Atelier: *Painter and Model*

## ATELIER

*An **attic**; a painting studio; the site where a poor artist's life unfolds.* Often juxtaposed to *en plein air* painting, *atelier* derives from the Old French *astelier*, carpenter's shop, a word that splintered off from *astele*, which meant, "splinter." Uncannily, I came across the connection when I spent an afternoon with the Grateful Dead's Jerry Garcia, who showed me around his music studio, in Marin County, California.

"This seems like an alchemist's lab," I joked. "No, it's just a carpenter's shop. We just build songs in here," he replied. "You can learn more in painting one street scene," wrote American painter George Bellows, "than in six months' work in an *atelier*." In *Barney's Version*, Canadian novelist Mordecai Richler writes, "A garage in Montparnasse served as Leo's *atelier*, and there he labored on his huge triptychs, mixing his paints in buckets and applying them with a kitchen mop." Companion words include *atelier nu*, a studio that features nude models, a wildly controversial innovation when it arrived in Paris in the nineteenth century.

## ATTIC

*A small uppermost room.* As someone who has great affection for both Greek and French culture, I'm fond of this word story since it connects both. *Attic* comes to us from *Attica* and its ancient capital, Athens, as if by a supply ship to medieval France, where it became *attique*, "a decorative architectural flourish consisting of a square decorative column," usually "in a low story above a building's main façade / above the main story of a building." Eventually, *attic* became shorthand for the area enclosed by such a structure and at the top of the building. Commonly, this consisted of square columns with bases and pilasters instead of pillars, which has been called the *Attic* order ever since. During the inevitable urban renewal of language we

Attic

lost the story, but kept the storage area. As early as 1560, the English began building structures capped by decorative structures called the *Attic storey*, which was later shortened to *attic* story. Both terms have survived in modern parlance, *attic* for the top level of a house or building, and in case you've ever wondered why floors are called stories, a *story* for each level. As a Greek word for architectural style and a French term for a secret, often hidden place to store our heritage, *attic* is rich with metaphorical possibilities. Sir Arthur Conan Doyle wrote, "I **consider** that a man's brain originally is like a little empty *attic*, and you have to stock it with such furniture as you choose." The English rock star Sting told an interviewer, "An uncle of mine emigrated to **Canada** and couldn't take his guitar with him. When I found it in the *attic*, I'd found a friend for life." Actor Lawrence Olivier: "I often think that could we creep behind the actor's eyes, we would find an *attic* of forgotten toys and a copy of the Domesday Book."

## AUTOLOGOPHAGIST

*Someone who eats his own words, usually on a dare.* Normally a figure of speech, but it became an actuality after a Danish writer, Theodore Reinking, wrote a scathing indictment of his country's defeat at the hands of the perfidious Swedes and was jailed in 1644. Years later, he was given the choice of life imprisonment or eating his own book, which he promptly did by slicing it up like so many vegetables and making a sauce for it, which he promptly devoured. Thus, he ate his own words. In 1980, German filmmaker Werner Herzog became a modern *autologophagist*, who was immortalized in Les Blank's 1980 documentary film *Werner Herzog Eats His Shoe*. The film depicts Herzog fulfilling his promise that he would cook and eat his shoe if fellow filmmaker Errol Morris actually finished his years-in-the-making doc, *Gates of Heaven*. Blank shows scenes from the completed film, plus scenes of Herzog boiling his shoes (the same ones he claimed to be wearing when he made the bet), with a mix of garlic, herbs, and stock for five hours, at Berkeley's famed Chez Panisse restaurant, alongside proprietor Alice Waters. The film closes with a triumphant final scene at the old UC Theater in Berkeley, which I watched in real time, in 1980, as Herzog acted the *autologophagist* and ate one of his shoes. Which just shows to go you, as Grampa used to say, you can have your shoe and eat it, too. Sir Francis Bacon: "*Some books* are to be tasted, others to be swallowed, and *some* few to be *chewed* and digested: that is, *some books* are to be read only in parts, others to be read."

## AVERAGE

*Typical, usual, the mean.* For much of my youth, this *average* word meant one thing—baseball. I spent Sunday afternoons memorizing virtually all of the major league batting *averages*, many of which I blush to say I remember to this day. (My boyhood hero, the Detroit Tigers' Al Kaline, hit for a .324 *average*, in 1962.) Little did I know that its origins were anything but *average*. Its roots lay curiously close to my own, the French Canadian tradition of *voyageurs*. This word sailed aboard the French *availe*, Italian *avaria*, Spanish *averia*, Dutch *avarij*, all possibly deriving from the Arabic *awariya*, and meaning "damaged merchandise." The French and Italian words entered the harbor of the English language around 1500, via a few Italian ports, as a maritime term for financial loss incurred by damage to goods during shipping. Some above-*average* explaining is in order here. The "loss from damage, over and above the cost of shipping freight … expenses were usually distributed proportionally among the interested parties in the venture—for instance, the ship owners and the cargo owners." According to the *American Heritage Dictionary of Word Origins*, "the idea of a mathematical *average*, or the arithmetic mean developed from the notion of distributing a sum among a number of persons, and the senses of the adjective *average*, 'typical' and 'usual,' are derived from this sense of a 'mean' figure." The mathematical meaning dates to 1755. The *batting average* calculations date back to Harry Chadwick (also inventor of the box score) in the late 19th century, and have taken on great metaphorical meaning. In the late Sixties, rock-and-roll star Chubby ("Let's Twist") Checker wondered why his phenomenal "rate of hits" in the Fifties was forgotten after the rise of the Beatles: "I [had] the best *batting average* in the music industry and I'm a byword."

## AZURE (ARABIC)

*Sky blue; the heraldic color blue;* figuratively, *cloudless, serene.* "Sky blue, unclouded vault of heaven, the bright blue pigment lapis lazuli," in the dulcet definition of the Concise OED. Herbert Coleridge, in his *Dictionary of the Oldest Words in the English Language* (1859), mines *azure* in Joseph Ritson's *Ancient Songs,* from 1792. This breathtaking pigment was so rare and so expensive Michelangelo couldn't even afford to pay for it himself. It is a word from the old Silk Road traders who carried the valuable lapis lazuli stone, *al-lazaward* in Arabic, during the early 14th century. The stone turned to paint and the word turned into Old French *azur.* "So called," writes the first official English etymologist, Walter W. Skeat, "from the mines of Lajward [in Turkestan] where lapis lazuli was found." Also attested to by Marco Polo, in his famous 13th-century journals. Most people only knew that it came on ships from lands far, far away, and so it became known as *azzurum ultramarine,* "azure from over the sea." The English photographer and fashion designer Cecil Beaton wrote, "More varied than any landscape was the landscape in the sky, with islands of gold and silver, peninsulas of apricot and rose against a background of many shades of turquoise and *azure.*" The blue-souled poet Arthur Rimbaud wrote, "I have bathed in the poem of the sea ... / Devouring the green *azures.*"

Azure: *Rimbaud at the Sea*

# B

## BAFFLEGAB

*Language that misleads readers either intentionally, through legalese, or unintentionally through confusion.* "Doublespeak [is] language that feigns to communicate, shifts blame and responsibility," according to Reuters, 1979. What does it say about us that we seem to have far more words in English to describe the mealy-mouthed malarkey that passes for communication than we have words for language that dances and sings? This ***smirkword*** harkens back to only the early 1950s, in the Golden Age of Madison Avenue ad campaigns. By combining **baffle**, confuse, with *gab*, speak, a **portmanteau** was created that expresses the goofiness of *gobbledygook* with the annoying *gabby*. The Legalese Hall of Fame, maintained by Adam Freedman, provides this classic knickers-in-a-twist sentence: "I am herewith returning the stipulation to dismiss in the above entitled matter; the same being duly executed by me." Baseball manager Casey

Stengel, "The Old Perfesser," delivers this curveball: "I wouldn't admire [recommend?] hitting against [Yankee fireballing pitcher] Ryne Duren, because if he ever hit you in the head, you would be in the past tense." Companion words are copious: *mellowspeak, gobbledygook, fimble-famble, jargonaut,* and *Bog Latin*, the derisive term for the gibberish of Irish farmers as perceived by city folk and foreigners. Speaking of which, *gibberish,* deliberate nonsense, derives from the **cant** language of thieves and gypsies called "Pedlar's French," sometimes attributed to the mystic language of Geber, the 13th-century Islamic alchemist.

## BALK

*Hesitate; ground left unplowed; sanctuary on a billiard table; an illegal move in baseball that deceives a base runner.* Speaking of **ball** words, here is a grounder, so to speak, a word grounded in the natural world that led to an expression in the game that most romanticizes its rural origins. The word comes to us from left field—or should we say, a field left behind, unplowed. In baseball jargon a *balk* is an illegal motion made by a pitcher that unfairly deceives a base runner by faking a throw to a base, which rewards the opposing team by allowing him or her to advance to the next base. In its verb form *balk* means to hesitate or be unwilling to accept an idea or undertaking. The connection for those of us doomed to love both words and baseball is thrilling. It harkens back to Middle English *balken,* to plow up in ridges, from *balk*, ridge, Old English *balca,* and Old Norse, *balkr,* beam. According to the lustrous *Concise Oxford Dictionary*, a *balk* is "a ridge left unploughed; stumbling-block, hindrance." The shift of speech to the ploughed field, which is what playing fields began as, is easy and poetic, a *balk* being the call of an umpire on a pitcher who doesn't stop long enough on the mound for the batter to adjust to the next pitch, or fakes and never ***throws*** at all. Incidentally, the ignominious major league record for *balks* is 90, held by Steve Carlton. Novelist Anne Tyler writes, "I can never tell ahead of time which book will give me trouble—some *balk* every step of the way, others seem to write themselves—but certainly the mechanics of writing, finding the time and the psychic space, are easier now that my children are grown." Motown legend Smokey Robinson says, "I don't ever *balk* at being considered a Motown person, because Motown is the greatest musical event that ever happened in the history of music." Companion words include *ballot*, voting by "*balls*" dropped—or ***thrown***—into a box or urn, and *blackballed*, from the black ***balls*** inserted into a box that signaled the *balking* of someone's participation.

## BALL

*A round object, something to **throw**; a fancy dance party.* A ball is what every *wordcatcher* needs: otherwise, how can you play with the language? If you are trying to communicate,

all words are *balls* that we use to ***throw*** meaning back and
forth. So let's get a grip on this one. Originally, *ball* derives
from the Old Norse *bollr*, referring to what we know as
an object used in sporting activities, a word that has been
rolling around since the 1200s. But its curious development—rolling out—from the object to the dance is what
we are delighted to share here. By the 1630s, the name for
a formal party or celebration featuring dancing emerged,
as evident in the Old French *baller*, to dance, from the Latin
*ballare*, also to dance, and the Greek *ballizein*, dance or
jump around. The word for a festive party and the overlap
between ***sports*** and dancing are traceable back to an Italian
custom, according to my leather-bound copy of Webb
Garrison's *Why You Say It*, which I inherited from my
father. The story goes (and don't they all?) that in Naples,
Italy, in the 17th century, during solemn occasions, the
city cathedral choirboys danced and sang slowly around
the dean, catching a *ball **thrown*** by a local dignitary to the
*belle of the ball* and her suitors in the *ballroom*. As the custom
of combining song and dance took hold, Garrison explains
that "any elaborate dancing party came to be known as a
*ball*." Do you **catch** my meaning? Companion words are
like a *ball bag* in a baseball dugout, including *ball*, **slang** for
testicles, first recorded only in the 14th century but surely
much older, and a few *ballsy* expressions, such as *to be on
the ball*, alert; *ball-point pen*; *ball of fire*, a glass of brandy;
*ballistics*, from *ball*-shaped bullets, *balling the **jack***, to go fast,
and *balling*, as in having sex, recorded as **jazz** slang in the

1940s. The list goes on, like the collection of thousands
of famous *balls* in the archives of the Cooperstown Baseball Hall of Fame: *parabolic,* **thrown** over; *symbolic,* **thrown**
together; and *diabolic,* **thrown** apart. And we can't forget
*having a ball*, which is what we're trying to do by tossing
these pitches.


## BANSHEE

*A female fairy whose bloodcurdling cry is thought to foretell death.*
A spectral word from Gaelic *bean sidhe* (pronounced "she"),
a female elf, from the expressive image of *bean*, woman,
and *sidhe*, earlier *sith*, fairy, or *sid*, fairy mound. So a *banshee*
beckons the spirits of dead ancestors or **heroes** from the
old megalithic mounds, still called fairy mounds in many
parts of Ireland to this day. The power to do so gave rise
to the belief in the *an sidhe,* the female fairy who foretells
death, which evolved around 1771 into *banshee*. Vividly
do I remember my **garrulous** neighbor, Mrs. Keaney, in
Ballyconneelly, Connemara, Ireland, back in the early
1980s, telling me with all due seriousness that *banshees*
were the drifting souls of women who died miserably—
fallen women who were recognizable by the rags that they
wore and their bloodcurdling screams. In her introduction to *Visions and Beliefs in the West of Ireland: Seers and
Healers*, Lady Gregory wrote, "This beginning of knowledge was a great excitement for me, for though I had heard
all my life some talk of the faeries and the *banshee* (having

indeed some reason to believe in this last), I had never thought of giving heed to what I, in common with my class, looked on as fancy or **superstition**. It was certainly because of this unbelief that I had been told so little about them." Companion words include *brownie, fay, pookah*, or the *sidhe* who appeared in bands of three—royally dressed, weeping, and foretelling a death. Over time they became associated with witches or supernatural beings. Some families are said to have their own *banshee*, who will let out a deathly wail before one of them dies. Ogden Nash turned the screeches into poetry: "What was it, anyway, that angry thing that flew at me? / I am unused to banshees crying Boo at me. / Your wife can't be a banshee— / Or can she?" And who can't still hear the cries of Siouxsie and the *Banshees*, the British postpunk rock band?

## BASK

*Laze, lounge, loll.* A "mirror word," one whose reflection is reversed, its meaning turned inside out over the years. It comes into English in the late 14th century as *basken*, to wallow in, as a warrior might in blood. These martial origins go back to the Old Norse or Viking words *baðask* and *baða*, which led to the word *bathe*, providing the steamy image of a sauna. Without engaging in bardolotry, it's helpful to point out that this is why Shakespeare borrowed words with metaphorical power and invested them with fresh meaning. *As You Like It* features the bard's update:

"soak up the warmth of," a bright reflection of how one might *bask* in sunshine. As lustrous as it is, the word can be used ironically, as Dan Castellaneta, the uproarious voice of Homer Simpson on *The Simpsons*, uses it: "Let us all *bask* in television's warm glow." Writing of the rise of civilizations, historian Arnold Toynbee describes the pattern of urban life emerging along rivers and seas: "The immense cities lie *basking* on the beaches of the continent like whales that have taken to the land."

### BAWDY

*Naughty, vulgar, dirty.* A ribald word with risqué roots. As lubricious as it sounds, *bawdy* reflects what linguists call a "sense evolution," or progress from the medieval *bold* to the modern **lewd**. Langland, in *Piers Plowman* (1362), groped around the language for a lecherous word and chose *bawd-strot*, a bold strut, which later picked up the connotation of **lewd** behavior. Although the great linguist Walter Skeat says its roots are unknown, he does provide a brilliant image, saying that it hails from the Welsh *bawaid*, dirty, from *baw,* mud. Old French *baudise*, ardor, passion, joy, but also boldness, and *fole baudie*, shamelessness. "Carting" was the punishment for *bawds*, who were carried through **town** in a wagon so "their person might be known." *Bawd* was a risqué Latin word for prostitute, shrouded in the late 15th century as a "**lewd** person," possibly from *baude-strote*, "procurer of prostitutes," from the Middle English *bawde*, merry, joyous, and the earlier Old French *baud*, gay, licentious, and Frankish *bald*, bold. The Online Dictionary claims, "It would not be the first time a word meaning 'joyous' had taken on a sexual sense." There is precedence, as Robert Cawdrey wrote in his 1604 dictionary, for *brothel* as a keeper of a house of *baudry*. **Consider** how the prickly journalist H. L. Mencken riffed on the word: "The opera is to music what a *bawdy* house is to a cathedral." Companion words include this brothel of naughty words: *bustlicious*, a delicious-looking bust; and "a covey of whores," the medieval collective noun for a *bawdy* house full of prostitutes.

Beguile

## BEGUILE

*To appeal in a mysterious way, enchant, attract—or to trick.* A "sonicky" word, as Roy Blount, Jr., calls them, dating back to the mid-12th century, but it's also one of those versatile words that seems to mean two different things but provides the beauty of subtle shadings between them. For Margaret Ernst, it is an example of a word metamorphosis, changing from *cheat* to *charm*. The Word Detective website provides help here, observing that *"*a similar softening of tone has been evident in *beguile* over the centuries, as the raw 'cheat and deceive.'" It goes on to say, "If there's a semantic difference between *charm* and *beguile*, it's the faint premonition that what we find 'beguiling' may not turn out as well as we'd hoped." To *beguile* is to *be* full of *guile*, to delude with deceit, to trick with cleverness. The Old Frisian roots dig down into *wigila*, sorcery, witchcraft. The OED explains the development: "To win the attention or interest of (any one) by willing means; to charm, divert, **amuse**." By the late 16th century, *beguile* meant "to pleasantly divert or amuse so as to make something disagreeable less unpleasant." Shakespeare writes, "Come, and take choice of all my library, / And so *beguile* thy sorrow." So what happened was what we might call a *wordflip*, like a backflip, but with words. What began as "trick or cheat" turned around to mean "charm and amuse." President Lincoln, in his famous Civil War–era letter to Mrs. Lydia Bixby, the grieving mother of five brothers who fell in battle on the Union side, wrote: "I feel how weak and fruitless be any word of mine which should attempt to *beguile* you from the grief of a loss so overwhelming." **Travel** writer Jan Morris reveals how she feels about Lebanon: "To the stern student of affairs, Beirut is a phenomenon, *beguiling* perhaps, but quite, quite impossible." Writing reelingly about the whorls of a seashell, Paul Valéry says, "It *beguiles* the eye, drawing it into a kind of controlled vertigo."

## BILLABONG (AUSTRALIAN)

*A streambed that fills with water during the rainy season in the Australian outback.* Every New Year's Eve of my youth my parents held a rollicking party that included a great deal of *carousing*, in the original sense of the word. Inevitably, my father would crank up the old Philco stereo and play Greek bouzouki music, and a few times over the years a record given to him by an Australian automaker of the country's semiofficial anthem, "Waltzing Matilda." There were so many exotic, melodic, iconic words in it that it stuck in my mind forever, and I quote it here in my father's honor, a tribute to introducing me to a new word every day of my youth, from crossword puzzles and exotic music to the sculptures of Angkor Wat and the *billabongs* of the Outback: "Oh, there was once was a *swagman* [an itinerant laborer] camped in the *billabong* / Under the shade of a Collibah [eucalyptus] tree, / And he sang as he looked at the old billy [kettle] boiling, / Who will come a-waltzing, Matilda [a swagman's bundle] with me?" Those incantatory rhythms are the heart of learning things by heart, the soul of poetry, songs of the soul. The swaggering detective Crocodile Dundee crowed in the eponymous movie, "I'll meet you at the Echo *Billabong* on Wednesday."

## BISCUIT

*Hard bread or cake.* A vestige of Roman shipping customs, a time when ships sailed farther and farther away from shore, necessitating longer-lasting food. Ship's cooks began to bake thin cakes or pastry that could be re-cooked, described in Medieval Latin as *biscoctus*, twice-baked, which evolved into *biscuit*. Companion words include *zwieback*, which was reheated as the English word for *cookie*. Poet Carl Sandburg bites off the word's crisp sound: "Poetry is the synthesis of hyacinths and *biscuits*." One of my informants, the legendary Knoxville tunesmith R. B. Morris, reports: "There was a fellow I worked with on the L&N Railroad when I was driving spikes and doing track maintenance for a living. I asked him how he got started with the railroad and he said he just went in to talk to the guy hiring and said, 'I got a little boy at home thinks the doorknob's a *biscuit*, and I gotta have work.'" Companion words include *biscuit*, the stage of pottery or porcelain that is post-baking and pre-glazing.

## BLACKMAIL

*Extortion for money in return for not revealing potentially compromising or harmful information.* Its root story is mailed to us from the Old English *mæðel*, meeting, council; *mæl*, speech; and *mal*, lawsuit, terms which when linked with *black* give us the image of meeting gone bad, rotten. *In a Word*, by Ernst, passes down the folk belief that it can be traced to English *black* and Scottish *mail*, rent or tribute. The backstory reveals a tale about "small farmers in the north of England and along the Scottish border who, in the *ol'* days, paid tribute to freebooter chiefs to gain immunity from plunder. This tribute was called *black* because it was often paid in black cattle. Rents paid in white cattle were called *white mail* ..." The first word portrait reveals a medieval knight sneakily painting his armor black to avoid having to polish it. The second portrait reveals a "protection racket," or extortion by English landlords from Scottish freebooter (clan) chiefs in hopes of protecting their cattle from plunder. By the early 19th century, the nasty practice was expanded to cover "any type of extortion money." In *The Dark Knight*, Batman's butler, Lucius Fox (Morgan Freeman), scoffs at their accountant's attempt to bribe the Batman: "Let me get this straight: You think that your client [Bruce Wayne, Batman's alter ego] one of the wealthiest, most powerful men in the world, is secretly a vigilante who spends his nights beating criminals to a pulp with his bare hands. And your plan is to *blackmail* this person? Good luck." **Sardonically** as ever, French filmmaker Jean Cocteau said, "Emotion resulting from a work of art is only of value when it is not obtained by sentimental *blackmail*."

## BLIMP

*A lofty word, a down-to-earth origin story.* It comes from the World War I military program to develop a supremely lightweight flying machine. When first launched it apparently looked so awkward it was said to "limp" along in the sky. Thus the first experimental model earned the nickname "A-limp," which barely got off the ground and needed extensive redevelopment. The winning design was the "B-limp," which soon became our beloved *blimp*. The soaring humor of Dave Barry helps us visualize the word in an unusual way: "A full-grown manatee, which can weigh more than 1,000 pounds, looks like the result of a genetic experiment involving a **walrus** and a Goodyear *Blimp*." Companion words include *dirigible* and *air light vehicle*; Colonel *Blimp*, of the English war novels; *blimp*, a pejorative name for an overweight person; and *zeppelin*, a shortened version of the German *Zeppelinschiff*, a Zeppelin ship, which was named after the German general Count Ferdinand von Zeppelin, who improved its design.

## BLOVIATE

*To speak verbosely; to discourse in a pompous, empty, preten-
tious, or boastful manner.* A magniloquent word for using
loquacious language; to be a *windbag*, a word that goes all
the way back to Homer's *Odyssey*, the leather bag carried
by the god of the winds. Now, there I go, being long-
winded, as opposed to speaking succinctly. **Laconically**.
Concisely. "To swallow a dictionary," as they said in Johnson's day, was a tasty way to describe the use of pretentious
language. Originwise, *bloviate* is a back-formation from the
noun *blowhard*. While it's wise to be chary about *bloviating*
about *bloviating*, it is safe to say it is a colloquial Americanism used to ridicule intellectual pretension among
politicians, academics, or talking heads in the media. *The
Oxford English Dictionary* indicates that *bloviate* derives from
adding a faux-Latin ending to the verb to *blow*, or boast,
"following a 19th-century fad of adding Latin-like affixes
to ordinary words." The prolific but not particularly prolix
American journalist H. L. Mencken tracks the vivid verb
to President Warren G. Harding. Known for using "a
notoriously ornate and incomprehensible prose," Harding
coupled together *blow* and *ate* to make "windy speech."
Poet e. e. cummings eulogized him as "the only man,
woman or child who wrote a simple declarative sentence
with seven grammatical errors." An 1872 issue of the *Over-
land Monthly* magazine in San Francisco described a scene
from 1860: "It was a pleasure for him to hear the Doctor
talk, or, as it was inelegantly expressed in the phrase of

the period, *'bloviate'*...." A competing theory comes from word columnist William Safire, who claimed that *bloviate* derives from combining the words *blowhard* and *deviation*. The US editor of the *Daily Telegraph*, Toby Harnden, trumpeted the sometimes "blamestorming" power of the word when he wrote: "[Donald] Trump's *bloviating* about [President Barack] Obama's birth certificate made him look very foolish indeed—but not as foolish as those who suddenly started reporting the Birther madness as if there was some substance to it." Companion words include *booboisie*, a Menckenism for the uneducated mob, a combination of *boobs*, as in dolts, and *oisie*, the people, possibly those who populate a "boobopolis," a hick ***town***, according to *Mrs. Byrne's Dictionary*. Its antonym would be *breviloquence*, brief but effective speech. In a word, **laconic** instead of verbose, pithy versus prolix.

## BOGEYMAN

*One of the things that go bump in the night.* Often used as a threat to keep children quiet. "If you don't behave, the *bogeyman* is going to get you!" is what many of us heard when we were young'uns. Sonically, the word is memorable enough, probably because of the *Boo!* at the front, and terrifying to young children; for adults fascinated with word origins the consensus is that it derives from the *Bugis*, the ferocious pirates of southern Sulawesi, characters who attacked the British East India Company and Dutch vessels bound for the Spice Islands in the 17th century, and who plague wayward ships and yachts to this day. *Bugis* came to the docks of Europe like so much cargo, in Dutch as *boeman*, in Danish as *bohmand*, possibly in Ireland as *puca* or *pook*, and in English as *puck*, the name of a familiar **character** in Shakespeare. Its bloodcurdling roots reach down into the graveyard of Middle English etymologies: *bogge/ bugge*, a bony word that provides us with another that is shiver-inducing for some, *bug*. Thus it is generally thought to be a cognate of German *bögge*, *böggel-mann*, which came hauntingly into English as our beloved *bogeyman*. Not only that, but some scholars surmise that *bogeyman* has the same origin as *bugger*, from ME *bougre* (heretic, sodomite). This root story is in dramatic contrast to the one I heard from a Filipino deckhand while on a ship traveling through the Spice Islands, a tale that sounded virtually unchanged from the one that European sailors brought back in their deliberately ***horripilating*** stories about the "bugi men," or pirates, they had encountered on the high seas. However, etymologists are spooked by this apparition, because words relating to *bogeyman* were in common use centuries before European colonization of Southeast Asia. In a mind-bending episode of *The Simpsons* Bart pshaws the spiritual dimension: "There's no such thing as a soul. It's just something they made up to scare kids, like the *bogeyman* or Michael Jackson." Companion words include *booger, bugaboo,* and *bugbear.*

## BONFIRE

*An outdoor fire; a charnel.* For centuries criminals, witches, and enemies of the state or the church were publicly burned at the stake. The morbidly curious who poked around in the ashes noticed that the condemned one's bones were often the last thing to burn. Hence, a *bone fire*. Later, Henry VIII, as part of his break with the Church, ordered that books, pamphlets, and ecclesiastical relics be burned publicly, out of doors, and these too became known as *bone fires*. Eventually, all outdoor or open fires came to be known this way. It was a *bone fire* for plague victims, witches, and books alike until Dr. Johnson arbitrated and decided it should be *bon fire* in his *Dictionary of the English Language* (1755). Kathryn Hulme, author of *The Nun's Story*, writes, "Lourdes was a *bonfire* of thousands of candles and burning cries and a week of rising suns over an esplanade where stretcher cases lay side by side, end to end, waiting for a priest to come over with a monstrance that gathered sun to its gold and blazed in the sign of the cross above the stretchers."

## BOOK

*A collection of words printed on paper and bound by covers.* Tracing the roots of such an elemental word reminds me of what art critic Bernard Berenson called "the **aesthetic** moment," which he defined as "that flitting instant so brief as to be timeless, when the spectator is at one with the work of art." That's what happened when I discovered that *book* comes from the Anglo-Saxon *boc,* the bark of a beech tree, traditionally believed to have emerged into German as *buch*, from *Buche*, beech. The page turns, and we're into Old English *boc*, book, any written document. The notion is of beech-wood tablets on which runes were inscribed, but the word may come from the tree itself. (People still carve initials in them.) Latin and Sanskrit also have words for "writing" that are based on tree names (birch and ash, respectively). *Book*, meaning "libretto of an opera," dates from 1768. The self-taught Cherokee scholar Tecumseh described books as "talking leaves." The irrepressible Groucho Marx said, "I find television very educational. Every time someone turns on a set I go into the other room and read a *book*." The first essayist, Michel de Montaigne, wrote, "*Books* give not wisdome where none was there. But where there is, reading makes it before." My father was fond of the bookmarks handed out by his favorite bookstore in Dearborn, Michigan, which featured the words of Thomas Carlyle: "Blessings upon Cadmus or the Phoenicians or whoever it was that invented *books*." The tea cookie inspired Marcel Proust to write, in *In Search of Lost Time*, "It seemed to be that they would not be my readers, but readers of their own selves, my *book* being merely a magnifying glass." The ultimate mythologization of *books* is Jorge Luis Borges's *The Library of Babel*: "On some shelf, in some hexagon, it was argued, there must be a *book* that is a cipher and a compendium of all other *books*." Companion words include *book* as a verb, "to enter for a seat or place, issue tickets," from 1841; betting *book*, from 1856; *bookmaker,* 1862. A *bookkeeper* was originally someone who never returns a borrowed book. And finally, *chapbook*, a smallish book of political essays, poetry, adventures, traditionally around twenty-four pages, sold by the *chapman*, a simple peddler. Wilfred Funk suggests that the chapbook is the forerunner of comic books.

Book: *Amber Memory*

## BOUQUET

*A bunch of flowers, the fragrance of a wine or liqueur.* A lovely old collective noun, a hint of spring. A borrowed word from Middle French, "a little piece of woodland," and from Old French *boschet,* little wood, and Latin *boscus*, grove, which leaves us with the rustic *bosky*, woodlike. Introduced to the English language in 1716 by the ubiquitous Lady Mary Montagu, the famous traveler and ***champion*** of smallpox inoculations. Edward Lloyd, in 1895, lends another view, which is that *bouquet* refers to any clump or plantation of trees. Figuratively, a *bouquet* is a bunch of **beauty**, a handful of perfume, as Fifties poet Richard Brautigan wrote: "I picked / a *bouquet* / of kisses / off her mouth … *A handful of flowers.*" Groucho Marx cracked,

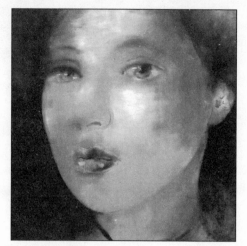

Bouquet: *Scarlet Shadow*

"In Hollywood, brides keep the *bouquets* and throw away the groom." "We sing and dance," wrote Pierre Bonnard, "make faces and give flower *bouquets*, trying to be loved. You ever notice that trees do everything to get attention we do, except walk?" Companion words include a mathematical term to describe the space built with the "wedge sum," a *bouquet* of circles.


## BUTTERFLY

*A nectar-feeding insect (superfamilies Papilionoidea and Hesperioidea, order Lepidoptera) with two pairs of large, typically colorful wings, held erect when at rest; active by day.* One of the most elusive of word origins; we'll need a *butterfly net* to **catch** it; or we'll need an entomologist to catch its etymology. Some say it derives from the Old English *buttorfleoge*, which at first blush resembles *butter* and *fly*, a lovely combination, lovelier than the other theory that traces the word back to the Old Dutch *botershitje*, butter shit. The latter possibly reflects a folk observation of exactly what it sounds like, the excrement left behind by an insect. One popular theory is based on an old superstition that butterflies are actually witches in disguise who eat uncovered butter or milk; the pale yellow color of many species' wings suggests the color of butter. I cast my net wide for the loveliest citation of this word and netted this one from the most famous lepidopterist of all time, the Russian novelist Vladimir Nabokov: "Literature and *butterflies* are the two sweetest passions known to man." The Hall of Famer Hoyt Wilhelm once described his famous knuckleball as "a *butterfly* with hiccups." Companion words and phrases include the *butterfly stroke*, in swimming circles dating back to 1936, and *butterflies*, "light stomach spasms caused by anxiety," from 1908. The "*butterfly* effect" was detected by an assistant professor in MIT's department of meteorology in 1961, Edward Lorenz, who created an early computer program to simulate weather and published his results in a 1972 paper, "Predictability: Does the Flap of a Butterfly's Wings in Brazil Set Off a Tornado in Texas?"

## BUXOM

*Bosomy, attractive, healthy.* Originally, *buxom* described the space embraced by the two outstretched arms, about six feet. The 12th-century Old English *buhsum*, humble, obedient, and *bugen*, to bend or comply, evolved together in a word that stretches out to mean robust, even lusty, health and comeliness, especially in women—and because of the wide girth of the embrace, a certain plumpness or **voluptuousness**. Altogether, a maternal, nurturing, warm clasp of a word that pulls you close, like a voluptuous (or what they used to call a *loveworthy* or *lovesome*) aunt hugging a bashful nephew. Poet John Milton wrote in *L'Allegro*, "There on beds of violets blue / And fresh-blown roses wash'd in dew / Fill'd her with thee, a daughter fair, / So *buxom*, blithe, and debonair." The original word has undergone linguistic cosmetic surgery. "Come to my *bosom*," people used to say," or in the safety of "Abraham's *bosom*." In *Othello*, Shakespeare writes: I shall bestow you where you shall have time / To speak of your *bosom* freely." In the 19th century people spoke of "*buxom* health," implying "cheerful comeliness," in the lovely words of the Irish writer Richard Trench. Companion words include *buxom bread,* the loaves of bread tucked inside the shirts of old-school stevedores; *bosom friend, a bosom buddy,* and *breastsummer,* a startlingly beautiful word for a *lintel,* the supporting block over a portal or door.

# C

## CAD

*A louse, cheater, **deadbeat**.* According to E. Cobham Brewer, in his indispensable *Dictionary of Fables* (1887), a *cad* is short for *cadaver*, a corpse. "Men, in university **slang**," he writes, "are sorted into two groups, those who are members of the university and those who are not. As the former are called *men*, the others must be *no men*, but they bear the human form, they are human bodies ('*cads*') though not human beings." So *cads* are dead weights, dead as a doornail. I'd be a *cad* if I didn't include a second root story, which gently rebukes the first one by suggesting that *cad* is short for *cadet*, someone who has never cultivated the so-called finer feelings, such as cultural ones like ***aesthetics***. Anthony West wrote in *H. G. Wells: Aspects of a Life*, "A *cad* used to be a jumped-up member of the lower classes who was guilty of behaving as if he didn't know that his lowly origin made him unfit for having sexual relation-

ships with well-bred women." *Death of a Cad* is a murder
mystery by M. C. Beaton published in 1987. Companion
words include *caddie*, a golfer's assistant, from the Scottish
*cadet*, the youngest son of serfs to serve in a manor house,
later drafted as *military cadet*. A caveat to golfers: hire a
caddie who is not a *cad*.

## CAFARD (FRENCH)

*Cockroach, depression, the blues. Avoir le cafard* is a colloquial
expression that means more than having a cockroach
problem in your **atelier**, and more than your standard
depleting depression. It's closer to B. B. King's blues, or
Simone de Beauvoir's existential **melancholy**. *To have the
cafard* has been an idiom since at least the time of the sple-
netic poet Charles Baudelaire, who used it in *Les Fleurs
du mal* to describe the **peculiar** pang of Parisian funk in
the city's smoky cafés, the zinc bar of loneliness. *Cafard*
conjures up a certain *je ne sais quoi*, such as a *poète manqué*
maundering away the day at La Coupole in Montparnasse.
Where there's smoke there's fire, as is the case with *cafard*,
which goes back to the Arabic *kabr,* a miscreant, nonbe-
liever, someone who only pretends to believe in God. How
could you use it today at Café Deux Magots? *Je ne peux
pas me concentrer aujourd'hui—j'ai le cafard*, which translates
as "I can't concentrate, I'm depressed; I have the blues."
Some cultures have built-in *remedies* for the blues, such as
the Scottish *tarantism*, the practice of lifting oneself out

of depression or melancholy by dancing the night away. Companion words include *mubblefubbles*, depression for no known reason, *blue devils,* demonic moods, or the *morbids*, as Edward Lear described the black cloud of depression: "I have the *morbids* again." *Chapfallen* is a "vaudible" word, visual and audible: dispirited, after the sad-sack look of a rooster with its dewlaps down.


## CAFÉ BEDOUINS

*A hip new breed of warrior-workers, neo-nomads fueled by caffeine, armed with laptops, camped out in the oasis of a café.* **Roaming** from café to café and borrowing a name from the nomadic Arabs who wandered freely in the desert, they've come to be known as *café Bedouins*, "café beds," for short. An article in the *San Francisco Chronicle* by reporter Dan Fost, on March 11, 2007, was a tocsin or a kind of Early Warning System for the new sightings in the city's bohemian quartiers: "where Neo-Nomads transform coffeehouses with laptops, cell phones, and **coffee**." Fost quoted Niall Kennedy, a 27-year-old San Franciscan, who dropped out of the system when he quit a good job at Microsoft to found a Web company, Hat Trick Media, which he runs out of a caravansary of cafés. "In *Lawrence of Arabia*," Kennedy said, "the Bedouins always felt like they were on the warpath ... They had greater cause." Kevin Burton, 30, declares, "At a startup, you're always on the go, plowing ahead, with some higher cause driving you. The San Francisco coffeehouse is the new Palo Alto garage" (referring to the legendary garage where Hewlett Packard was born). Burton runs his Internet startup Tailrank without renting offices. "It's where all the innovation is happening," he says. Companion words include *café tan*, the pallor of someone who has spent too much time indoors, and *bobo*, a, bourgeois bohemian; and *bobo*-a-go-go, the place where they congregate and gentrify.

## CAMOUFLAGE

*To disguise, mask, or hide.* Visual subterfuge. Concealment by blending in to make indistinguishable with the surroundings. Rarely can **slang** be tracked down to a single time or place; it usually sets up smoke screens to keep word warriors from discovering its ruses. Oddly enough, we can see through this *camouflage*. For years Parisians used to play a little social game in parlors or cafés called *camoufler*, French slang for "disguise," possibly a contraction of *capo muffare*, to muffle the head, from *camouflet*, puff of smoke. When the smoke clears we see an impudent social practice of literally blowing smoke in someone else's eyes to bother them—or provide a momentary smoke screen for something they want to hide. During World War I, Allied ships used smoke to disguise their whereabouts, and later flags and paint, which the British navy dubbed "dazzle painting." Singer Gloria Gaynor once used it figuratively: "That's why you find a lot of entertainers are

insecure, because it's the perfect *camouflage* for insecurity."
Companion words include *masquerade,* masking through
mummery or mimicry.

## CANTER

*A relaxed pace for a horse or a pilgrim.* Curiously, it is short for
*Canterbury pace*, or *Canterbury gallop*, reflecting the leisurely
speed of medieval pilgrims riding on the Old Kent Road
to Thomas Beckett's shrine in Kent. Let's not *lollygag*, or
*dawdle*, about this definition; let's get moving. The truncated version, *canter*, appears in Johnson's epic *Dictionary*,
in 1755, where he defined *Canterbury gallop* as "the gallop
of an ambling horse, commonly called a *canter.*" In *Canterbury Tales*, Chaucer's famous poem, a company of pilgrims
*canter* toward Beckett's shrine with *Canterbury bells* on their
horses, flowers resembling jangling bells on pilgrim horses,
a ritual that gave us the *Canterbury story*, a roundabout tale
trotted out for entertainment. Companion words include
**saunter**, walking slowly to the *Sainte-Terre* (Holy Land);
*progress*, walking a circuit of sacred sites; *ramble*, wander
around; and *caravan*, a group of travelers or pilgrims who
rest after their long day's journey (another **travel** word)
into night at a *caravansary*, an inn for travelers. "The *canter*
is a cure for every evil," said Benjamin Disraeli.

## CAPRICE

*A whim, an impetuous act.* An impulsive act that makes
people bristle. The word jumps at us from the Latin
*caprum*, of a goat, and *caprice*, free, fantastic style, from, of
course, beautiful island of Capri, famous for its gamboling
goats. Originally from the Greek *caper*, to move antically,
frightened or startled, *caprice* bounded into English from
the Italian *caporiccio*, from *capo*, head, and *riccio*, hedgehog.
A shiveringly clear image of someone scared—or exhila-
rated. Visualize a hedgehog and, ahem, you'll feel the true
roots of the word. What sets that frizzy animal apart from
all others is its spines or bristles, which resemble the ***horrip-
ilation*** of human hair standing on end when someone is
scared—or in awe, as when witnessing an impressive leap of
imagination. This frisky word inspired the French *cabriolet*
wagon (from *capriole*) that rolled over cobblestones, and the
Italian *capriole*, rolling over like a somersault, and *capriccio*,
which in Italy still refers to a startlingly spontaneous act, as
well as a musical term to describe improvisational playing.
Goya's *Los Caprichos* was a series of eighty aquatint prints
that satirized 17th-century Spanish mores and prefigured
modernism. The risible Oscar Wilde said: "The only
difference between a *caprice* and a lifelong passion is that a
*caprice* lasts a little longer." The capaciously minded historian Barbara Tuchman wrote, "Reasonable orders are easy
enough to obey; it is *capricious*, bureaucratic or plain idiotic
demands that form the habit of discipline." Companion
words include *capricious*, from the French *capricieux,* whim-

sical, liable to leap from one thing to another, idea to idea, lover to lover, like a goat kicking its heels in a stony field.

Caress

## CARESS

*To touch softly, feel with care, fondle.* As early as the 1640s, the seductive French word *caresse* appeared, from Italian *carezza*, from *caro*, dear, from Latin *carus*, **cant** for whore. The verb is 1650s, from French *caresser*, from Italian *carezzare*, endearment, from *carezza*. The last time I ventured across the ***garrulously*** green land of Ireland I was welcomed at the Ennis Inn with this traditional greeting from the pintman, "May the Irish hills *caress* you." Of all the writing instructions I've heard, my favorite is from Vladimir Nabokov, in his *Lectures on Literature* (1980): "*Caress* the details, the divine details." Companion words include the ***onomatopoeic*** *cosset* with its soft and sibilant "*ss*" sounds, like a lover's whisper, and the Irish *croodle*, to cuddle.

## CARIBOU (ALGONQUIAN)

*An Arctic deer with impressive antlers in both females and males, otherwise known as a reindeer.* One of a herd of American Indian words, including thousands of place names from coast to coast, plus hundreds of everyday English terms that have been absorbed into English over the last five hundred years. Dating back to the 1660s, *caribou* hails from the Micmac *kalpu* (Algonquian *kaleboo*), a pawer, scratcher or scraper, so called from its habit of kicking snow aside so it can feed on moss and grass. "I also don't trust *caribou* anymore," says Joss Whelan, the writer of *Buffy the Vampire Slayer*." They're out there, on the tundra, waiting ... Something's going down. I'm right about this." Companion words from our American Indian heritage include *moose,* from the Abenaki *mos*; *pecan,* from Illinois *pakani*; and *anorak*, from the Greenlandic Inuit *annoraq.*

## CARNIVAL

*A riotous ritual celebration of public revelry during the week before Lent.* A Saturnalia by any other name, a fest, a feast, a feat, a fête, all in one, over a night or a week. Feasting before fasting. Debauchery before deprivation. For *carnival* carries within it the period of "merrymaking in the days before Lent." The vegetarian-sounding Latin *carnem levare,* to remove *meat* from one's diet, provides the clue. Over time it has evolved into a word that describes any regular celebration, such as summer *carnivals* across America, but also orgies so salacious that *masks* are worn to protect the reputation of the revelers. After one such **bawdy** spree, Truman Capote wrote: "Venice is like eating an entire box of *chocolate* liqueurs in one go." Originally, it referred to the period in the Roman calendar when the faithful sacrificed meat for the forty days of Lent. Arianna Huffington posts, "The economic game is not supposed to be rigged like some shady ring toss on a *carnival* midway." Playwright David Mamet barks like a *carny,* "Films have degenerated to their original operation as *carnival* amusement—they offer not drama but **thrills**." Companion words include *carnival barker, carnal,* and *carrion.*

〜〜〜

## CAROUSE

*To party hearty; celebrate and jubilate.* The English expression *till all get out* lends a colorful hint to the curious roots of this vivifying verb. It stems from the German custom *trinken garaus,* from *gar,* completely, and *aus,* out, as in to "drink completely." Figuratively, it has come to mean, to put it bluntly, "Get out!"—of the bar or any other establishment that's closing. So *trinken garaus* evokes a rowdy drinking bout where everyone drinks everything in the house.

Carouse: *A Slip of Time*

Around 1567, it turned it into the elating word it is today. To this day, in England you might hear its equivalent, "Time's up, lads." In Ireland, "Drink up, lads, drink up." Compare the old *toast* "Bottoms up!" which is another exhortation to drink up and be gone with ye. All these exhortations are compressed into *carouse*, which is a hazy linguistic memory of those last few minutes of carrying on till closing time at the pub, bar, bierkeller, taverna, or café. *Carouse* goes beyond celebrating and takes the urge to drink and party to the limit—*until all get out*. D. H. Lawrence captured the roistering spirit of the spirits within the word when he wrote: "Temperance: Eat and *carouse* with Bacchus, or munch dry bread with Jesus, but don't sit down without one of the gods." Companion words include the archaic but still rollicking *mallemaroking*, the *carousing* of seamen on board Greenlandic whaling ships.

## CAROUSEL

*A merry-go-round; a revolving display case; a continuously turning conveyor for airport luggage.* This roundelay of meanings all evolved from a medieval tournament that will make your head spin. Around the 1640s, a *carousel* was "a playful tournament of knights in chariots or on horseback." The English word derived almost intact from the French *carrousel* and the Italian *carusiello*, both of which referred to a tilting or jousting match. Look closer and you'll **catch** a blurred image of the earlier Latin *carro*, or chariot, which was tapped for the English *car*. What couples these words is that they all **run** in a circle. The French linguist Emile Littre defined it as "a great festival solemnized with a [race] of chariots, horses, etc." The English lexicographer John Kersey wrote in 1772, "A tournament in which knights, divided into companies, distinguished by their liveries and dresses, engaged in various plays and exercises; to this were often added chariot races, and other shows and entertain-

Carousel: *World's Edge (Carousel, Santa Monica Pier)*

ments." For usage, we turn to one of the most prominent books in my own library, an early edition of J. D. Salinger's *Catcher in the Rye*: "Then the *carousel* started, and I watched her go round and round … All the kids tried to grab for the gold ring, and so was old Phoebe, and I was sort of afraid she'd fall off the goddamn horse, but I didn't say or do anything. The thing with kids is if they want to grab for the gold ring, you have to let them do it, and not say anything. If they fall off, they fall off, but it is bad to say anything to them." The irrepressible Erma Bombeck asked, "Did you ever notice that the first piece of luggage on the *carousel* never belongs to anyone?" Companion words include the now sadly anachronistic photographic *slide carousel,* and the wistful *Merry-Go-Sorry*, a story that conveys **happiness** and sadness at the same time, like one of those old chestnuts, jokes that begin with "I have good news and bad news." Spin the wheel and you find the British *giddy-go-round* and the Irish *merry begotten,* a **love** child.

## CARRYTALE

*Raconteur, spinner of **yarns**, tale-teller.* One of my ***carnivalesque*** candidates for word revival. Has a storyteller ever been better described than as someone who carries a tale or two or three in his satchel? Johnson defines one as a "tale-bearer," citing Shakespeare's *Love's Labour's Lost,* which reads: "Some carry-tale, some please-man, some slight zany, some mumble-news, some trencher-knight …" Across the

Irish sea the poets of old called him or her a *banaghan*, "a marvelous tale-teller." As Francis Grosse writes in his 1811 book on **slang**, "He beats Banaghan; an Irish saying of one who tells wonderful stories. Perhaps Banaghan was a minstrel famous for dealing in the marvelous." A *seanachie* is one who carries tales from *town* to town. Grosse also records the equally evocative *bowyer,* or bow man, and defines the word as "One that draws a long bow, a dealer in the marvelous, a teller of improbable stories, a liar, perhaps from the wonderful shots frequently boasted by archers." Companions around the hearth of this word include *anecdotist, annalist, fabulist, litterateur, mumblenews, mythmaker, penwoman, sagaman, scenarist, word painter, **yarner**,* and for some **peculiar** reason other than a perennial distrust of storytellers, a *Satan* or *Father of Lies!*

## CATAPHILE (FRENCH)

*A lover of catacomb crawling.* If you crossed a *pub crawler* with a *spelunker*, someone who explores caves, you would create a new breed, an urban adventurer who surreptitiously explores the underground world of modern cities. They are *cata,* cavern, and *philes*, lovers, self-described seekers who defy the warning above the entrance to the Paris catacombs: "Abandon hope all ye who enter." Over the past couple of decades they have snubbed the search for natural caves and searched the underbellies of New York's subways, Detroit's salt mines, and those tunnels cut into the basement of Paris, the much ballyhooed "Empire of Death." *The Week* magazine, July 1, 2011, describes the new hobby thus: "Down is the new up, in the City of Light, as locals and tourists are finding new ways to enjoy the underground maze of tunnels, caves, crypts, and abandoned quarries that lie below street level—sometimes far below … Paris' most intrepid spelunkers, known as *'cataphiles,'* treat the vast subterranean underworld as a playground." Companion words include *catanyms*, or cave handles, nicknames, for those who explore the catacombs, such as "Lézard Peint," or "Painted Lizard." *Cataclysmic* might refer to the experience of a *cataphile*, a lost soul in the *catacombs* of life.

## CHAMPION

*The winner in a game or competition; one who triumphs over all comers.* The triumphant noun is a trumpet blast of celebration, rooted in the very ground of France, the *champs*, or field. A citing from 1895 says it originally referred to "one who lives on open ground." Later, it came to refer to one who stands up to deny all who challenge the throne. In *Altered English,* Jeffrey Kacirk cites Low and Pulling (1904), who wrote, "The *champion* of England is an officer whose business it is to appear at the coronation of a sovereign, and challenge all comers to deny the new ruler's title. The office is an ancient one, popularly supposed to have been instituted by William the Conqueror." Slow your pronunciation of the word and allow it to echo in your inner ear: you might hear Freddie Mercury's soaring voice singing the worldwide anthem "We Are the *Champions*." Companion words include *champ*, to chew or bite, which is what a *champion* does when the game is on the line. A *champion* champs at the bit of victory.

## CHAPARRAL

*A close, dense thicket of small evergreen oaks and other shrubby plants characteristic of Southern California and Baja California.* Where the land is dry and studded with shrub it makes for fertile grazing. The Basques shepherded the word into English. The old-as-stone Basque word for dwarf evergreen trees, *txaparro,* grew into the Spanish *chaparro*, and immigrated to America with the Basque shepherds, many of whom now work in the remote *chaparral* countryside of the American West. The popular TV show *High Chaparral* featured this exchange between two cowboys in its first season: Killian: "I've got a sister that can out rope and out ride the best man High *Chaparral* ever saw." Joe: "Oh, I'll admit your sister's a better man than you, Killian." In *The Pacific Coast Trail*, William R. Gray writes, "Fragrant with sage, a rippling breeze played among low hills blanketed by *chaparral*."

Chaparral: *Le Piedras del Cielo*

## CHARTREUSE

*A pale apple-green* **color***; an aromatic liqueur produced by French Carthusian monks.* In 1866 the monastery of the Grande-Chartreuse, so called because of its proximity to the nearby Chartreuse Mountains, concocted an herbal liqueur called *Les Pères Chartreux* from their apple orchards. The proceeds from its sales went to the maintenance of the monastery and the rest to charity. Eighteen years later, 1884, the liqueur went into commercial production producing a **color** as **intoxicating** as the drink, distilling a new word in honor of the monks' delectable work. *Blue Cats and Chartreuse Kittens* is a book by Patricia Lynn Duffey that explores the **strange** and wonderful ways that synesthetes "color their world." Companions include the illuminated medieval Book of Hours "The Grand *Chartreuse*," by the Limbourg Brothers, and "The Grande Chartreuse," a poem by Matthew Arnold. And colorwise, *incandescent*, glowing, from *candescere*, to make white.


## CHASTITUTE (IRISH)

*A celibate layperson.* A much-needed word to describe those who not only choose the celibate life, but claim moral superiority for having done so. Irish novelist John B. Keane used this word in *Letters of A Love-Hungry Farmer* to describe the "name given by the local parish priest ... to those without orders who chose celibacy before marriage, love affairs or promiscuity, and were **peculiar** only to country places in Ireland, Spain, Portugal, etc, where the Catholic tradition of lifelong sexual abstinence was encouraged." The humor writer Peter De Vries cracked, "Celibacy is the worst form of self-abuse." The magnificent Mae West murmured, "I used to be Snow White, but I drifted." Companion words include *chastitution*, abstinence, as in "The whole countryside is reeking with *chastitution*," as one informant, Jaz Lynch, cracked to me at The Stag's Head, in Dublin.


## CHECKMATE

*The clinching move from which there is no escape in a game of chess.* The winning move, which has come to mean figuratively to outwit, foil, or beat back a challenge. To follow the word's meandering course is to retrace the evolution of English itself and the mysterious force behind words that imply movement. Its ultimate source is the Persian *shah mat*, "The king is dead!" or alternatively, "The king is left helpless, the king is slumped over." Its penultimate source is the Old French *eschec mat,* and as the game became more popular the term moved into Spanish and Portuguese, where it was translated as *xaque mate*, which is only a few letter-moves on the Scrabble board or keystrokes on your laptop away from *checkmate*. Leave it to our court jester Stephen Colbert to find humor in the word: "As God said to Job, '*Checkmate!*'" Isaac Asimov, arguably the record-holder for most books published in a lifetime (over four hundred), wrote: "In life, unlike in chess, life continues after *checkmate*." Companion words include *woodpusher*, a poor chess player.

## CHIAROSCURO

*The dramatic treatment of light and shade in art.* Hearing or reading this melodic word, most of us think of Rembrandt's paintings or Chandler's books rendered in film noir. Both are *achieved* by strong contrasts and bold arrangements of light and shadow, or having the light fall in a **skewed**, uneven, or even dizzying direction, like the shots in *The Third Man*, or Da Vinci's use of it to create an uncanny sense of *volume* or three-dimensionality. According to James

Smith Pierce's clarion-clear definition in his architectural dictionary, *From Abacus to Zeus, chiaroscuro* is "the treatment, especially gradation, of light and dark in a picture." English novelist Somerset Maugham used the word figuratively in *The Gentleman in the Parlour*: "Mandalay has its name; the falling cadence of the lovely word has gathered about itself the *chiaroscuro* of romance." In *Leonardo da Vinci*, art historian Kenneth Clark defended the master's experiments in painting, "Much of Leonardo's most sensitive and unacademic use of *chiaroscuro* dates from long after his investigations into its nature." Companion words include *skiography*, which derives from one of the few names of Greek painters that have miraculously survived, Apollodoros Skiagraphos, an artist who flourished in the 5th century BCE. None of his paintings survive, but his technique lives on in the word *skiagraphia*, literally shadow writing, which shows the flickering nature of immortality. *Sfumato* is Italian for "gone up in smoke," a smokier *chiaroscuro*, "a sensuous softness," writes Pierce, "and at times a tantalizing ambiguity," such as Mona Lisa's smile. Companion words include *sfumaiezza*, the blending of colors.

## CHOCOLATE

*For lovers of the beatifically brown bean it is* theobroma, *the drink of the gods.* A delicious word brought back to the Spanish court by the conquistador Hernán Cortés around 1520, a word he encountered in the courts of Aztec nobility who

Chocolate: *Portrait of Yareli Arizmendi (Like Water for Chocolate)*

accepted cacao pods as tribute from the farthest reaches of their empire. The delectable drink made from the paste of roasted cacao seeds spread across Europe. Its fame is echoed in the Spanish proverb "Like water for *chocolate*," a **metaphor** for the boiling point of human emotions. The word has been boiled down from the Nahuatl *xocaliai,* to make bitter, and *atl*, water, a reminder of how it tasted before sugar and milk were added. On November 24, 1664, Samuel Pepys recorded a visit in his pointillistic *Diary*, "To a **Coffee**-house, to drink *jocolatte*, very good." Companion words include *chocolatier*, attested to in 1888; *chocolate chip*, in 1940. A sexy tribute comes from Marilyn Monroe, who was dining with Fred Astaire, Clark Gable, and Arlene Dahl and overheard them talking about Walt Whitman. "Oh, Whitman," she cooed, "I just love his *chocolates*."

## CHUTZPAH

*Spunk, daring, fearlessness; brass balls.* This audacious Yiddish word derives from *khutspe*, impudence, gall, from Hebrew *hutspah*. Only a *schmendrik*, foolish, clueless, naive, would object. In the immortal words of Oscar Levant, often attributed to Leo Rosten, *chutzpah* is "that quality enshrined in a man who, having killed his mother and father, throws himself on the mercy of the court because he is an orphan." In his commencement speech to the 1980 class at Connecticut College actor Alan Alda urged the students to live a bold life: "I want you to have *chutzpah*. Nothing important was ever accomplished without *chutzpah*. Columbus had *chutzpah*. The signers of the Declaration of Independence had *chutzpah*. Don't ever aim your doubt at yourself. Laugh at yourself, but don't doubt yourself. Whenever you wonder about yourself, look up at the stars swirling around in the heavens and just realize how tiny and puny they are."

## CLIMAX

*An exciting result, epitome, acme.* From the Latin, originally used in the late 16th century in a rhetorical sense; as the OED has it: "a series of propositions rising in force and effectiveness." This rising sense of effectiveness is a reflection of its Greek roots in *klimax*, literally a ladder. The painted word here provides a vivid picture of ideas or emotions rising, climbing rung by rung to the top, hinted at in its ultimate source, *klinein*, to slope, to lean, like a ladder against a wall. These associations led to the English meaning of a "series of steps by which a goal is achieved," and then onward and upward to "escalating steps." Curiously, this popular, bordering on jocular, refining of the word around 1789 to mean the highest point, the top rung of the ladder, the acme of pleasure, was described rather puritanically by the OED "from popular misuse of the learned word." The sexual rise or descent, depending on your proclivities, into the verb *to climax* is recorded in 1835. Over the next few decades the word gets more and more excited until it peaks with *climaxing*, in 1918. That was the year that Scottish birth-control pioneer Marie Stopes chose it as a more accessible and vivid word than *orgasm* for the culmination or consummation of climbing the ladder of pleasure. A dramatic use of the word was coined by famed producer Samuel Goldwyn, who once said, "We want a story that starts out with an earthquake and works its way up to a *climax*." On the musical side, Jim Morrison of the Doors crooned, "When play dies it becomes the Game. When sex dies it becomes *Climax*." Charlotte Brontë wrote in *Jane Eyre*, using the word in its earlier sense, "This was the *climax*. A pang of **exquisite** suffering—a throe of true despair—rent and heaved my heart." Companion words include *anticlimax*, which actor Scott Roeblen uses to admit, "I'm a terrible lover. I've actually given a woman an anticlimax."

## COBALT

*A spritely blue, an otherworldly bluish-green pigment.* For centuries the mineral used as a glaze for ceramics, decorative beads, statuary, and frescoes, most famously in ancient Egypt, Persia, and Pompeii. Ironically, *cobalt* is often said to resemble the **color** of the sky on a clear day—ironic since the word comes from the silver mines of Germany, where smelted ore that didn't give up any metal was traditionally ascribed to a *Kobold*, a mischievous spirit believed to hex the life of miners because of their presence near the ore. The lustrous word shines a flickering blue light on the path that some words take, beginning as one thing and then taking on another thing altogether. The Irish recipient of the Nobel Prize in Literature Seamus Heany writes unforgettably of "the living *cobalt* of the afternoon." Companion words include *kohl*, the Egyptian mineral used for eyeliner millennia ago.

## COFFEE

*A tree, a beverage, a way of life.* A beverage and a word that seems to have been around forever, but dates back only to 1598, when it appeared on the doorsteps of Europe as the Turkish *kalve,* from Arabic *qalwa,* and eventually Italian *caffè.* The crop grows in the tropics; the beverage is made in a café by percolation, infusion, or decoction from the roasted and ground seeds of any of several Old World tropical plants (genus *Coffea,* especially *C. arabica* and *C. canephora).* Its storied roots lie in the hills of Ethiopia, where, it is said, a goatherd noticed his flock capering about one afternoon. Wondering what had made them so *capricious,*

Coffee

goatlike, he watched them chewing a red berry from a bush. The roots of the word *coffee* probably come from the soil of Dutch *koffie*, from Turkish *kaveh*, and earlier from Arabia, where it was considered a kind of wine. Recently, when the *Washington Post* ran its annual contest in which readers are asked to provide alternate meanings to familiar words, the hyperfamiliar *coffee* was redefined as "a person who is coughed on." Companion words include *coffee-housing*, a reputedly invidious mind-game tactic of replicating café chatter in the world of competitive Scrabble, popularized by Stefan Fatsis, in *Word Freak*; and *a cup of coffee*, a brief time in the major leagues. Coffee entered the Western world during the Siege of Vienna, in 1529, when the marauding Turkish soldiers left their sacks of *coffee beans* behind when they were repelled at the gates of the city. The next day the victorious Austrians celebrated with **croissants**, as a tribute to the crescent moon that shone above the city the night of the attack. *Coffeehouse*, in merry old England, was vulgar **slang** for a woman who was taken advantage of, suggestive of "coming and going and spending nothing."

## CLEW

*Thread; hint; the way out.* An unfamiliar word that suddenly sounds familiar the minute you enunciate it, *clew* refers to the gold thread that the Minoan princess Ariadne handed as a **ball** of **yarn** to the Greek **hero** Theseus to help him escape the **labyrinth** after he slew the dreaded Minotaur. If you follow the long thread of this backstory far enough, you not only escape ancient Crete but eventually reach England and the English word *clue*, which is defined as a *ball* of thread, from the Old English *cleowen*, and then on into Modern English: "evidence that helps solve a problem; to roll into a *ball*, direct, guide, as if by a thread." The OED defines *clew* as a "ball of thread or *yarn*," which when unraveled goes back to a northern English and Scottish relic of Old English *cliewen,* a sphere, ball, skein. Its spelling changed to the more familiar form around the same time that *blew* became *blue*, and *trew* turned to *true*. Sir Arthur Conan Doyle provides his detective Sherlock Holmes with this insight into the powers of deduction: "Singularity is almost invariably a *clue*. The more featureless and commonplace a crime is, the more difficult it is to bring it home." Companion phrases include "I haven't got a clue," which is to say, "I haven't got a way to get out of the labyrinth that I'm in." Another way to think about the *clew* is "the ineluctable theme of the spiral," as Paul Valéry writes, the path to the center.

## COLLECTIVE NOUNS

*A special class of words used to colorfully describe groups of objects, people, emotions, and concepts, but most memorably and notably, animals.* The English language is studded with terrific group nouns, which faintly echo the terminology of

Collective Nouns: *The Existentialist Seeking His Essence (Portrait of Cassiel Chadwick)*

medieval hunters, originally called *terms of venery,* or *venery nouns.* The first known collection appeared in an 1801 book by Joseph Strutt, *The Sports and Pastimes of the People of England;* another appeared in the classic by Eric Partridge, *Usage and Abusage: A Guide to Good English*, in 1942. More recently, James Lifton published *A Parliament of Owls*, which has proved wildly popular and gone through several new and expanded editions. Classic collective nouns for animals include *a crash of rhinoceros, a parliament of owls, a skulk of foxes, a skein of geese, a zeal of zebras*; human ones include *an oversight of academics, a trove of libraries, an essence of existentialists, a discord of experts, a conjunction of grammarians, a banner of knights, a drift of lecturers, a lapsus of linguists, a logorrhea of lexicographers, an **abomination** of monks, a walk of **peripatetics**, a gloss of philologists, a brood of researchers, a scrum of philosophers*, and *a bliss of unicorns*. Recent coinages include *a **sandlot** of Little Leaguers, a couch of video game players*, and *a cuddle of homecoming queens*.

## COLOR

*The sensation produced by the effect of light waves striking the retina of the eye.* Webster offers a poetic definition: "The phenomena of light ... that enables one to differentiate between otherwise identical objects ..." But if we turn to a poet and painter, William Blake, we find a more succinct and mysterious description: "Colors are the wounds of light." This is the essence of poetic paradox, imagery and incisive psychological insight. It's technically true that "the *color* of something depends mainly on which wavelengths of light it emits, reflects, or transmits; the hue of something." But it isn't as psychologically true as the quote by the *colorstruck* Blake, cited above, or the *lightstruck* Pierre Bonnard's definition-defying description of *color*: "It's *color* but it's not yet light." Tracing the word back to its origins is like sending a satellite to orbit

Color: *The Wounds of Light*

the sun to investigate the origins of light. The word *color* dates back to the early 13th century, when it was used to describe the shades of skin color, hueing from Old French *color*, color, complexion, appearance, whence it came into Modern French *couleur* from Latin *color*, from the earlier Old Latin *colos*, a covering, akin to skin, from *celare*, to hide, conceal. So *color* reveals our fascination with something as elemental as the complexion of skin, which hides or covers, from the Sanskrit *varnah*, covering (and **varnish**), and *vrnoti*, cover, and eventually *chroma*. Not until the early 1300s did *color* refer to the visible hue in English, and only later did it become the name for a "substance, such as a dye, pigment, or paint, that imparts a hue." Incidentally, a hue is a *pure color,* and *chroma* is the strength of the *color.* Georgia O'Keefe told the filmmakers who made the 1977 documentary *O'Keefe*, "I found I could say things with *color* and shapes that I couldn't say any other way—things I had no words for." Impressionist Claude Monet was haunted by it: "*Color* is my day-long obsession, joy, and torment." **Fascinatingly**, there is a word for the study of the reactions of people to various *colors* of the spectrum, which is, wonderfully, *prismatism.* Or as the Irish folksinger Luka Bloom croons, "It's a rainbow day ..."

## COMEDY

*A humorous performance; a funny celebration.* Rarely do word origins provide immediate comic relief, but this one, by definition, does, rooted as it is in the Greek *kome*, village, and *ode. Comedy* comes from "village songs" or "the songs of the village," which must have originally been humorous, even **bawdy.** This is a reference to the origins of comic theater itself, the communal and ritual merrymaking in ancient Greece. The **encyclopedic** E. Cobham Brewer defined *comedy* as "village merrymaking in which songs take central place." Cultural historian Joseph Meeker, in *The Comedy of Survival,* writes, "*Comedy* promotes survival not merely as a continuation of existence, but also as an affirmation of life and joy, despite the disasters that may occur." The last word goes to Charlie Chaplin: "Life is a tragedy when seen in close-up, but a *comedy* in long shot."

Consider: *Under the Lapis Sky*

## CONSIDER

> *To think over; to divine from gazing at the stars; to think under the heavens.* The Romans, like the Greeks before them, had a multitude of divination techniques. One of the most popular was astrology, referred to in Latin as *considerare*, from *con* with, *sider*, stars, which involved charting the course of the stars and planets and drawing **augurs** from the findings, what Cawdrey adeptly called *auguration*, "guessing or conjecturing at things to come." By language's own natural attrition it came to mean simply *observe*, but, hmm, with a little nudge it could again take on its earlier meaning of "deep contemplation under the stars." Henry Beston writes in *The Outermost House*, "*Consider,* the marvel," and then proceeds to unfold the marvelous world of the Eastern seashore. *"Consider this, consider this …,"* REM pleads in their anthem "Losing My Religion": think hard, think hard about the immortal questions.

## COPACETIC

> *In excellent condition, satisfactory, edging toward* **cool**. Unswervingly **hip**. Theories abound, its origins confound. It is *copacetic* for us to review a few. First recorded in 1919, in Irving Bacheller's biography of Abraham Lincoln: "As to looks I'd call him, as ye might say, real *copasetic*." Though there is little consensus, it is probably rooted in 19th-century American English and Southern black **slang,** when it meant "as it should be." The linguist Robert Chapman suggests that

❦

Copacetic

it "may have been acquired by the black customers of a Jewish merchant." Origin theories include Latin, Yiddish, Italian, and playwright David Mamet's contribution that it is a contraction of "All is well, for the Cop is on the settee." Others believe it derives from the Hebrew *kol b'seder*, "All is in order." The French phrase *"comme c'est sympathique"* has been tossed around for its melodic echo as a possible source for *copacetic*, but if you can cope with more possibility, my vote is for the Cajun French *coupe-setique*, able to cope with. Word maven Eric Partridge believed that *copacetic* is a **portmanteau**, joining *cope* and *antiseptic* to create a rhythmic slang word for "excellent, all right," or "all safe or all clear." A syncopated though unattributed theory suggests its origins lie in black speech, underscored by song-and-dance man Luther Bill "Bojangles" Robinson's claim to have coined it while working as a shoeshine boy in Richmond, Virginia. Mr. Bojangles claimed to have used it so often in his performances that he gave a kind of finger-snap approval to it, but many Southerners have since chimed in that their parents or grandparents used it long before this. John O'Hara wrote in his huge 1934 novel, *Appointment in Samarra*, "You had to be a good judge of what a man was like, and the English was *copasetic*."

## CRAQUELURE (FRENCH)

*The pattern of cracking in paintings; art's stress marks.* Another *whatchamacallit* word. For anyone who has ever peered closely at an Old Masters painting and wondered if there was a word to describe the alligator skin–like patterns that sometimes appear all over the surface or in a few areas, you can rest assured that a sonicky one does exist. *Craquelure* sounds already ***varnished***, a word dignified and elegant we can wedge into English because we don't have one that even approximates the subtlety. Art historians tell us that the pattern of cracks is the result of aging paint, and depends on whether the painting was laid down on canvas or wood, as well as the type of paint. In *The Forgery of Venus,* Michael Gruber fictionalizes the story of a fake Velasquez, using the fractured word to reveal the secret of the forger: "He shrugged impatiently. 'Oh, Christ, anything can be faked. Anything. But as a matter of fact I painted it in 1650, in Rome. It has genuine 17th-century Roman grime in the *craquelure.* The woman's name is Leonora Fortunati.' He turned away from the posters and looked at me. 'You think I'm crazy.' 'Frankly, yes. You even look crazy. But maybe you're just drunk.'" Companion words include *craquelure anglaise*, notably present in the paintings of 18th-century English painters such as Sir Joshua Reynolds.

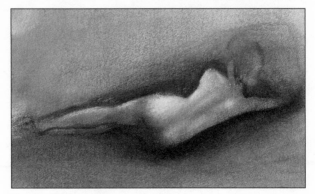

Craquelure: *The Forgery of Venus*

## CROISSANT

*A buttery, crescent-shaped bread.* This leavened puff pastry consists of butter and yeast dough, growing into a crescent shape when baked, like the moon each month. The correspondence is no mere coincidence. Although there are scattered breadcrumbs of evidence that crescent-shaped loaves have been around for centuries, legend has it that birth of our beloved *croissant* occurred in 1839, when August Zang, an Austrian artillery officer, established Boulangerie Viennoise, a Viennese Bakery, at 92 rue de Richelieu in the heart of Paris. Zang's specialty was a scrumptious connection, Viennese *kipferl*, the Vienna loaf, which became the talk of the **town**, spurring other bakers to imitate Zang's pastries and breads, which were called *viennoiserie*. Soon, Parisian bakers had their own version of the *kipferl*, so named for its crescent shape, an echo of a crescent moonlit night on which Austrians repelled the Turks. Musing about the humorous side of the noble bread in New York, Fran Lebowitz writes, "Do you know on this one block you can buy *croissants* in five different places? There's one store called Bonjour Croissant. It makes me want to go to Paris and open up a store called Hello Toast."

## CURFEW

*A law or regulation requiring people to extinguish fires at a set time, or the said hour at which church bells tolled.* A blazing origin from the Old French *couvre feu*, to cover the fire, dating back to 1608, when it was written, "Tis time to ring *curfew*." Over time the word lost some of its heat, though its original meaning was never extinguished. Even today it refers to the strict time people are required to retreat inside, such as during war or a state of emergency. To give teenagers a *curfew* is a signal that if their fire isn't put out by midnight, figuratively speaking, there will be hell to pay. The English poet Thomas Gray wrote, "The *curfew* tolls the knell of parting day, / The lowing herd winds slowly o'er the lea. / The ploughman homeward plods his weary way, / And leaves the world to darkness and to me." Psychologist James Hillman issues a caveat: "All we can do when we think of kids today is think of more hours of school, earlier age at the computer, and *curfew*. Who would want to grow up in that world?"

## CURRICULUM

*A career; a running list of accomplishments.* The Old French *carière* was a road used to carry things, stemming from the Latin *carrus*, a car. It also referred, in falconry, to the flight of a bird of about 120 yards; a higher flight was called a *double-career*. When a term was needed to describe the courses offered in schools, which often **run** with a learning curve, *curriculum* was the obvious choice. A course on which a race is **run**. Every careening **pun** intended. The word dashes down to us from classical Latin *curriculum*, "a running course, a career," which is also related to *careering*, as in a fast chariot or race car, *a currere*. To say that one's career is in the fast lane, then, would be redundant. Its usage is collegiate, dating back to Scottish universities of the 1630s. Hence, it is not too much to say that a *curriculum vitae* reveals the current of one's life, one's curve of learning. The earliest modern reference is 1824. Companion words include *curriculum vitae*, in common parlance a list of one's jobs or expertise or grades, but literally *the running of one's life*, or the *way one's life has **run***: one's career, which may be either racing ahead or running behind. The lonely starlet Marilyn Monroe expressed doubt about her fame when she said, "A *career* is wonderful, but you can't curl up with it on a cold night."

# D

## DAISY

*A diminutive grassland plant whose flower* (Chrysanthemum leucanthemum) *features a yellow disk and bold white rays.* Generations of acute folk observation revealed that the petals of this lovely flower close tight at night, then open again at dawn. Early on, this realization led to its Greek name, *khrysanthemon*, golden flower, and then the Old English name *dægesege*, from *dæges eage*, or *day's eye*. Combining the two we can see a flower that resembles the daily beauty of the golden eye of the sun. Its Latin roots sound like an architectural feature, *solis oculus*, eye of the sun. Here is a poetic observation of the yellow "eye" staring out of the center of the plant, as if Mother Nature herself was looking at us—and winking. Companion words include the name *Daisy,* a pet form of Margaret. The colorful term *daisy-cutter* goes back to 1791 and described horses that trotted with low steps, and was later picked up by cricket players around 1889, and later by baseball players to describe hits that skip and skim along the ground. The phrase "pushing up daisies," presumably referring to what a corpse does in a cemetery, has been pushed up into usage and can be traced all the way to 1842. Finally, the flower inspired the popular lover's game of plucking its petals, while chanting "He loves me, he loves me not," which sounds even more romantic in French, "*Effeuiller la marguerite*," literally, *"to rip off the leaves of the daisy."*

## DANDELION

*A brilliant, many-rayed yellow flower (Taraxacum officinale) with notched, toothlike foliage, often used to make wine or a garnish in salads.* A shepherd or a poet must have noticed its resemblance to teeth, let's say of an angry open-mouthed beast. Hence, *dandelion*, from the Old French *dent de lion*, which derived from Latin *dent*, tooth, *de*, of, *leonis*, lion. Altogether we get one of our most colorful painted words. Henry Ward Beecher described the flowers with flair: "You cannot forget if you would those golden kisses all over the cheeks of the meadow, queerly called *dandelions*." Emily Dickinson poetizes: "The *dandelions*' pallid tube / Astonishes the grass, / And winter instantly becomes / An infinite alas."

## DEADBEAT

*A worthless, sponging idler.* Ironically, this spineless word has a strong linguistic spine that helps it stand up straight in the history of words. Socially lethal, it harkens back to the American Civil War, when *beat* meant swindle or cheat, or referred to soldiers who shirked duty, or worse, avoided battle, by faking illness: shirkers who *beat* the system, then *beat* a path home. Galway's *Valiant Hours* (1862) sets the type: "The really sick and the habitual *deadbeats*, anxious to escape duty, are marched from each company by a sergeant to the Surgeon." Around 1877, *deadbeat* is recorded as American **slang** to describe someone completely beaten, dead tired, from *dead* and *beat*. Inevitably, folks recognized its metaphorical possibilities, and soon it came to mean someone who fails to pay personal debts. A century later, the term *beat* took on a new rhythm when it was immortalized by the *San Francisco Chronicle's* beloved columnist and Pulitzer Prize winner, Herb Caen. On April 2, 1958, he made the first reference to the bongo-beating poets of North Beach: "*Look* magazine ... hosted a party ... for 50 *Beatniks*, and by the time word got around ... over 250 bearded cats and kids were on hand, slopping up Mike Cowles' free booze. They're only *Beat*, you know, when it comes to work." Companion words include *deadbeat dads,* **deadpan,** and the mordant barroom term *deadfall,* to describe the drop through a trapdoor into a chamber where drunk sailors were stowed until they were **shanghaied** by disreputable ship captains.

## DEADLINE

*The cutoff point, finale, limit, the time when time is up.* A magical word for me, since I've been writing against *deadlines* since I was a sixteen-year-old cub reporter. Furthermore, I was haunted enough by them to name one of my early books *Deadlines: A Rhapsody on a Theme of Last Words.* Little did I know, less did I appreciate, that a *deadline* is a Civil War term for the seventeen-foot limit on the battlefield beyond which a soldier would be shot and behind which soldiers *hightailed* it out of danger. This *No Man's Land* was a **rhapsody** on the printer's term *no man's line,* which applied to the guideline on the bed of a cylinder printing press over which the prepared type surface should not pass. The American press captured the expression to denote the time by which all copy had to be ready for inclusion in a particular issue of a publication—or a story would be "killed" or "spiked," morbid newsroom expressions with unfortunate echoes of war. Nowadays the term is applied to tasks or payments that have strict time limits. Feminist icon Rita Mae Brown suggests, "A *deadline* is negative inspiration. Still, it's better than no inspiration at all." Off-Hollywood director Francis Ford Coppola said, "It's ironic that at age thirty-two, at probably the greatest moment of my career, with *The Godfather* having such an enormous success, I wasn't even aware of it, because I was somewhere else under the *deadline* again."

Deadline: *Drum Taps*

## DEADPAN

*Straight-faced; emotionless; dry* **wit**. Have you wondered, as **laconic** comic (lacomic?) Stephen Wright has, "How come *abbreviated* is such a long word?" If you have, and if you just laughed, then you appreciate *deadpan* humor, an expression whose meaning comes alive when you *consider* its *deadly* origins, in *dead,* lifeless, and *pan,* **slang** for the face. A lifeless face, but a livelier word, even a painted word, nonpareil. *Deadpan* dates back to the 1920s as a theater term for a form of comic delivery in which humor is presented without a change in emotion or body language, usually speaking in a casual monotone or in a solemn manner. Sometimes blunt. Other times disgusted. Delivered in a lethally matter-of-fact voice. Unflappably **calm**. If you're not laughing anymore, let's return to our regularly scheduled program featuring more of the droll genius of Stephen Wright: "Why are there five syllables in the word *monosyllabic*?" Often when I think of *deadpan*, I think of my late friend Danny Sugerman, the Doors biographer, who once groaned while we were drinking double Scotches at Cafe Figaro, in Hollywood, "I'm so tired I couldn't play dead."

## DEBACLE

*Disaster, collapse, an explosive incident.* A percussive word that *sounds* ominous, as is vindicated by its violent backstory. Today a *debacle* refers to a sudden breaking loose or bursting forth that destroys barriers; a violent dispersion or disruption; an impetuous rush; an explosive outburst. Each of these images reveals an aspect of how it burst into English from the Middle French *débâcler*, to unbar or unblock, as in the breaking up of ice on a river. For me, *debacle* is one of those vivid "observation words" that resulted from countless generations noticing the **caprices** of nature, in this case the often violent consequences of a springtime thaw of river ice that releases tremendous amounts of water downriver. Eventually, this image of violent destructive forces led to its figurative meaning of "downfall" or "disaster." Czech novelist Milan Kundera writes, "Mankind's true moral **test**, its fundamental test (which lies deeply buried from view), consists of its attitude toward those who are at its mercy: animals. And in this respect mankind has suffered a fundamental *débâcle*, a *débâcle* so fundamental that all others stem from it." To describe the disastrous drop in DVD sales, a September 2011 article in *Market Watch* was titled "Netflix and Qwikster, a deliberate *debacle*? Brand confusion may be a way to rapidly kill DVDs."

## DECREPIT

*Aged, weak, muted.* The only time most modern people ever hear or use this word is when it is coupled with "old," as in the usually pejorative phrase "old and *decrepit*." A closer look reveals a literary palimpsest, a word underneath the original form, with tinctures of real beauty: the Latin *decrepitus,* old, infirm, from *de*, away, and *crepare,* break down, and *itus*, a noise. As defined by Edward Lloyd in his 1895 *Lloyd's Encyclopaedic Dictionary, decrepit* is being "unable to move or stir, or make a noise, broken down by age or infirmities." Now what we find is a poignant image of the decrepit as broken down and unheard, which is to say feeble and silent. A skeletal word now takes on flesh and blood, as heartbreaking as it may be, perhaps one of Rembrandt's broken beggars on the cobbled streets of Amsterdam, or Käthe Kollwitz's concentration camp prisoners. Ironically, this enfeebled word is a strong **meta-phor** used to describe our urban environment, as in a *decrepit* building, which sounds close to *derelict* and is just as silent when abandoned. Companion words include *decrepitation*, the crackle of burning wood or coal.

## DELIRIUM

*A state of unrest, unsteadiness, craziness.* Someone swept up in a *delirium* is unsteady, emotionally and physically, which eerily corresponds to the unsteady lines in a plowed field left behind by a staggering plowman. The term dates back to Roman farmers who took as much pride in their straight and narrow furrows as Roman road makers took in their straight roads, or a swordsmith in the straightness of his blades. To be *delirious* means to be crazy, mad, raving, from *deliriare*, literally to "go off the furrow," which is what a farmer does when his plowing isn't straight, or is *de lira*, off line, away from the furrow of earth thrown up by the plowing. Eventually, those looking to describe irregularities in everyday behavior saw the **metaphor** and borrowed it to become *delirium.* The painter Philip Guston captured just this sense of the coming-and-going, back-and-forth movement of inspiration when he wrote, "I am a night painter, so when I come into the studio the next morning the *delirium* is over." The great cellist Jacqueline du Pre said, "Playing lifts you out of yourself into a *delirious* place." Companion words include *delirium tremens*, Latin for *shaking frenzy*, referring to severe alcohol withdrawal, also called "the shakes," "horrors," and "DTs." The delirious *boustrophedonic* is another fieldwork word, from *bous*, ox, and *strephen*, to turn, which reflected how Greeks plowed their fields, first one direction, then back again, which was also the name for an ancient form of writing in which the lines run right to left, then left to right, over and over again, like a long day of plowing.

## DENOUEMENT

*The untying of a knotted drama; its outcome.* The final act of every play, movie, novel, or narrative leads inexorably to a conclusion where the knots of the plot are either pulled apart and the dramatic issues resolved—or they aren't, in which case the audience, viewer, or reader feels ineffably let down. To follow our **metaphor** to its conclusion, the lack of *denouement* leaves the reader or viewer all knotted up with unresolved tension. The roots of the word, first recorded in the 1750s, reveal why. It stems from *dénouer*, untie, from *des*, un, and *nouer*, to tie the knot, from Latin *nodus*, a knot. If you want to follow the thread even further back, it reaches to the Proto-Indo-European (PIE) *ned- "to bind, tie, as in a net." To come full circle, a *denouement* is the untying of the knot of tension that comes with every dramatic situation; by unbinding the threads tension is relieved and the story resolved. In *The Name of this Book is Secret,* Pseudonymous Bosch writes, "One dictionary defines *denouement* as 'a final part in which everything is made clear and no questions or surprises remain.' By that definition, it is exactly the wrong word to describe this chapter. This chapter will make nothing clear; it will raise many questions; and it may even contain a surprise or two. But I say we call it the *denouement* anyway because the word sounds so sophisticated and French." Companion phrases include its mirror image "tying the knot," an 18th-century term for marriage.

## DEXTEROUS

*Right-handed.* On the other hand to the commonly used *sinister*, left-handed, or the medieval *widdershins*, the suspicious left-handed path. *Dexter* is the Latin root, a seldom-used description for the right-hand side. A much-needed word, considering how unbalanced the language is with so much attention given to the sinister side of life. Irony of ironies, *Dexter* is the name of a cult cable television series about a man who believes he does sinister things—kills people—for the right reason, because they are evil. In *Oh, the Places You'll Go!*, Dr. Seuss writes, "Step with care and great tact and remember that Life's a Great Balancing Act. Just never forget to be *dexterous* and deft. And never mix up your right foot with your left." Companion words include *diabolical*, devilish, from diabolic, "pulled or ***thrown*** apart"—as opposed to symbolic, employing a sign by which one infers meaning, from Greek "***thrown***

Dexterous: *Potsdamer Platz*

together"—and the archaic but worthy of revival *infaust*, to make trouble for others, according to Webster's, 1913.

## DRAGONFLY

*A flying insect of the genus Libellula.* The word flies at us with surprising celerity, being here and then gone again. We think we know what we've seen, then it's gone. *Dragonfly*, we say, then we wonder, why a *dragon*? Did our ancestors imagine fire-breathing beasts of yore? The clue is in the name of the genus, *Libellula*. If you remember your Latin, you'll recall that it means *little book,* which opens the book on this fleet insect whose wings reminded country folk of the leaves of a book. The word reminds us of a talent for observation that we are rapidly losing as the world becomes more and more urban, that is, the *genius* for *correspondence*. A *dragonfly* corresponds to an open book, which is honored in this case by the scientists who first named it. In his poem "Silent Noon" Dante Gabriel Rossetti writes, "Deep in the sun-searched growths the dragonfly / Hangs like a blue thread loosened from the sky." Companion words include Komodo dragons and Globe dragons, those flying serpents drawn on the empty spaces of maps and globes with the Latin banner *Hic sunt dracones*, Here live dragons, or Here be dragons.

## DRAGOON

*A medieval carbine or musket; the act of coercion.* The fire-breathing presence of a *dragon* in *dragoon* is no mere coincidence, nor is the sonic shadow you might hear when you say it out loud. The painted word appears on the canvas of etymology as a fabulous dragon because medieval minds who heard or saw the guns were ***galvanized*** by their ability to spit fire. Over time the word for those early *muskets* evolved into *dragoon musket*, then fastened onto the soldier actually firing it, a *dragoon*, and eventually what the soldier did, *to force, persecute, seize*. The metamorphosis of meaning is a marvelous example of *sense evolution*. The earliest evidence comes from the Greek *draco*, to see clearly, from the belief of the preternatural ability of the airborne or cavebound serpents. Ambrose Bierce slays the *dragoon* in *The Devil's Dictionary*: "DRAGOON, n. A soldier who combines dash and steadiness in so equal measure that he makes his advances on foot and his retreats on horseback." Companion words include *Draguignan*, a **town** in Provence once haunted by dragons; and the Dragoo Family Association (DFA), a genealogy association for families who share variations of the surname Dragoo, including Draggoo, Dragaud, Drageau, Drago, and so on.

## DROMOMANIA

*Crazy about* **travel**. The Greek *dromos* means "running," but has come to suggest "compulsive traveling," from *travail*, "hard work," and *trepalium*, "the medieval rack." I tell you those word stories to tell you this one. The lapidary word *travel* simply means "to journey," but is essentially the same word as *travail*, from, as Skeat writes, "the toil of traveling in olden times." Moreover, it suggests that those on long *journeys* (from French *jour*, day) are not running away from home, but are rather pilgrims seeking something they're uncertain about, like those Irish rover-pilgrims, the *gyro-*

*vagi*, staying at the occasional *hospice*, or traveler's inn **run** by a religious order. And so it is with the words that have meandered across history to us, as if by caravan across an endlessly long desert. These are the frankincense, myrrh, and damask of words, redolent of faraway times and lands, adding a little spice to our everyday lives, which are all the poorer without them. Companion words include *white line fever, travel bug, wanderlust*, and my favorite, *drumble*, to move slowly, sluggishly, like a mumbling teenager on any school morning.

Dromomania: *Deutch Traum (German Dream)*

# E

## EASEL

*A painter's prop; an instrument for holding a canvas; a tripod.*
There is old proverb that goes, "If an ass goes abroad it
shouldn't expect to return a horse." But what if an ass
just galumphs out into the countryside? It might expect
to return with a painting. That's the surprising Dutch
sense of *ezel*, a donkey or ass, which was for centuries the
animal of choice for carrying a painter's burden of a sketch
box, paints, brushes, and canvas. Eventually, the name for
the carrier became the thing carried, *ezel* evolving into
*easel*, the stand or frame. The *easel* made it *easier* to paint
outdoors. Those without one became *ill-at-easel*. Action
painter Jackson Pollock said, "I continue to get further
away from the usual painter's tools, such as *easel*, palette,
brushes, etc. I prefer sticks, trowels, knives and dripping
fluid paint or a heavy impasto with sand, broken glass,
or other foreign matter added." Hockey player Jeremy

Roenick uses the word in the figurative sense to describe the craft of skating: "This is our canvas. Our *easel*. This is how we paint, on fresh sheets of ice." Companion words include *ease*, which suggests a certain comfort, pleasure, and ***opportunity***.


## EAVESDROPPER

*Someone who intentionally overhears what others are saying; an aural voyeur.* Apparently the **sneaky** habit isn't new, since its first recorded use since is a 16th-century word from the Old English, *yfesdrype*, for the space close to a building where the rainwater drips off the roof and onto the ground. Court records from 1487 in Nottingham, England, reveal the act as a crime: "Jurors say that Harry Rowley is an *eavesdropper*." This evolved into the sense expressed by 18th-century writer Sir William Blackstone, who tells of those Nosey Parkers who hover under walls and eaves to listen for juicy gossip that they can use to their advantage. Captain Grosse defined the word in his indispensable book of **slang**, in 1811: "one who lurks about to rob hen-houses, also a listener at doors and ***windows*** to overhear private **conversations**." Not all *eavesdropping* has nefarious motivations, however, as anyone knows who has read the ***deliriously*** romantic *Cyrano de Bergerac* by Edmond Rostand (1897) or seen *Roxanne*, Steve Martin's heart-thumping movie version. The contemporary drama critic Kenneth Tynan explains the curious origins of a theater writer: "A dramatist is a congenital *eavesdropper* with the instincts of a Peeping Tom." Speaking of the perennial temptation to listen in on gossip, *scuttlebutt* is an old nautical term that recalls the habit of sailor's huddling over the *butt,* barrel or water cask, on the *scuttle*, the deck, to spread **rumors** or gossip. Speaking of *butts*, there is recorded a Scottish proverb from 1721: "A bit *butt* and bit bend make a moy maiden at the board's end." In plain English: A piece of beef and a draught of drink make tender **lady** sated by the end of the meal. Companion words include *auditor,* one who listens and reports, and *wiretapper,* one who listens and tape-records.

## ELIMINATE

*To put something or somebody out.* An ordinary word that proves extraordinary with a little digging. The act of *elimination* points back to the days when thresholds were vitally important, both in architecture and symbolism. To cross the threshold of a house was hugely symbolic, bringing with it a host of responsibilities, such as hospitality from the householder and responsibility from the guest. Figuratively, crossing over suggests moving to a new level. All of this is inherent in *eliminate*, which has in its heart the word *limn* or *liminal*, an earlier way to signal a threshold. Legendary radio D. J. Casey Kasem says: "They thought talking movies might *eliminate* radio as well. But radio just keeps getting stronger." Sir Arthur Conan Doyle explained his hero, Sherlock Holmes's, method of deduction: "Once you *eliminate* the impossible, whatever remains, no matter how improbable, must be the truth." Companion words include *limn*, to depict or describe, even highlight with more **color**, as we are offering to do here; and *liminal*, the boundary line, as between dream and waking, the sea and the sky.

Eliminate: *Time's Shadow*

## ELOQUENCE

*The practice or art of using words aptly and with fluency.* Note the emphasis on practice and fluency, as in fluid, flow, ease. *Eloquence* is a lesson in luscious locution. If it doesn't *flow* it isn't beautiful, which may mean it doesn't pay to speak out. This is suggested in its derivation, from Latin *eloquens*, the faculty of speech, and *eloqui*, to speak out, from *ex*, out, and *loqui*, to speak. While the origins flow easily, what is unexpected is the number of distributaries from this strong river, including the melancholic *tristiloquence*, which refers not the beauty of Tristan's pillow talk with Isolde, but to sad or alarmed talk. **Consider**, too, *magniloquence*, the magnificent flow of words, or *stultiloquence*, the foolish flow, and while we're at it, let's suggest *iridescequence*, the colorful, rainbow-hued flow of words. William C. Bryant captured its essence: "*Eloquence* is the poetry of prose." Companion words include *locution*, one's style or expression, and *tardiloquent*, talking slowly.

## EMBARRASS

*To shame, humiliate, as if imprisoned by one's emotions.* There is a curious connection here between all three elements of this red-faced word. The prefix *em*, to, is followed by *bar*, as it looks and sounds, a word from the Bastille, as evident in the French word *embarrer*, to be put behind bars. The third syllable, *ass*, we can suggest more playfully than linguistically, is what someone feels like when shamed or humiliated. Though better than a death sentence, ***incarceration*** was shameful and humiliating, as is still hinted at in the expression *bare-assed*, naked, vulnerable. Together, these three components evolved into an eviscerating verb that captures the pain of humiliation. An early philosophical use of the word comes from the 16th-century French novelist Jean de la Bruyère, who wrote, "At the beginning and at the end of love, two lovers are *embarrassed* to find themselves alone." The charismatic president of the Philippines Corazon Aquino said, "I'm not *embarrassed* to tell you that I believe in miracles." Companion words include *abash, discombobulate.*

## EMBOLALIA

*The nervous, I mean, stammering habit of, you know, inserting, I mean kinda **throwing** meaningless words into, you know, a sentence, when you're, ah, talking.* Tossing in the word *throw* was no accident, as evident in its root word, the Greek *emballein*, from *em*, in, and *ballein*, to throw in or at, which makes it another "***throwing*** word," such as **hyperbole**, to throw over somebody's head, or *parabola*, to throw beside or near. So *embolalia* turns out to be a sixty-four-dollar word to describe the habit of throwing around words without thinking, or as the phrase goes, talking before thinking. The habit is characterized by often uncontrollable utterances (*hmm, umm, errr*), and is a cringeworthy nervous tic in languages everywhere. The cause may be a general deterioration of the spoken word, or a lack of respect for it, sheer nervousness, or a disdain for proper, poetic, or colorful use of the language. Who knew there was actually a word to describe what is otherwise known as "Valley Speak," the bubblegum-blowing, petulant, goofy way of talking that is regularly mocked in television shows like *Saturday Night Live*, or any beach movie. In this sense *embolalia* is a near-perfect word to describe *what we all do* at some point in our lives—*we **throw** words around without thinking about them. It's human nature to occasionally stutter and hesitate* in our **conversations**. All of which leads us to this startling thought: *embolalia*, you know, can also be an affectation, an emblem of someone who disdains not just, um, proper English, but kinda colorful language, as, you know, pretentious. The disdained "filler words" might be filigreed words, an emblem of language rebellion. Companion words include *chavish*, the annoying prattle of people in public.

## ENSŌ (JAPANESE)

*A calligrapher's circle drawn for meditation purposes.* An example of *simplexity*, deceptively simple complexity, or is it complex simplicity? Originally, *ensō* simply meant circle in Japanese. But in its context of Zen Buddhism the simple act of drawing one is infinitely complex in its implications. In true Zen fashion, it is a symbol not a **character**, though it can *reveal* character by illustrating the state of mind at the moment it is drawn. The *ensō* tradition is a venerable one in Buddhism, and reveals the Japanese **aesthetic**. For some monks and many artists the creation of an *ensō* is a daily centering ritual of using a calligrapher's brush to draw a circle on silk or rice paper—in one fell swoop, one continuous, spontaneous broad stroke. First thought, best thought; first move, best move. No chance to edit or touch up. One stroke. The belief is that the very spirit of the calligrapher is revealed moving across the paper at that one moment. In that spirit, the exercise illustrates the emphasis of living in the now, which is expressed in the Zen saying, "Present moment, perfect moment." The *ensō* is an elegant expression of minimalism in Japanese art, a reflection on the ironically named *stress* on the mind being free enough to actually create something. The daily ritual is also intended to act as a kind of spiritual Rorschach Blot, free **jazz** with an ink brush, revealing the artist's character, and in a mysterious way the very nature of the universe. Used correctly, the *ensō* or circle symbolizes and maybe reveals enlightenment, strength, and due to the empty space in the center of the circle, the void of existence. Zen Buddhism teaches that only someone who is spiritually whole can create a true *ensō*. Companion words include *surrealist automatism*, writing or sketching without censorship.

## ENSORCELL

*Bewitch, enchant, hypnotize.* An archaic but astonishing *Aha!* caliber word, it emerges from the magic wand of the Middle French *ensorcerer,* from *en,* in, *sorcier,* sorcerer, and *sorcellerie,* enchantment. It is one of a charming number of *magic* words that survive the Middle Ages, its earliest citation back in 1541. The journalist Nat Hentoff writes in *Speaking Freely*: "I have been a journalist too long to be **ensorcelled** by conspiracy theories." Companion words include *enthrall,* to enslave, put in thrall; **beguile**, to hold spellbound, mesmerize, and enrapture.

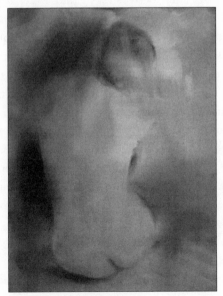

Ensorcell: *The Rose of Time*

## ESPONTANEO (SPANISH)

*Spontaneous, voluntary, willing behavior; a spectator or **fan** who suddenly leaps into a bullring.* In his memoir *Out of League,* George Plimpton wrote about his unique form of participating in **sports**, comparing himself to the "*Espontaneo*, the guys who charge into the bullring." I personally witnessed this **crazy** but inspired act in the Lisbon bullring, in 1991, when *six* men leapt out of the stands and lined up in front of a charging **bull**, each of them taking turns to "catch the bull by the horns" and leap over it, which evoked for me the bull-leapers portrayed in the Knossos frescoes. Curiously, a few years later, between a jig and a reel at O'Connor's pub in Doolin, Ireland, I thought of the *espontaneos* when a young lass stood up in the middle of the hubbub, hands at her side, an age-old signal that she wanted to sing *sean nos*, unaccompanied. The pub went silent as she sang a heartrending version of "The Lass of Aughrim." Education innovator Maria Montessori wrote, "If an educational act is to be efficacious, it will be only that one which tends to help toward the complete unfolding of life. To be thus helpful it is necessary rigorously to avoid the arrest of *spontaneous* movements and the imposition of arbitrary tasks." Companion words include *impulsive, unprompted, instinctive.*

## ETAOIN SHRDLU

*Typesetter's terms for jammed keys on a linotype machine. E-t-a-o-i-n s-h-r-d-l-u* is the approximate order of frequency of the twelve most commonly used letters in the English language, and is a now known as a nonsense phrase that sometimes appeared in print in the days of "hot type" publishing due to a custom of Linotype machine operators. If a sequence of letters jammed on a linotype machine, the entire "slug," or block of letters, might drop right into the family newspaper, something I recall seeing right up until a few years ago. Let's say it's a story about the discovery of a new Paleolithic cave teeming with rock paintings: "… and as recent discovery at Le Chauvet in France reveals etaoin shrdlu three dozen charcoal images of gamboling gazelles."

Since my days as a journalism student at the University of Detroit, it has been my metaphor for any accidental words dropped into the middle of a story. Technically, it is created when the Linotype setter makes a "temporary marking slug" by running a finger down a bank of keys of his machine to use as a placeholder, never intended for publication. Sheer embarrassment has forever impressed the memory of my introduction to the chockablock word, because my college journalism teacher, Judy Serrin, mildly mocked a run-on sentence of mine. "All the words are running together," she wrote in the margin of my paper, "like an *etaoin shrdlu* down at the *Free Press*." *Antoine Sherdlioux* would be a memorable name for a mixed-up journalist.

## EXQUISITE

*Of exceptional* **beauty**, *or rare quality; characterized by discriminating taste.* In its own *exquisite* way it means more: "affectedly delicate and concerned with appearance; marked by flawless craftsmanship or by beautiful or elaborate execution; acutely or painfully beautiful." Lyly's memorable phrase in "Euphues," in 1579, may still be the finest definition: "consummate and delightful excellence." To say that this entry has been carefully chosen, selected for its sound and beauty, is to give a hint about its origins. It derives from the early 15th-century *exquirere*, to search out thoroughly, from *ex*, out, and *quaerere*, to seek. The French philosopher Voltaire playfully wrote, "Ice-cream is *exquisite*—what a pity it isn't illegal." The painter Georgia O'Keefe: "It was in the 1920s, when nobody had time to reflect, that I saw a still-life painting with a flower that was perfectly *exquisite*, but so small you really could not appreciate it." And how can we forget the camp usage of Freddie Mercury, lead singer of Queen: "I want to lead the Victorian life, surrounded by *exquisite* clutter." Companion words include *Exquisite Corpse*, the French parlor game invented by the Surrealists, which derived from *cadavre exquis*, or turning corpse, wherein words or images are gathered spontaneously and juxtaposed, often on sequentially folded paper, with someone else's to produce surprising results.

## EXTRADICTIONARY

*Beyond the book of words.* Dr. Johnson's own definition is painfully powerful considering how much of his life he dedicated to words: *"Not consisting of words but realities."* I can't resist adding his citation of Brown's *Vulgar Errours:* "Of these *extradictionary* and real fallacies, / Aristotle and logicians make six; but we / observe men are commonly deceived by four / thereof." Likewise, Jiddhu Krishnamurti reminded his followers of the limitations of language, in *The Book Life*, "To understand each other, I think it is necessary that we should not be caught in words; because, a word like God, for example, may have a particular meaning for you, while for me it may represent a totally different formulation, or no formulation at all." Companion words include *live dictionaries*, the name that Wild West cowboys gave to young women teachers who taught in one-room schoolhouses.

# F

## FAFFLE

*Stammer, hesitate, waste time, waver.* One of my prime candidates for revival, for the sheer sound of it but also as a tribute to my dictionary-diving father. Growing up in the suburbs of Detroit, I became aware of this unusual word due to the way he used to comment on the way I did my chores. Every summer morning he posted a series of tasks on the refrigerator door, such as mowing and weeding the lawn and carting home dirt from the nearby woods for the family garden. When he came home from work at the Ford Glass House the former Army sergeant would emerge in the way he examined my work, and if it wasn't satisfactory he would say, "Stop *faffling*, and do it again." To *faffle* is to falter, stumble, or just take too much time with a job or a piece of work. There are few words that combine its gruff "f" sound at the start of the word and its middle "f"s, with the hint of goofing off. W. H. Auden used the archaic word, which had last been defined in a dictionary in 1913, in the figurative sense to describe how flags might "stammer," which is to say to wave hesitantly, when he translated the German Romantic poet Friedrich Hölderlin's quotation: "The walls stand / speechless and cold, the banners / *faffle* in the wind." Companion words include *famble*, *maffle*, *sputter*, and *wobble*.

Faffle: *Lorca's Tree*

## FAN / FANATIC

*A devotee, follower; a zealot.* In 1st-century Rome there
flourished a sect of the war goddess Bellona, whose
followers were so crazed that the Roman general and
consul Sulla was forced to build a new temple, known
then as a *fanum*. Over time the crazed behavior of frenzied devotees and war-besotted priests in front of the *fanum*
became more and more **peculiar**, including the shredding
of their clothes and slicing themselves with sword cuts
in a frenzy of divine inspiration. There is an echo of the
word as well in *profane*, less than respectful or even sacri-
legious behavior committed in any sacred place, from *pro*,
before, and *fanum*, temple. Crazed behavior of **sports** fans,
whether at a Manchester United soccer match, a San Francisco Giants World Series game, or a Beatles concert circa
1964, all earn the **moniker** of *fan* behavior, though it can
also have more affectionate connotations. The sportswriter
Arthur Daley wrote, "A baseball *fan* has the digestive appa-
ratus of a billy goat. He can, and does, devour any set of
diamond statistics with insatiable appetite and then nuzzles
hungrily for more." The English playwright Simon Gray
wrote, "I'm *fanatical* about **sport**: there seems to me something almost religious about the fact that human beings
can organize play, the spirit of play." From the star's point
of view onstage, Lady Gaga writes, "So the real truth
about … my *fans*, my little monsters, lies in this sentiment:
They are the Kings. They are the Queens. They write the
history of the kingdom and I am something of a devoted

Jester." Novelist Pat Conroy opines, "Baseball *fans* love numbers. They love to swirl them around their mouths like Bordeaux wine." Companion words include *crank*, an archaic word for *fanatic*, and the preferred term in the 19th century for a *baseball fan*.

## FARRAGO

*A **strange** mix, a confused mixture, an odd medley.* First recorded around 1630, the Latin *farrago* derived from *farr*, grain, and the earlier Indo-European *bhares*, animal fodder made of a mix of grains, a mishmash, we can safely say. The barnyard word eventually became a **metaphor** for a confused mixture, or conglomeration. If we were to be playful in our description, we might say it's a word or work that only makes sense in a "far-ago world," or mention the bumper sticker I saw during a film shoot in Fargo, "*Farrago* is not a city in North Dakota." Film critic David Denby writes in the *New Yorker*, "Darren Aronofsky's *Black Swan* is a luridly beautiful *farrago*—a violent fantasia that mixes the tensions of preparing a new production of *Swan Lake* with sex, blood and horror-film flourishes." Companion words include *mingle-mangle, hodgepodge, salmagundi.*

## FARTEUR (FRENCH)

*A professional, even musical farter, an auteur of farts.* A *farceur* is someone who indulges in farce, mystification, which is not exactly what's happening here, for this word refers to something as real as it smells. Its etymology likely lies in a play-on-words of **flâneur**, a stroller, and *fart*, the emission of intestinal gas from the anus, or in the vernacular, to break wind. As unlikely as it sounds (or smells), there were famous *farteurs*, the most famous being La Pétomaine, the stage name for Joseph Pujol, the French "flatulist," or "professional farter." Pujol "played music" through his backside—professionally—onstage at the Moulin Rouge in Montmartre during the Belle Époque years in Paris. Incidentally, Pétomaine derives from *péter*, to fart, and *mane*, maniac, which combines to mean "fartomaniac." While still a professional baker Pujol began "imitating musical instruments, and claimed to be playing them behind the counter" for his customers, which led to his stage debut, where he squeezed his butt cheeks like a concertina in Marseille in 1887, and then went on to play the legendary louche nightclubs all over Paris in 1892. A little pinched-nose odiferous research reveals that Pujol's stage routine, which included explosive cannon fire sounds, the boom of thunderstorms, and operatic performances, was augmented by a judiciously placed ocarina and amplifying tube so he could perform standards like "O Sole Mio" and "*La Marseillaise*." Beyond Montmartre's usual habitués the illustrious clientele that came to see him included the Prince of Wales, King Leopold II, and Sigmund Freud. There is some precedent for such anatomical shenanigans. In medieval Ireland the *braigetoir* was a professional farter employed to **amuse** the local chieftain or king. And who can forget the Icelandic proverb, "Every man likes the smell of his own fart." Companion words include *catch-fart*, a footboy, so called from the practice of such servants following close behind their master or mistress; and *fartiste,* someone so adept at farting they are *considered* an artiste. A *fartlek* is a rigorous Norwegian athletic training regime embodied by distant runners like the legendary Paavo Nurmi.

Fascination: *The Source of Words*

## FASCINATION

*Intensely interested, deeply attracted, in awe, even terror.* An old concern to the point of fear in the ancient word, stemming from the timeless fear of being out of control. First recorded in the 1590s, it stems from the Medieval French *fasciner* by way of Latin *fascinare,* bewitch or enchant. A tantalizing possibility is that its roots stretch back even further, to Greek *baskanos*, **sorcerer**, and reflects the ancient belief that witches, warlocks, and certain species of serpents could cast spells over people with a single glance. By 1815 the word had reversed direction, shape-shifting from terror to delight, fear to attraction. There is a marvelous Irish expression, *take to the fair*, which holds centuries of folk *fascination* with "the fancy life." Psychologist James Hillman writes, "The sexual *fascination* is the soul trying to get out and get into something other than itself." Companion words include *fascinator,* a headpiece, whether a fancy feather or a lacy headdress used strategically to attract—or *fascinate*—a possible suitor.

## FATHOM

*To understand the depths; the measure of comprehension; to stretch out and embrace. Fathom* this startlingly romantic backstory. The Old English *fæðm* was a legal term that referred to the length of two outstretched arms, which **averages** about six feet, "or the length of a man's embrace of his lover"; *fæðmian*, the verb form, meant to embrace, surround, envelop. Originally, *fathom* was, in the sweet cadences of Webb Garrison, "a combination of an embrace, a bosom, and the object of one's affection." By inference, a *fathom* is a distance that is within arm's reach, and figuratively something that we can grasp because we can embrace it. On the other hand—or arm—*unfathomable* refers to something or somebody beyond our reach, our grasp, our understanding. The OED adds the subtle but visual dimension of "spreading out," as a person spreads her arms to embrace a friend or greet the morning sun, which is a picturesque way of saying that we *fathom* the world. *Sixteen Fathoms Deep*, a submarine movie from 1948 starring Lloyd Bridges, points us toward the maritime or naval dimension of the word, which has come to refer to measuring depths at sea in six-foot increments. To "take soundings" dates to around 1600, and soon afterward took on the figurative sense of getting to the bottom of something, to understand and comprehend it. Personally, I scarcely *fathom* the genius of Shakespeare's rhythmic alliteration in *The Tempest*: "Full *fathom* five thy father lies; Of his bones are coral made; Those are pearls that were his eyes." Actor Michael Caine confesses, "For all my education, accomplishments, and so-called wisdom ... I can't *fathom* my own heart." Companion words include *fathometer*, an instrument for measuring depths, and *unfathomable*, beyond measure.

## FEISTY

*Touchy, testy, quarrelsome.* A word that possesses all the nervous energy of an exuberant puppy, which makes sense since it derives from *feist,* a Southern term for a small and specifically snappy, nervous, belligerent, little dog. Where *feist* comes from helps us sniff out its more nuanced meaning: *fice*, fist, which was short for *fysting curre*, or stinking cur. The smelly dog reference goes all the way back to the 16th-century *fysten*, to break wind. Do you get the picture? Originally, the word overlapped with *fart*, from the Middle English *fist,* related to the Old Norse *fisa*, to blow, as in wind. This lexicographer leaves it to the *feisty* imagination of the reader to determine if there is a connection between the need to pass gas and a person who is snappy, nervous, or belligerent. Colorado senator and vice-presidential candidate Geraldine Ferraro wrote, "The polls indicated that I was *feisty*, that I was tough, that I had a sense of humor, but they weren't quite sure if they liked me and they didn't know whether or not I was sensitive." Companion words include *fiery* and *frisky*; also *spunky,* which harkens back to an archaic word for the tinder that sparks the fire.

## FIASCO

*Trouble, disaster, problem.* A word with transparent, see-through origins. Think of the Murano glassworks, in Venice. On a recent visit I learned that *fiasco* is Italian for "flask or bottle," and that Italian wordsmiths believed it dates back to Venetian glassblowers who tossed their flawed glass aside, work that was considered a *disaster*. Out of the discarded glass came the innovation of making the common bottle. Today we've kept the "disaster" part of the word without redeeming the full value of the bottle, as if we don't like recycling our failures. The Italian phrase *far fiasco* means "to make a bottle," and figuratively to fail in a performance. Speaking of which, actor Orlando Bloom delineates failure in the movie business: "There's a difference between a failure and a *fiasco* ... a *fiasco* is a disaster of mythic proportions." The former Prime Minister of Spain José Luis Rodríguez Zapatero writes: "I will listen to Mr. Bush, but my position is very clear and very firm. The occupation [of Iraq] is a *fiasco*. There have been more deaths after the war than during the war." Companion terms include The *Fiasco* Theater Company, which emphasizes the actors, text, and audience over the *fiasco* of overly-**glamorized** art and the high ticket prices that go with it.

**FIB**

*A harmless lie.* "A lie," says Bierce, "that has not cut its teeth. A habitual liar's nearest approach to truth; the perigee of his eccentric orbit." Without engaging in too much *fimble-famble*, a *fib* is most likely a natural contraction of *fibble-fable*, which was, according to Charles Funk, an injunction against children telling outright nonsense. However, behind the warning was a slight berating of those who told *fables*. The dismissive phrase "Oh, it's just a story" contributes to the diminishment of the imagination, the source of all creative thinking. Contrast the punitive tone above with Pablo Picasso's maxim "Art is the lie that tells the truth." Similarly, the fable is the soft lie about moral truths usually told by animals (as in "The Tortoise and the Hare") to illuminate human foibles. The real *fib* is telling children that there are no truths in fables. *Larry-Boy and the Fib from Outer Space!* was a sci-fi flick from 1997. Companion words include *fabrication*, a made-up story, or *atrial fib,* short for *atrial fibrillation*, an involuntary muscle twitch in the heart.

## FIDO

*A faithful dog; popular name for a pet dog.* Good reason: it derives from the Latin *fido,* meaning "I trust, put confidence in, rely upon"—all common sentiments that dog owners know well. Secondarily, Eric Partridge tracks the word to the Italian and translates it as "trusty." Folklore attributes the name for dogs to Abraham Lincoln, who named his dog *Fido.* The frenetically funny Eddie Izzard says in one of his routines, "Picasso, he should have been a taxidermist! 'I've done your dog. It's got nine eyes down the side. I made his head all square, fifteen legs. What do you think of that?' *Fido* looks a bit weird."

## FILLIP

*To snap the fingers, or propel an object with a flick of the fingers.*
A snap or light blow made by pressing a fingertip against
the thumb and suddenly releasing it. Figuratively, a *fillip*
has come to mean an embellishment, a stimulation, or sign
of approval. The 15th-century Latin word *philippen* was
probably imitative, meaning to flip (a coin or cards) with a
snap of the fingers—picture Robert Redford flipping cards
in *The Sting*. The noun form, *fyllippe*, can be attested to
from the 1520s. Philosopher Blaise Pascal complained, "I
cannot forgive Descartes. In all his philosophy, he would
have been quite willing to dispense with God. But he
had to make Him give a *fillip* to set the world in motion;
beyond this, he has no further need of God." Companion
words include the sonicky Scottish *thrip*, a *finger snap*, *phil-
lipen*, to flip coins or cards, and *Flip*, short for *Philip*, a nickname coined by Wayne, Michigan's own Ruth Garvey for
yours truly, her favorite writer.

## FIRST STRING

*The starting player on a **sports** team; a regular player, not a
second stringer.* For a competitive **athlete**, there can be no
substitute for *first string*; it's *first string* or the bench. Only
the best get to play. If you want to hit the bulls-eye, say
top-flight archers, aim just a little high with your first
string, your first shot. The **metaphor** is apt. Originally,
it's an archery term that bends back like a bow to the 12th

century to describe a marksman's favorite, his *first-streng*, which was kept in reserve for mandatory Sunday longbow competitions ordered by Edward III in the 13th century to assure primacy for English archers. Eventually it was adopted, in 1863, from the archer's practice of carrying extra bowstrings in his quiver. The modern sense of being on the "first team" was first used in 1915. Andy Hill, who played for legendary UCLA basketball coach John Wooden from 1969 to 1972, said, "It didn't matter how good the player was. It didn't matter if you were on the bench or *first string*. We were, we are, and we always will be Coach's boys. His players know the titles didn't make Coach great. What the titles did was get all of you to notice how great he was." Companion words include *first violin*, a **rhapsody** on the theme of *first string,* or *first four strings*, the violinists who can play loudest and softest in the orchestra.

## FLABBERGAST

*To amaze,* **astonish**, *surprise.* First recorded in a Sussex magazine article in 1772 and described as "a new vogue word … perhaps from some dialect," possibly an arbitrary formation that linked *flabby* and *aghast*. Ogden Nash wrote these confounding lines: "First / Let the rockets flash and the cannon thunder, / This child is a marvel, a matchless wonder. / A staggering child, a child astounding, / Dazzling, diaperless, dumbfounding, / Stupendous, miraculous, unsurpassed, / A child to stagger and *flabbergast*, /

Bright as a button, sharp as a thorn, / And the only perfect one ever born. / Second / Arrived this evening at half-past nine. / Everybody is doing fine. / Is it a boy, or quite the reverse? / You can call in the morning and ask the nurse." In *Harry Potter and the Chamber of Secrets*, J. K. Rowling writes, "'Ginny!' said Mr. Weasley, *flabbergasted*. 'Haven't I taught you anything? What have I always told you? Never trust anything that can think for itself if you can't see where it keeps its brain?'" Columnist Anna Quindlen adds, "The world is full of women blindsided by the unceasing demands of motherhood, still *flabbergasted* by how a job can be terrific and tortuous." Companion words include a cheeky adjective that I heard a few years ago in Drimoleague, County Cork, Ireland, from a wee lad named Luka when I told him I lived in the same city as famed children's author Lemony Snicket: "Well, I'm positively *gobsmacked!*"

## FLAMBOYANT

*Colorful, theatrical, fiery.* The French *flamboyant,* essentially "flamelike," took three hundred years to catch fire, but it was worth the wait. Originally an architectural term, early in the 15th century *flamboyant* referred only to architectural style with "flame-like curves," from French *flamboyant*, flaming, wavy, from the Latin *flammula*, flame. Finally around 1879 the word had "metaphorized" to mean "showy" or "ornate," to describe a certain kind of person or their behavior, one who tends to "attract attention because of their exuberance, confidence, and stylishness." Rock-and-roll legend Little Richard once said, "I would wear *flamboyant* clothes and long hair, and most singers at the time didn't." Novelist and aviator Beryl Markham: "If a man has any greatness in him, it comes to light, not in one *flamboyant* hour, but in the ledge of his daily work." Companion words include *flambé*, flaming dessert.

## FLUMMERY

*A bland meal; empty talk; hokum.* Of uncertain origin, but possibly from the Welsh *llymru*, a low-grade, soft, but sour oatmeal boiled with the husks. Its figurative use echoes the empty feeling after the meal, coming to mean empty words, the very definition of flattery, or an empty meaningless ceremony, from the 1740s. Around that time, the Dean of Dublin, Jonathan Swift, penned this description of the common meal, consisting of "food much used in Scotland, the north of Ireland, and other parts. It is made of oatmeal, and sometimes of the shellings of oats; and known by the names of sowins or *flummery*." In *The Devil's Dictionary*, Ambrose Bierce writes: "HOVEL, n. Down upon the middle of his legs fell Twaddle / And astonished Mr. Twiddle, / Who began to lift his noddle / Feed upon his fiddle-faddle *flummery*, unswaddle a new born self-sufficiency and think himself a mockery." Companion words include *flummer*, the archaic back-formation that referred to a way to fool, coax, or ***beguile*** someone.

## FOYER

*A lobby, anteroom, entrance hall, or vestibule of a theater or hotel.* If you've ever stood in a lobby and warmed your hands before, during intermission, or after a performance, or watched members of the audience warming up with a cup of *coffee* or a hot toddy, you have experienced what led to the creation of this warm word. In old Europe theaters were not very well heated and often the only warmth was found in the vestibule, where people socialized and warmed up. After the Old French *foier*, fireplace, from the earlier Latin *focarium*, *focus*, the hearth, for fire. The early French *foyer* sounds like it's as old as fire, but its first appearance in print is only in 1859, in reference to the 19th-century equivalent of the "green room," where actors gather and prepare for their performance. Apple founder Steve Jobs said, "That's been one of my mantras—focus and simplicity. Simple can be harder than complex: You have to work hard to get your thinking clean to make it simple. But it's worth it in the end because once you get there, you can move mountains." Companion words include **focus**, *keen* concentration, what an actor engages in between stage entrances, or theatergoers of old did to keep warm.

## FUN

*An amusement or diversion; leisure activity that is enjoyable or exciting.* A word that embodies *simplexity*—so simple and yet we make it far more complex than it needs to be. Leave it to Dr. Seuss to keep it lighthearted: "*Fun* is good." Good for the heart, good for the soul. This is a *boustrophedonic* move, a turnaround from its earlier meaning, attested to in 1727: "cheat, trick, **hoax**," from the 1680s verb *fun*, which is of uncertain origin, though possibly a variant of Middle European *fonnen*, befool. **Stigmatized** by Johnson as "a low **cant** word." The older sense is preserved in the phrase *to make fun of* (1737) and *funny money*, counterfeit bills (1938, though this may be more for the sake of the rhyme). Walt Disney's secret was believing that "It's kind of *fun* to do the impossible." Basketball legend Michael Jordan said, "Just play. Have *fun*. Enjoy the game." Likewise, Hollywood legend Katherine Hepburn reminded us, "If you obey all the rules, you miss all the *fun*." Companion words include *funambulist* from 1793, a tightrope walker or rope dancer, from Latin *funis*, rope, and *ambulare*, to walk.

## FUNGIBLE

*Interchangeable*. A **delightful** alternative to "equivalent," or "identical," that is, if you can remember it. A late 17th-century word deriving from medieval Latin *fungibilis,* from *fungi,* to perform, enjoy, serve in place of. It is hard for a wordcatcher to admit, but this is possibly the word I've looked up more times than any other. Is there a word for *that*, words on the tip of our tongue? Why is this such a delightful—but hard to remember—word? Maybe it's the first syllable, so immediately recognizable as *fun*, but a

**false friend**, a word that looks like something you think you know, but you don't. Still, it is used occasionally, as it was in the *Boston Legal* episode "Head Cases": "Everyone is *fungible*." Ouch; just when we thought we were unique. Still, after hunting down this snark of a word in a dozen dictionaries, I want to know, what rhymes with fungible?

## FUNKY

*Bluesy, soulful, sexy.* The backstory takes us way back to the 1620s and the French *funkier,* "to smoke." By 1787 it was a deft descriptor for smelly old cheese. Captain Grosse is helpful, defining *funk* as "to smoke," and by extension "to smoke or stink through fear." Eventually it took on the connotation of anything that reeked of the earth, was musty, or grounded, but at least smelled *real*. If you came of age in the 1960s, it's hard not to hear the echo of Sly and the Family Stone's *funkadelic* song "Play that *funky* music right, boy!" in 1969. Having seen him at Baker's Keyboard Lounge in Detroit in the early 1970s, I can still recall the intensity of Miles Davis's smoky, bluesy, funky searching trumpet, and was grateful to later hear him say, "Those dark roads of Arkansas, that's what I'm trying to reach in my music." Companion words include *funk music,* a 1960s innovation that blended soul, jazz, and blues, leaving room for some *vamping*, or improvisation.

Funky

# G

**GADGET**

*A playful term for a nameless tool or instrument.* A *gadget* is a small specialized mechanical or electronic device, from French *gagée*, a seaman's term for things even the sailors forgot, what they used to call *a gill-guy, timmy-noggy, wim-wam*, among a toolbox of names. The word's heritage traces back to the French *gâchette*, a 15th-century word for the catchpiece of a mechanism, the lock of a gun, from *gâche*, the staple of a lock. The modern sense dates to 1886 and was used early in the 20th century by the Dadaist and Surrealist French painter and illustrator, Francis Picabia, who is infamous in artiste circles for claiming, in typical *épater le bourgeois* fashion, "A new *gadget* that lasts only five minutes is worth more than an immortal work that bores everyone." More recently, the cleverly contrived *Inspector Gadget* was an animated television series featuring an oafish, half-cyborg, gabardine-wearing detective hero endowed with bionic *gadgets* built into his body that he activated by uttering the word "Wowsers!" then naming the gizmo. To wit: "It's the top secret *Gadget* phone!" "Go-go-go, Gadget-mobile!" Recently, I overheard at Caffè Trieste in North Beach, "Get real, dude, you've got *gadgetitis*." Companion words include *contraption, gimmick, jigger, widget*.


## GALOOT

*A lout, an oaf; an awkward, boorish, or **strange** person.* Two competing etymologies vie for our attention, one from Old Irish for an elf, a clumsy man, or, as Shaw defines it in *Slanguage,* "a **crazy** person," probably, I might add, from "Ballygobackwards." The other suggests it derives from an 1812 term from nautical lingo for an innocent recruit, or is a sailor's contemptuous word for soldiers or marines. *Dictionary of American Slang* proposes *galut*, Sierra Leone creole form of Spanish *Galeoto*, galley slave, or even the Dutch slang *kloot*, testicle, *klootzak*, scrotum, a common insult. In the 1972 movie *Bad Company*, a soldier shouts: "Then this big *galoot* come chargin' at me with a knife. See what he did?"


## GALORE

*Bountiful, plenty, sufficient.* A lovely Irish contribution to English, rarely credited, as David Cassidy discovered in his research into Irish American **slang**. He traces it back to the 1670s to the Irish *go leór,* corresponding to the commodious Gaelic *gu leóir,* more specifically "till sufficient, till enough, till clarity." Actress Winona Ryder used it humorously in an interview: "In high school, I dressed up as every James Bond girl. I was a teenager Pussy *Galore.*" Shel Silverstein writes in *The Land of Happy*, "There's no one unhappy in Happy. / There's laughter and smiles *galore.* / I have been to the Land of Happy / What a bore!" Companion words include *abundance; good and plenty.*

## GALVANIZE

*To shock, excite into action; to form a coat of protective zinc over iron or steel.* The kind of word that is to etymology what euhemerism is to the study of mythology, a definition connected to a real person. The name of Euhemerus, a 4th-century Greek mythographer, lives on because he explained the myths as distortions of historical events. This entry dates to 1802, from the French *galvaniser*, from *galvanisme*, named after the Italian scientist Luigi Galvani. He invented the process of coating metal with protective zinc to prevent rusting and corrosion, which is accomplished by dipping the metal directly into a bath of molten zinc. When Galvani was just twenty-six he was named Professor of Anatomy at the University of Bologna, in Italy. Shortly after his appointment, his wife was watching him dissect a frog and was amazed to notice that it twitched every time her husband's scalpel touched a nerve, which they discovered had "become charged with electricity by an adjacent electric machine." Subsequent experiments led to daring new research into the phenomenon of electricity. Hence the verb *galvanize*, "to subject to the action of an electric current especially for the purpose of stimulating physiologically." Fifty years is all it took for folks to find the **metaphor** in the exciting new word, which they used to describe exactly that—excitement. In 1853, *galvanize* was first recorded as a synonym for stimulation as if by electricity and became one of our most enlivening verbs. Using the term in the scientist's original sense, poet Phillip Levine writes, "On the *galvanized* tin roof the tunes of sudden rain." Seafaring novelist William McGee used it for electrifying effect: "There are some men whom a staggering emotional shock, so far from making them mental invalids for life, seems, on the other hand, to awaken, to *galvanize*, to arouse into an almost incredible activity of soul." Companion words include *catalyst*, a stimulator, and *catalytic converter,* a device that changes the rate of chemical reaction, as in an automobile engine.


**GARRULOUS**

*Talkative to the point of prattling.* The Latin *garrulus*, from *garrire*, to chatter is where the word begins, but perhaps eventually it devolved into the notion of talking only of commonplace or **trivial** things; perhaps inspired by descriptions of birds as "loud, harsh note; noisy." The 1828 edition of Webster's laconically defines it as "talkative, prating." By the 1913 edition, Webster's has harshened its description but clarifies in a useful manner: "A *garrulous* person indulges in long, prosy talk, with frequent repetitions and lengthened details; *talkative* implies simply a great desire to talk; and *loquacious* a great flow of words at command. A child is talkative; a lively woman is loquacious; an old man in his dotage is *garrulous*." In 2002, Allan, a loquacious Galway coach driver, confided to me, "Ireland is a green, greedy, and *garrulous* land." Companion words include the *garrulous roller*, a noisy chatterbox of a bird.

## GEMÜTLICHKEIT (GERMAN)

*Cozy, easy living. Gemütlichkeit* is to words what slippers are to footwear. The painted word here could be the depiction of a berobed Bavarian couple sitting by the fire, a glass of schnapps in hand, discussing Schiller's poetry and Mahler's music. What I hear when I hear the word are the voices of Ella Fitzgerald and Louis Armstrong singing "Summertime": "… when the livin's easy / fish are jumpin' / and the cotton is high." *Coziness* is arguably the closest **translation**; picture a small, warm, nicely furnished flat. *Gemütlichkeit* also captures the elusive feeling of belonging, social acceptance, nonstressful living. Scholars credit Queen Victoria, whose relatives were German, with popularizing *gemütlich* in English.

The website Skadi Forum: A Germanic Online Community advertises **travel** to Namibia: "The former German colony of Namibia has become an attractive destination for German tourists and expats looking for a new home offering a touch of Teutonic *Gemütlichkeit*—or hospitality." Companion words include Czech *pohoda*, which Wikipedia defines as "cozy, ease, tranquillity, well-being."

Gemütlichkeit: *Der Himmel Draußen (The Sky Outside)*

## GENIZA (HEBREW/YIDDISH)

*A sacred storehouse for holy books in Jewish culture.* A recent *New York Times* article recounts the discovery of the "Living Sea Scrolls" in the lost world of the Cairo *geniza*, a depository in a synagogue or cemetery for "worn-out Hebrew-language books and papers on religious topics ... before they could receive a proper cemetery burial." The word is ancient Hebrew for "storage," from the Persian *ganj*, meaning "hoard" or "hidden treasure." Generally, it refers to the storeroom for religious books or papers, *since it is "forbidden to throw away writings containing the name of God (even personal letters and legal contracts could open with an invocation of God)."* But in practice writings of a more secular nature were also given the sacred ritual of being buried in synagogue cemeteries, the Jerusalem synagogue burying the *geniza* every seventh year. Moreover, the place and the practice of burying the *geniza* is a powerful **metaphor** for the recognition of the sacredness of the written word and the need to preserve it in a respectful way; even more, it embodies a teaching from a beloved sage: "Turn it and turn it ... everything is in it." This teaching alerts us to the holographic nature of the "sacred scraps" found in the Cairo *geniza*; to look at them closely reveals the entire universe. According to the *New York Times Book Review*, it is an "ultimate statement about the worth of words and their place in Jewish life," which must have "either a sacred or a subversive **character** ... both must be hidden, concealed away, out of view, inaccessible." A *geniza* serves a twofold purpose—preserve good things from harm, bad things from harming. In an age in which books are very unceremoniously dumped into landfills, and entire collections of newspapers such as the *St. Louis Post-Dispatch* are destroyed for lack of storage space, the word *geniza* with its attendant meaning is included here for its metaphorical power. "*Geniza* is a barely translatable Hebrew term that holds within it an ultimate statement about the worth of words and their place in Jewish life." Elkan Nathan Adler, who visited the Cairo *geniza* in 1888, wrote: "There is no **sport** quite equal to the hunt for a hidden **manuscript**." Companion words include **thesaurus**, Greek for a treasury or storehouse, of gold, shields, weapons—or words.

### GERONIMO (MEXICAN-SPANISH)

*An exclamation of success; the shout of paratroopers; the name of an Apache freedom fighter; an expression denoting "mission accomplished."* Most Baby Boomers grew up shouting it—jumping off diving boards or while skydiving—but had *zilch* idea of why. Hence, it is a *Where did that come from?* Well, surprise, surprise, it traveled from the arroyos of New Mexico to the green fields of France—a long haul, but there's a good reason why the shout came up. The story unfolds like this: In 1940, some American paratroopers training in drop school watched a new movie titled *Geronimo*, with the legendary Apache warrior Geronimo (Spanish for "Jerome") played by the fierce-faced Chief Thundercloud.

Legend has it that a GI named Aubrey Eberhardt promised he would shout out the chief's name, *Geronimo!* (originally Goyathlay, Apache for "The One Who Yawns"), when he jumped. He shouted and was so impressive that the rest of the paratroopers adopted the fierce call. In spring 2011 the Naval SEALS Team Six mission to assassinate Osama Bin Laden was code-named "Operation *Geronimo*." When the minute-by-minute accounting of the details of the operation was sent by satellite to President Barack Obama, members of the military and his cabinet cheered when they heard "*Geronimo*," the code word for the mission's success. In Saratoga, Wyoming, I found this sign at the old Trading Post: "Life is not a journey to the grave with the intention of arriving safely in one pretty and well preserved piece; but, skid in broadside, thoroughly used up, worn out and defiantly shouting '*Geronimo!*'" Companion terms include the ironically named *Geronimo!* Balloon Company, which employs a word for falling to celebrate the art of rising!

### GLOAMING

*Twilight, dusk, candlelight.* An expressive Old English word for the light that **roams** at dusk, ye olde "roaming in the *gloaming*." Originally, it was *glōmung,* having **roamed** from *glōm,* related to Old Norse *glāmr,* moon, which Brewer suggests depicts the movement of lunar light from "gloom to darken." Evocative as that may be, it only captures half the charm. Adventurer and founder of the Sierra Club,

Gloaming: *Pegasus Night*

John Muir (from *muir*, Old Gaelic for a "sweet, **calm** sea"),
wrote, "The grand show is eternal. It is always sunrise,
somewhere; the dew is never dried all at once; a shower is
forever falling; vapor is ever rising. Eternal sunrise, eternal
dawn and *gloaming*, on sea and continents and islands, each
in its turn, as the round earth rolls." Vladimir Nabokov,
in *Speak, Memory*, cites the lovely Russian word *soomerki*,
for "dusk." The venerable Scottish song "Roaming in the
Gloaming," with lyrics by poet Meta Orred, popularized
by Harry Lauder in 1874, captures the other half of the

charm, the long sigh of a setting sun, the romance of the ruins of day, in the lyrics: "I was roaming in the *gloaming*, / with a Bonnie near the Clyde. / Roaming in the *gloaming*, / with a lassie by my side." Companion words include the Irish phrase "owl-light," to describe dusk.

## GOBLIN

*A mischievous, often demonic creature.* Originally, a *goblin* was a cobbled-together underworld spirit, hovering somewhere between a furtive phantom and an annoying dwarf, naughty just this side of noxious. Our English word comes via the Anglo-Norman *gobelin*, in Middle Latin *gobelinus*, from the German *kobold*, still the name in Deutschland for creepy little creatures [see **cobalt**]. That *goblin* bears passing resemblance to the illustrious Gobelin tapestries, from Paris, is no **false friend**, as the French describe similar words from different languages that have no meaningful connection. Early in the 15th century there appeared a new, deeper, nearly shocking shade of red in the tapestries that was so unsettling common folk suspected the Gobelin brothers, owners of the factory, must have sold their souls to the devil for the formula. "Profits on the exchange are the treasure of *goblins*," wrote the frighteningly prolific Spanish playwright Lope de Vega. "At one time they may be carbuncle stones, then coals, then diamonds, then flint stone, then morning dew, then tears." For Isaac Bashevis Singer, "They still believe in God, the family, angels, devils, witches, *goblins*, and other obsolete stuff." Companions include *brownies, Erl-king,* and *Billy Blind.*

## GONGOOZLE

*To stare, gape, gawk for long periods of time.* Originally, the word referred to any long, dreamy gaze, the kind of look that humorist James Thurber referred to when he said that a writer is someone who has to convince his wife he's working while staring out a **window**. Mrs. Byrne in her humorous dictionary of preposterous words defines a *gongoozler* as "Someone who stares for hours at anything out of the ordinary." Lately it has come to refer to a special breed who gather around maritime locks or stand on bridges, staring longingly. A hobby that is to canals and boats what trainspotting is to tracks and trains. *Gongoozler* is said to have originated with the **cant** of canal workers to describe an observer or an entire crowd gathered, usually quietly, along the towpaths. The term once had a sharp edge of mockery to it, but today it is used with pride by the *gongoozlers* themselves to describe their own harmless hobby. Etymologically, the word is like a canal boat whose name has been rubbed away by time, but one theory traces it back to *gawn* and *gooze*, from Lincolnshire dialect, essentially to gape at boats, during the heyday of canals in the 19th century. *Narrow Boat*, a 1944 book about life along the canals by L. T. C. Rolt, recounts the life of the *gongoozlers* with affection. As my son points out, *Gongoozle* is also the name of a fictional character in *World of Warcraft* and *Runescape*, two of his favorite online games. When I think of this kind of intense staring I can hear an old bartender in Knoxville, Tennessee, describing how his customers had been looking at a troublemaker at the end of the bar: "They stared at him like he was bad weather." Companion words include *gawkery*, the practice of *gawking* at car wrecks, and *gove*, to stare absentmindedly; but to make a finer point, *goving* is that nuanced form of staring halfway between absentminded and gazing fixedly in the distance in hopes that you will be struck by a bolt-out-of-the-blue thought. A *gobemouche* is literally "one who swallows flies," open-mouthed, naive, gullible.

## GROAK

*To stare at somebody else's food in the hope that they will share it.* An anamorphoscope of a word, like a distorted painting that appears **normal** when looked at through a special lens. Rather than a dreamy **gongoozling** stare, this one is dripping with longing, like your Labrador puppy's hangdog staring at the last piece of Thanksgiving turkey, the look that makes you laugh and cry at the same time. Everybody has an Uncle Jimmy who owns a humongous appetite and finishes before everyone else, then stares at the half-eaten food around the table without saying anything, hoping it will be shared. *Stare* is a word too **vanilla** to capture the humor and longing of this scene, whereas *groak* sounds like the thing being done. "All right, would you like this last slice of pizza? Anything to make you stop *groaking* at my food! Here take it, take it!" *Cassell's Dictionary of Slang* defines it as "to look longingly at something, esp. of a child or dog begging for food." A void-filler of a word. Companions include *grok*, Robert Heinlein's 1960 coinage for "understanding, getting it."


## GROCER

*Owner or operator of a food and household products store.* A venerable old word that came ashore in English with the Norman invasion to describe a merchant who bought and sold food items in "gross," from Anglo-French *grosserie*, a wholesaler, which came from the Latin *grossarius*. By the 15th century, *grocers* built *grocery stores* where their goods were sold, such as Grocer's Hall in London. The contemporary usage of "a *grocer's* shop" dates to 1828. The Great American Tea Company, founded in 1859 by Huntington Hartford and George Gilman, morphed into the Great Atlantic and Pacific Tea Company, which became the more familiar A & P *grocery chain*. Companion words include *grocery coupons* and *grocery lists,* which often included a *dollop*, a packet of tea.

## GROTESQUE

*Ugly in a twisted, strangifying way.* Why do so many of our vivid words describe the stranger side of life? This word was first a noun, in the 1600s, from the Middle French *crotesque*, and earlier Italian *grottesco*, of a cave, from *grotta*. The usual explanation is that the word first was used of paintings found on the walls of basements of Roman ruins, from the Italian *pittura grottesca*, a colorful suggestion that the OED finds "intrinsically plausible." Originally "fanciful, fantastic," it turned pejorative after the 18th century. In Italian architecture, *grotte* are ancient buildings featuring murals known as *grottesca* because of their **peculiarity**, and their perverse popularity eventually evolved into the English word as we know it. Satirist Mark Twain asks, "Why was the human race created? Or at least why wasn't something creditable created in place of it? God has His **opportunity**. He could have made a reputation. But no. He must commit this *grotesque* folly—a lark which must have cost Him a regret or two when he came to think it over and observe its effects." Dorothea Lange, exploring the ambiguity of her art, wrote, "Photography today appears to be in a state of flight, the familiar is **made strange**, the unfamiliar *grotesque*. The amateur forces his Sundays into a series of unnatural poses." Companion words include the 1960s term *grotty*, possibly a combination of *grotesque* and *snotty*.

## GYMNOPHORIA

*The queasy feeling that someone is mentally undressing you.* Undressing the word, we find the odd thing that there is no common word for such a common suspicion, from *gymno*, naked, and *phoria*, state. The Urban Dictionary describes it as a discomforting but invaluable "gap word" that means the **horripilating** feeling that results from someone's unwanted and lascivious staring. Companion words include **gymnasium**, a place for exercising naked, *apodyopis*, which is likely to occur in an *apodyterium*, a word that the OED defines as an ancient Greek term for "the apartment in which clothes were deposited by those [athletes] who were preparing for the bath or *palaestra* [wrestling school]; hence *gen,* a dressing room, a robing-room." And who can forget the *gymnosophists*?—those "naked philosophers," as the shocked Greeks called Hindu ascetics or forest hermits, who were infamous for abstaining from wine and sex and who subsisted on nothing but rice, plant food, and meditation.

Gymnophoria: *Das enherne Zeitalter (The Age of Bronze)*

# H

## HACKNEY, HACKNEYED

*A carriage horse; tired, old,* **clichéd**. Originally, a *hackney* was, according to the OED, a "horse of middle size & quality for ordinary riding; a drudge, hireling." Over time, the word was hitched to the carriage it pulled, turning into an adjective by 1769, *hackneyed*, referring to the practice of hiring a horse-drawn carriage. As *hackneys* became replaced by more sophisticated carriages they lost business and couldn't be updated, their paint fading, their cushions threadbare, the horses that pulled them older and wearier. The sudden deterioration from luxurious **travel** to drudgery led to the word's figurative sense of becoming older, wearier, duller, insignificant, and finally *hackneyed*. Through overuse it devolved into that most dreadful of English descriptions— "common." The term *hackney* was first hired out to mean "a paucity of originality" around 1745. One **cliché** led to another, and the stereotype kept repeating itself until it came to describe those bromide-dispensing pen-for-hire writers, uninspired and unoriginal ones who get by with a concatenation of clichés. Hence, *hacks*. The novelist John Gross was fond of puncturing pretentious writing: "The cliché is a *hackneyed* idiom that hopes that it can still palm itself off as a fresh response." Companion words include *Hackney pony*, a high-stepping breed descended from the *Hackney horse*, originally bred to haul carriages, but today bred as show ponies.

## HA-HA

*A fence sunken in a ditch; a barrier or boundary to a park or garden, unseen from a distance.* The design is impressive, but the response is hilarious. So much so that the country walkers who stumble upon one of these hidden ditches or fences tend to instinctively cry out, "Ha!"—often followed by the duplicative *"Ha-ha!,"* a kind of side-slapping cry of laughter upon seeing someone fall into the ditch or hole. Known from Norman times in England, *ha-has* first appeared in deer parks, such as Parkside Farm, on the road between Dover and Canterbury, established by the brother of William the Conqueror; parts of it can be seen today. In the early 1970s, the archaeologist Richard Reece uncovered an 18th-century *ha-ha,* a moatlike ditch designed to protect the abbey from roving cattle, while excavating on the pilgrimage island of Iona, Scotland. After the terrorist attacks of 9/11, a dramatic ditch was dug around the

Washington Monument to protect it from future assaults. In his urbane essay "City and Soul," psychologist James Hillman digs deeper into the implications of creating *ha-has*. "The eighteenth century took care of this need of the soul for indirection in a canny manner," he writes. "Into the walking areas there were constructed what the common people called '*ha ha's*,' surprising sunken fences, hidden hedges, boundary ditches which, when come upon suddenly, called forth a 'ha ha,' stopping the progress of the walk, forcing the foot to turn and the mind to reflect. How **strange** this is to us today." Hilarious, really. Like all good jokes, it makes you stop and think. Imagine that. Companion words include "Aha!," the rapscallion philosopher Alan Watts's "Eureka!"

### HALIBUT

*A white fish, famous fodder for fish and chips.* If we cast a wide net for its origins we pull up the Middle English *halybutt*, holy butt, which doesn't refer to a saint's buttocks, but to the old word *butt,* for any flatfish. The holy part of the butt, so to speak, of the enormous **flounder**, which was usually set aside for eating on holy days, hence "holy flounder," then "holy butt," then scaled down to *halibut.* In Monty Python's *Life of Brian*, the condemned Matthias moans, "All I did was say to my wife, 'That piece of *halibut* was good enough for Jehovah!'" In a 1996 essay that I caught on the Fine Fishing website, "How and Where to

Catch **Trophy** *Halibut* from 40 to 800 Pounds," Christopher Batin writes, "Biological studies show that predatory species are often prey selective, meaning if crabs are the predominant item in an area, and *halibut* have been feeding on them, and the crabs have hit a sweet tooth, *halibut* will continue to search out crabs." After a shot of Glenlivet one night in Honolulu, Joseph Campbell uttered the only two **puns** I ever heard slip from him, as he was saying farewell to me: "Years ago, I went to Ireland for the whiskey, and to England for the *halibut*." Shaking my hand, he added with slightly swithered Gaelic **glee**, "Abyssinia," pronouncing it like "Ah'll-be-seeing-ya."

## HAREM (TURKISH)

*A room where a sultan keeps a bevy of wives.* In early Arabic *haram* referred to the wives and concubines of the sultan, and *harim* was a forbidden place, from *harama*, to prohibit. They blended together like spices from the Istanbul bazaar to describe both the place and the people, the part of a Muslim house reserved for women and the women who lived there with their husband, or master of the household. Eventually, the sense evolution gave us the *harem* we know today, usually used titillatingly to describe a group of women at the beck and call of a powerful man. In the *Dreams of Trespass: Tales of a Harem*, Fatima Mernissi writes **arabesquely**, "Sometimes, she said that to be stuck in a *harem* simply meant that a woman had lost her freedom of movement. Other times, she writes, a *harem* meant misfortune because a woman had to share her husband with many others." Irrepressibly, the irreverent Brendan Behan wrote, "Critics are like eunuchs in a *harem*; they know how it's done, they've seen it done every day, but they're unable to do it themselves." Ralph Waldo Emerson saw the sensuous poetry of the word: "A man's library is a sort of *harem*." Companion words include *seraglio*, the room for the harem, from Persian *serdi*, residence or palace, which supplied us with *caravansary* and *zenana*, from the Persian *zan*, woman.

## HEARTBREAKER

*A woman's fetching lock of hair.* A **gorgeous** word dating back to at least 1630, which Dr. Johnson in his *Dictionary* defines as "a **cant** name for a woman's curls, supposed to break the heart of all her lovers." He cites the obscure poet Hudibras: "Like Samson's *heartbreakers*, it grew / In time to make a nation rue." By 1863, those curls had grown to refer to mean a person and not just the hair, a woman so radiantly beautiful or lovable she could break your heart. Companion words include the name of a rock band, Tom Petty and the *Heartbreakers*, and a song by Pat Benatar, "Heartbreaker," with lyrics like these: "You're a *Heartbreaker* / Dream maker, love taker / Don't you mess around with me, no, no, no …"

## HECTOR

*Shout loudly; scold.* George Orwell once commented that fine prose should be as clear as a pane of glass. I would add fine words as well, such as this one, which derives from one of the most famous stories of all time. The Trojan prince Hector, in the *Iliad*, is the oldest son of King Priam and Queen Hecuba and the older brother of fair Paris, the doomed lover of Helen of Sparta. He is an honorable **hero** whose unassailable reputation, other than a brief boast after his slaying of Patroclus, is remembered not for his *heart-breaking* words to his wife, Andromache ("No man can escape his destiny") but because of this blustering word. His own good name derives from the Greek *hektor*, holder, stayer, from *ekhein*, to hold fast, which is contained in the allusions to his tight grip on the glory that was Troy's and his steadfast **character** in staying to defend his city even in its darkest hour. Until the 14th century *hector* echoed Homer's sense of "a valiant warrior," but for reasons barely worth shouting about. By the 1650s, the word had turned cowardly, yielding Dr. Johnson's definition "a blustering, turbulent, pervicacious, noisy fellow." Thus, a tragi-cally inverted word with soft-spoken origins. It is a short chariot ride around the walls of Troy to get to the odd reversal, which might be in Shakespeare's *The Merry Wives of Windsor*: "Said I well, bully *hector*?" Scholars suggest this isn't a typo, or an elision, but a "contraction of the common idiomatic expression *bully hector*, suggesting a "swaggering warrior," but not necessarily a bully. No doubt Achilles did "bully Hector," which could be the source of the confusion between the two heroes. Michael Madrone suggests the modern sense may derive from "a group of seventeenth–century London street toughs known as *Hectors*. These sword-wielding ***window***-breakers probably gave themselves this name, flattering their own prowess; but everyone else in the city regarded them as blustering bullies." Companion words include *Apaches*, a gang of street toughs in Paris in the early 20th century, urban warriors waging war against the dreaded bourgeoisie.

## HIFALUTIN

*Pretentious, trying to stand out or above it all.* Americans have had a long and lacerating suspicion of education and educated people, as well as of pretentious social behavior. The latter disdain of privilege is memorialized in this Mississippi River–inspired word, first recorded in 1848, from the observation of tall, fluted smokestacks on fancy steamboats, presumably from the perspective of small boats, canoes, even rafts. Eventually, the term became a sterling example of *synecdoche*, where one thing stands for another, in this case the passengers on board who were flaunting their money or education. Hence the common epithet in Westerns, where a fast-talking greenhorn is called "hifa-lutin" because he is showing off his education. Competing theories have the word being cut down to size from *high-flying*, or meaning a *high-pitched flute*. Companion words include *hoity-toity*, a rhyming compound from *hoit*, archaic English for fool.

## HILLBILLY

*A resident of the hills and hollers of Appalachia.* A badge of honor for some, a city slicker's insult to others. Always a combustible term and a source of debate for word scholars. Some believe it to be a remnant of William of Orange, "King Billy," some of whose followers settled in the hills of southern Appalachia. What in tarnation did you expect other than *hill-billy*? The word goes through what Appalachians call *twistification* to arrive where it is today. By April 23, 1900, the *New York Journal* was writing: "In short, a Hill-Billie is a free and untrammelled white citizen of Alabama, who lives in the hills, has no means to speak of, dresses as he can, talks as he pleases, drinks whiskey when he gets it, and fires off his revolver as the fancy takes him." The word became more popular worldwide due to its use in folk music, the earliest reference being in 1924. Loretta Lynn said: "Once in a while I get inspired and finish my act with the *hillbilly* hoedown." Country and Western legend Hank Williams: "You got to have smelt a lot of mule manure before you can sing like a *hillbilly*." Companion words include *rube, hayseed,* and the ever-faithful Irish *clodhopper.*

## HOBNOB

*To keep fancy company.* A far cry from Captain Grosse's original explanation of the question "Will you *hob* or *nob* with me?"—which meant, back in 1611 when he published his early dictionary, a request to imbibe either a beer on the *hob* (warm) or a beer on the nob (cold). Webb Garrison's marvelous *Why Do They Call It That?* says: "Originally, Old English, *haebbe*, have, *noebbe*, have not—an old **toast**, Will you have warm or cold beer, i.e. beer from the hob (from inside the hearth), or from the nob, cold from the table?" In *Twelfth Night*, Shakespeare writes this exchange: "Viola: I pray you sir, what is he? Sir Toby: He is knight, dubb'd with unhatch'd rapier, and on carpet consideration, but he is a devil in private brawl. Souls and bodies hath he divorc'd three, and his incensement at this moment is so implacable, that satisfaction can be none but by pangs of death and sepulchre. *Hob, nob,* is his word; give't or take it." Companion words include *hobnocker*, a loser who performs gross, illegal, sometimes public acts, and *Nob Hill,* in San Francisco, where this book is currently being completed. Recently, I overheard one of an old couple at Big 4 Restaurant say, "My mother used to say that on *Nob Hill* a man counts his carriages not his expenses."

## HOLY MOLY!

*An epithet of surprise!* A conundrum of a phrase, with roots ramifying out into both mythology and herbology. If you look in *The Odyssey*, you will find it is the name of Hermes's magical herbal potion; in an herbal dictionary you will find *Alium moly*, a wild member of the lily family, garlicky in flavor. The *Concise OED* traces *holy* back to the Old English *halig*, dedicated to a religious purpose, and *moly* to an herbal mixture with magical powers used by Circe to turn men into pigs, which lends itself to no end of scurrilous jokes. Moving to the modern mythic world of comic books, specifically *Captain Marvel*, the epithet *Holy moly!* was often used by the eponymous **hero** in his battle against the forces of evil during World War II. Linguists deem it a "reduplicated rhyming compound," like *killer-diller, hokey-pokey,* and my grandmother's favorite, *fancy-schmancy.* Companion words and phrases include, as Rocky Reichman writes in his word blog, *legal eagle, hokey-pokey, super-duper, razzle-dazzle,* and most memorably, the Sixties pop lyric "She wore an *itsy-bitsy, teenie-weenie yellow polka-dot bikini.*"

## HOMER

*A big hit of a word; a poet, a four-base hit; a measure of about three pints.* In Leviticus, it is written, "An *homer* of barley-seed shall be valued at fifty shekels of silver." Homer was the legendary blind Greek poet, an early kind of wandering minstrel, who flourished around 850 BCE, author of the *Iliad* and *The Odyssey*. In baseball, a four-base hit; also *homer*, a pigeon trained to fly home, hence a *homing* pigeon; *homer*, unit of capacity used by the ancient Hebrews, equal to 10 ephahs (about 10 bushels) or 10 baths (about 100 gallons). Babe Ruth described his approach to hitting: "I swing big, with everything I've got. I hit big or I miss big. I like to live as big as I can ... I never heard a crowd boo a *homer*, but I've heard plenty of boos after a strikeout." The polymath Isaac Asimov, in *Words from the Myths*, defines *Homeric* as a synonym for "sublime," or "majestic." Companion words include *home-run monkey* and *Homer*, Alaska.

## HONORIFICABILITUDINITATIBUS

*The state or condition of being able to achieve honors.* It holds the honor of being the longest word in Shakespeare's prodigious collected works, used once in *Love's Labor's Lost*, Act V, Scene I, and spoken by the comic jester Costard: "O, they have lived long on the alms-basket of words. I marvel thy master hath not eaten thee for a word; for thou art not long by the head as *honorificabilitudinitatibus*: thou art easier swallowed than a flap-dragon." Among the anti-bardologists who believe Francis Bacon is the author of those works, there is a **rumor** that the word is an anagram for *hi ludi F. Baconis nati, tuit orbi*, or "These plays, F. Bacon's offspring, are preserved in the world." The word has scarcely been honored since. Companions include the truncated version *honorific*, a name that confers esteem and admiration.

## HOODLUM

*A punk, a criminal.* You could stir up a good street fight among linguists if you brought up its word history, which no one knows for sure because it has vanished like a crime witness. But we have found some clues. Writing from North Beach, across Broadway from San Francisco's Chinatown, it's intriguing to **consider** that this slightly gangsta word may have arisen in my own neighborhood. Charles Funk's sleuthing suggests that it was lurking in the city's underground around 1870, while Bartlett tracks it down via anecdotal evidence to 1877: a "gang of ruffians" and their leader, Noodlum, whose name was spelled backward by a reporter in fear of reprisals—then an errant typesetter misspelled it *hoodlum* anyway. Other theories, Funk points out, include Pidgin English *hood lahnt,* very lazy mandarin, a bastardization of the speaking habits in Chinatown. James Cagney, who helped **immortalize** *hoodlums* in movies such as *White Heat*, was troubled by the possibility that his vivid acting may have led to tolerance of underworld crime. As he wrote in his memoirs, "Though I soon became typecast in Hollywood as a gangster and *hoodlum*, I was originally a dancer, an Irish hoofer, trained in **vaudeville** tap dance. I always leapt at the **opportunity** to dance in films later on." Companion words include *hoodlum knife,* a survival blade.

## HORDE

*An army of uncivilized marauders, a mob.* Out of our ancient word hoard comes another kind of invader, this time from the West Turkic or Tatar *urda, horde,* or royal residence or camp, combined with the Turkish *ordu,* camp, army, from the 1550s. As time and troops marched across Europe they carried words with them, including the Mongol *orda* and the Russian *opð,* which transformed into the Polish *horda,* Middle French *horde,* and German *Horde* before reaching the shores of England. The American Da Vinci, R. Buckminster Fuller, is known more for his geodesic domes than for his poetry, but here's one anyway: "Let architects sing of **aesthetics** that bring rich clients in *hordes* to their knees; / Just give me a home in a great circle dome / where stresses and strains are at ease." Social historian Camille Paglia writes: "Teenage boys, goaded by their surging hormones, **run** in packs like the primal *horde.* They have only a brief season of exhilarating liberty between control by their mothers and control by their wives." Companion words include *hordeolum,* an infection of the eyelid.

## HORNSWOGGLE

*To cheat,* **bamboozle**, **hoax**. An old seafaring term, first recorded around 1829, for being tossed around the ship or into the water. Better known to moderns to mean "being taken advantage of or fooled." The cartoon Hercules, Popeye, once cried out after being roughed up by Brutus,

"Well, I's bin *hornswoggled!*" In the 1988 mock sci-fi flick *Killer Klowns from Outer Space*, Farmer Gene Green shouts out like Gabby Hayes in a 1950s Western horse opera, "Well, I'll be *hornswoggled!*" Companion words include *Hornswoggle*, a professional wrestler who was Cruiser-weight **champion** from 2007 to 2009.

## HORRIPILATION

*Goose pimples or bristling hair brought on by fear or cold weather.* Oh, the horror of it all! A horrendous word, one that makes the hair on your head stand up. When my son Jack was about five he called it the "creepy-crawlies." The Latin origins would terrify you, from *horripilere*, with its roots showing in *horrere*, to bristle, and *pilus*, hair. A rather *circumlocutionary* citation comes from Dick Cavett in his *Talk Show: Confrontations, Pointed Commentary, and Off-Screen Secrets*. Of the literary life, he wrote, "A good example is the great but frequently wounded quote of Mark Twain's on writing, a quote that causes, when done right, my forearms to *horripilate*." He was referring to Twain's letter to Fred J. Hall, August 10, 1892, in which he said: "I conceive that the right way to write a story for boys is to write so that it will not only interest boys but strongly interest any man who has ever been a boy. That immensely enlarges the audience." Companion words: *goose bumps*, *chicken flesh*, and the hair-raising *piloerection* and *pilomotor reflex*.

## HORS D'OEUVRE (FRENCH)

*An appetizer; a simple dish served before or aside from the meal.*
Literally, it means "outside the work," from the French
*hors*, outside, and *oeuvre*, work. Figuratively, it means "aside
from the main course." One's *oeuvre* is the full course, the
full meal, especially when served with spicy *hauteur*, while
an *hors d'oeuvre* is an extra, an appetizer. Speaking of the
difference, comedian and *musician-manqué* Jack Benny gave
this definition: "*Hors d'oeuvre*: a ham **sandwich** cut into
forty pieces." In 1925's *The Great Gatsby,* F. Scott Fitzgerald
serves up this beautifully painted description: "On buffet
tables, garnished with glistening **hors-d'oeuvre**, spiced
baked hams crowded against salads of harlequin designs
and pastry pigs and turkeys bewitched to a dark gold."
Companion words include *canapé, finger food, munchies.*

## HUCKSTER

*A* **phony** *seller; an untrustworthy politician.* It's an old practice
and an old word, at least eight hundred years old, dating
back to the 13th-century Middle Dutch *hokester,* peddler.
Around 1225, John of Garlandia (Johannes de Garlandia),
the medieval English grammarian, used it memorably in
his *Dictionarius:* "Today I saw a *huckster* peddling table
knives, carving knives, and daggers, scabbards small and
large, styli, and stilettos ... *Hucksters* send out servants,
male and female, to entice scholars to whom they sell,
much too dearly, cherries, white and black plums and

unripe apples and pears and lettuce and cress." The pejorative dimension came later, around the 16th century, and the modern sense of an advertising con man can be dated to the 1947 novel by Frederick Wakeman, *The Hucksters*, peddled by MGM into a movie directed by Jack Conway, starring Clark Gable. Then comes the notion, from one of the most deftly named writers of all time—the jurist Learned Hand—of the snake-oil salesman: "What seems fair enough against a squalid *huckster* of bad liquor may take on a different face, if used by government determined to suppress political opposition under the guise of sedition." A learned and handy description of a hawker, if there ever was one. Companion words include the ever-lyrical *colporteur,* costermonger, and the simply hustling *street vendor.*

## HUNKY-DORY (FRISIAN-DUTCH)

*Okey-dokey, all's well, satisfactory.* A catchy example of a reduplicative word, As recounted in John Russell Bartlett's 1877 edition of *Dictionary of Americanisms*, the catchphrase came from a **vaudeville** performer in New York named Japanese Tommy during the 1860s and is based on *Honchodori*, a street expression for sailors' diversions in Tokyo. But as Allan Metcalf points out in *The World in So Many Words* it was probably a play on words within words, riffing off the New York **slang** word *hunk*, which once meant a safe place or position, in the lingo of its day, from the Danish word for "goal" or "home" in a ball game, which in turn derived from the Frisian *honck*, house or safe place. Hence, *hunky-dory* truly means a safe hiding place. Companion words include *hunker down*, settle in, take shelter.

## HUSH PUPPY

*A delectable Southern specialty: a **ball** of deep-fried cornmeal batter.* According to legend, invented by hunters who threw the treats to their noisy dogs to **calm** them down. First attested to in 1918. We learn from this delicious word *recipe* from 1939, in *The Southern Cook Book:* "Tallahassee Negroes ... sugar cane grinding ... around open fire ... iron pot for cone pone cooked in fat ... spell-bind each other with tall stories ... hounds whimpering, Hush, puppy." Companion words include *hushbuster,* something difficult to keep secret, and the soft shoes *Hushpuppies,* from 1961, presumably as comfortable to wear as the food was to eat for the hunting dogs. Recently, I discovered in an old journal, from 1987, notes I took from a conversation with my grandfather Horace Cousineau at a Southern-style restaurant in Casselberry, Florida, where he said to me, "Pass them *hush puppies* before they bark."

## HWYL (WELSH)

*Emotional outburst of fervor, such as the **eloquence** expressed by a poet or actor; sudden spark, **enthusiasm**, **fun**; wind in your sails.* One of the more unusual and hard to pronounce words (*hew-ell* or *ho-eel*). An **untranslatable** from Wales that describes a sudden emotional eruption of eloquence. It's tempting to think that this Celtic phenomenon is a direct descendent of the *warp spasm* that came over the old **heroes** like Cuchulain, who, according to Cahill, "became possessed when confronting an enemy." Think of the pearls of poetry that came over Dylan Thomas at the White Horse Tavern, or Richard Burton at the Royal Shakespeare Company. Of unknown derivation, other than that the tantalizing *hwyl* originally meant "sail, journey, course, mood, fervor." In Celtic witchcraft *hwyl* is used to describe the blessing of the ancestors. It is also credited with describing what it means to be Welsh, all compressed and condensed, like Richard Burton's performance of *Hamlet*, in one four-letter word. The Durham, North Carolina, *Herald-Sun* reviewed a band with the self-same name that played at the Carrboro Music Fest 2006: "*Hwyl* brings new culture to North Carolina."

## HYDRODAKTULOPSYCHICHARMONICA

*The glass harmonica, the bowl organ.* Have you ever wondered if there was a word for the musical practice of rubbing one's fingers along the rim of a glass or glasses? Next time someone pulls this trick at a bar or a party you can tell them what a great *"armonica"* player they are, from *harmonia*, Greek for "harmony." Or if you're daring enough, try to pronounce the whole thing: *hydro (water)—*

*daktulo (fingers)—psychic (soul)—harmony.* For full effect, "the music of the soul played by fingers dipped in water." The earliest references date back to the Renaissance, and Galileo wrote about the *armonica* in *Two New Sciences*, but it was the Irish musician and inventor Richard Poekrich, in 1740, who is credited with the first public exhibitions of his newly-forged, cut-glass talent. Our own Benjamin Franklin was so fond of this parlor trick he invented his own version, simply called the *armonica*, Italian for "harmonious," and Wolfgang Mozart created a few pieces of music for the intrepid to play. The sounds are created by using cups or bowls of glass in increasing and decreasing size to produce different pitches by the sheer friction of the fingers. There were rumors that the instrument drove listeners mad. The German musicologist Johann Friedrich Rochlitz wrote: "The harmonica excessively stimulates the nerves, plunges the player into a nagging depression and hence into a dark and melancholy mood that is apt method for slow self-annihilation. If you are suffering from any nervous disorder, you should not play it; if you are not yet ill you should not play it; if you are feeling melancholy you should not play it."

## HYMN

*Song of praise.* A word as beautiful as it sounds and as ancient as the **beauty** it evokes. All cultures have sung *hymns* in one frame or fashion, but our English word dates back to around 1000 CE, from Old French *ymne* and Old English *ymen*, both leaning back to the Latin *hymnus*, a song of praise, and the Greek *hymnos*, a song or ode in honor of the gods or **heroes**, inspired by *Polyhymnia*, the **muse** of religious music. The word is familiarly used in the Septuagint for various Hebrew words meaning "song praising God." One anecdotal origin story suggests it is a variant of *hymenaios*, a wedding song, from Hymen, Greek god of marriage. "I wrote a big *hymn* on a train from Kyoto to Tokyo," wrote Allen Ginsberg to Gary Snyder from Japan, on August 29, 1963. Companion words include *doxology*, a *hymn* of praise to the Almighty, uncannily employed by songwriter R. B. Morris in "Emily," and *hymnody*, the singing or composing of hymns, as in Van Morrison's "I sing my *hymns* to the silence."

Hymn: *Passing View of Shohei Bridge*

## I

## IGNORAMUS

*A person not in the know, an ignorant **cad**.* The Latin translation leads us in the right direction: "We do not know," the response of medieval juries when there was not enough evidence to convict someone on trial. This sense was immortalized by playwright George Ruggle in his play *Ignoramus*, in 1615, which he said was "written to expose the ignorance and arrogance of common lawyers." In the Talmud, we read: "When a scholar goes to seek out a bride he should take along an *ignoramus* as an expert." In *The Devil's Dictionary,* Ambrose Bierce features this definition that Beelzebub himself would have relished: "IGNORAMUS, n. A person unacquainted with certain kinds of knowledge familiar to yourself, and having certain kinds of knowledge unfamiliar to yourself, and having certain other kinds that you know nothing about." Companion words include *moron*, Latin for "fool," and *"You block-*

*head!"*—Lucy's shout-out at Charlie Brown in *Peanuts*.

## IMMORTALING

*Working on one's own fame, sorting out one's lot in life, cadging for immortality.* Immortalize, but with some gallop in its step. Actually a lost Greek verb that vividly describes the self-conscious process of working on one's immortality, as did Plato, or Achilles in the *Iliad*. This unquenchable thirst for everlasting fame was called *kleos*. Companion words include the lofty *ensky*, to make immortal by way of funeral pyres sending the smoke of **heroes** into the heavens. Books of quotations, such as Bartlett's or the OED's, are *immortaling* efforts in the world of words. The frontier hero Davey Crockett said when it reprinted the hundredth time his words, "I would rather be politically dead than hypocritically *immortalized*."

## INCARCERATE

*To imprison, to jail.* For the ancient Romans, gladiator fights were the gory center of the infamous Blood and Circuses spectacles designed to feed the bellies and bloodlust alike. The gladiators were slaves and prisoners who fought each other as well as the occasional hungry lion, and lived in underground rooms not unlike the cages where the animals were kept until battles were waged. The cages were called *carceres*, as were the gladiators who were trained to fight to the death, as if they were one and the same. So sharp was the image of living behind bars and at death's door that the word gave rise to the Latin *carcer,* prison, the foundation stone for *incarcerare,* to imprison, the vengeful English verb. Comedian, actor, activist Bill Cosby asks, "The *incarcerated*? These are not political criminals. These are people going around stealing Coca-Cola. People getting shot in the back of the head over a piece of pound cake, and then we run out and we are outraged, saying, 'The cops shouldn't have shot him.' What the hell was he doing with the pound cake in his hand?" Companion words include *incarnadine,* flesh-colored, crimson, not unlike the blood spilled in the *arena* (Latin for "sand") by the *incarcerated* ones.

## INDIGO

*A blue powder or dyestuff; deep shade of blue, one of the seven prismatic colors.* This transmarine dye, coming from across the sea, or ultramarine, from beyond the sea, derives from the India plant *Indigofera tinctoria.* The Anglo-Saxon word is much hardier: *woadstuff.* Together, the **color** and the sound converge in this heavenly-hued word. The earliest uses can be traced by following the 16th-century trade routes: the Spanish *indico,* Portuguese *endego,* Dutch *indigo,* each rooted in the Greek *indikon,* from *indikos,* Indian dye. All these words refer to the lusted-after blue dye from India. When rubbed, this dark-blue plant reveals what's been called "a copper-violet luster." The equally colorful novelist Tom Robbins, in his jazzy and redolent novel *Jitterbug Perfume*, takes advantage of the word's wonderful inner rhythms: "Hold on to your divine blush, your innate rosy magic, or end up brown. Once you're brown, you'll find out you're blue. As blue as *indigo*. And you know what that means. *Indigo. Indigoing. Indigone.*" Companion words include *Indigo children,* a New Age designation granted to children believed to possess paranormal or supernatural abilities such as telepathy, but also a general sensitivity.

## INFANT

*A baby or small child, one that hasn't found its voice yet.* Although it appears obvious what an *infant* is, its inner meaning startles and surprises. The word means what it says, or better yet, what it *doesn't* say, deriving from the Latin *in-fant*, unable to speak yet. Strictly speaking, though we don't want to be too strict with babies, a newborn baby is an *infant* for a few weeks from birth, defined in medical books as *neonate*, Latin, *neonatus*, newborn, for twenty-eight days after birth. Humorist Dave Barry makes a rib-tickling distinction: "The difference between men and women is that, if given the choice between saving the life of an *infant* or catching a fly **ball**, a woman will automatically choose to save the *infant*, without even considering if there's a man on base." English poet William Blake: "Sweet babe, in thy face Soft desires I can trace. / Secret joys and secret smiles. Little pretty *infant* wiles." Legendary *New Yorker* movie critic Pauline Kael found the dark streak of the word when she gave a rather left-handed compliment to Steven Spielberg for his *Close Encounters of the Third Kind:* "A kid's movie in the best sense," but later **kvetched**, "It's not so much what Spielberg has done, but what he has encouraged. Everyone else has imitated his fantasies, and the result is an *infantilization* of the culture." Companion words include the obvious *infantile*, and the less obvious *vocation*, from Latin *vocationem*, a calling, as in hearing your inner voice, which is what *infants* and children need to do to grow into adults.

## INKHORN

*The term for an over-intellectualized word.* A painted word borrowed from the horn-shaped pot used to store ink for old quill pens. The 16th-century author Thomas Wilkes wrote, "Among all other lessons, this should first be learned, that wee should never effect any straunge ynkhorne terms ... using our speech as most men do, and ordering our wittes as the fewest have done." Melvyn Bragg defines them in his indispensable *The Adventures of English* as "new, usually elaborate, classically based terms," which transformed our language into one "honeycombed of English with Latin and Greek terms that disturbed some scholars." Moreover, he adds, the "*Inkhorn* Controversy" triggered what he considers to be the first and most vigorous dispute about what is considered to be the True and Proper

English. Eventually, the ink in the *inkhorn* dried up, leaving only the stains of memory of a time when newly coined words, especially recondite or obscure ones, were received with deep contempt. After all, didn't Shakespeare, the inventor of some 2,000 words, describe himself, in *Love's Labour's Lost*, as "A man of fire-new words"? Ironically, some words that sounded pretentious when coined, such as those by Francis Bacon (*catastrophe)* and Thomas Moore (*exaggerate*) are commonly used now. A sobering thought for those who still despise neologisms—oops, I mean new words. Some are actually clever and useful, such as the recent *moasting*, boasting about what makes us moan. Companion words include *inkling* (see below), *inkstain*, and *Inkscape*, which is, according to Wikipedia, a free software vector graphics editor.

## INKLING

*Slight evidence.* A *euphonious* but obscure word, recorded only once, in Middle English *nyngkiling*, a whisper, an undertone. When I was late with a story at my first newspaper job I didn't have an *inkling* about **deadlines**, until my editor Roger Turner told me, "Son, when it's *ink*, it's real." Grosse defines *inkle weavers* as "supposed to be a very brotherly set of people, as great as two *inkle weavers*, being a proverbial saying." The *Inklings* were a bevy of University of Oxford dons, authors, and book lovers, who met for nearly twenty years at a pub in Oxford, England, to discuss epic narrative and fantasy. Among the enthusiasts were J. R. R. Tolkien and his son Christopher, C. S. Lewis and his older brother Warren, linguist Owen Barfield, Charles Williams, South African poet Roy Campbell, and other noteworthies. "Properly speaking," wrote Warren Lewis, "the *Inklings* was neither a club nor a literary society, though it partook of the nature of both. There were no rules, officers, agendas, or formal elections." The Inklings Society of Aachen, Germany, has published a journal, *Inklings Jahrbuch für Literatur und Ästhetik*, since 1983 focusing on fantasy literature and mythopoetics. "The American's **conversation** is much like his courtship," writes Donald Lloyd. "He gives an *inkling* and watches for a reaction: if the weather looks fair, he *inkles* a little more." During the building of the Transcontinental Railroad, in the 1860s, *ink-slinger* was a common name for newspaper reporters: "Everybody who could sling *ink* became correspondents." And of course there is *ink* all by its lonesome, here from Emerson: "I dip my pen in the blackest *ink*, because I'm not afraid of falling into my *inkpot*." In the fall of 2011 I read in the shadows of a medieval **scriptorium** at Clonmacnois the Irish proverb "A scholar's *ink* is worth more than a martyr's blood." Companion words include *inkle*, to utter in an undertone, still used in the game of bridge, as in "She *inkles* a club."

## INTIMISM (FRENCH)

*The practice of painting intimate, often sensual, paintings.* Coined by the French painter Pierre Bonnard, and practiced also by Edgar Degas and Edouard Vuillard, it affectionately describes Bonnard's *intimate* works of women, mostly his wife, Marthe, who posed for him in such sensuous settings as bathtubs and, *en deshabillé,* undressed, before mirrors. Naturally, he based it upon the familiar word *intimate,* from Latin *intimatus,* "closely acquainted," and the earlier *intimus,* inmost, implying a close friend. A much-needed word to describe particularly *intimate* art, such as Vermeer's *Woman in Blue Reading a Letter,* and to distinguish it from

Intimism: *The Mirror Dreams*

the often unintended sexual connotations of *intimate*. The Latin *intimare* lends us the curious root, which is "to make known, impress." Companion words include the Victorian fig leaf *intimates*, for women's underwear. An art historian might help revive the word by writing, "The *intimist* work of the 19th-century photographer Julia Cameron was hugely popular in Paris."

## INTOXICATE

*To make drunk, poison with alcohol, or exhilarate beyond control.* If you've ever been under the influence of alcohol or drugs, you have been "smeared with poison," the OED's reminder of the word's toxic origins. During both the ecstatic and the agonizing moments you have unwittingly felt a visceral connection to the curious continuity of words that have traveled through time. During Roman times some scalawags began to dip their arrows in poison. An archer's bow at that time was called a *toxon*, and anything related to a bow was *toxikos*; the poison over the arrow tip became *toxikon*. By the Middle Ages, the word had become separated from the bow and arrow, but the poison lived on in the word *toxic*, like a lingering fever, as some words are fever dreams. Figuratively, Anaïs Nin writes, "I only believe in *intoxication*, in ecstasy, and when ordinary life shackles me, I escape one way or the other. No more walls."

## IRIDESCENT

*Rainbow-colored, brilliant, luminous.* Luminous colors that appear to change when viewed from different angles. From one angle, the ordinary dictionary, it is defined monochromatically and platitudinously as merely "colorful." From another angle it is mythopoetic, harkening back to *Iris*, the winged messenger goddess of Greek myth, who swooped down from Mount Olympus and left a trail of colors in her wake. Similarly, *iridescent* is far more than colorful; it describes how hues appear to change when seen from a variety of views. Surprisingly, the word dates back only to the late 18th century, rainbowing down to us from the Latin *iris*, from *irid*, rainbow, plus the suffix *-escent*. To lend a sense of the ephemeral beauty and the sobering passing of *things* evoked by this *bubblescent* word, let's give the writer William Osler the floor: "No bubble," he wrote, "is so *iridescent* or floats longer than that blown by the successful teacher." Companion words include *prismatology*, the study of the effects that different colors have on people.

# J

## JACK

*One of the most versatile words and names in the language; a pet name for John.* If you think you know the extent of this capacious word, then "You don't know, *Jack,*" as people say about someone they think knows nothing at all. But let's go back to the beginning, as Walter Skeat does by defining him as "a saucy fellow, a sailor ... often used as a term of reproach, as in *Jakke foole*, in Chaucer." Also, he adds, "a coat of mail." Skeat tracks the etymology back to the Hebrew Ya'akov, Jacob, "one who seizes by the heels." Since my son is named Jack, my alert is on for any mention. Charles Earle Funk speculates that *Jack* is commonplace because it became the familiar form of the most common name in Old English, John—so common, in that place, so to speak, that *Jack* evolved into the nickname for common youths, then disreputable youths, symbolized by the *knave* on playing cards, and finally common laborers.

Commonly, they became synonymous with the jobs they performed, since common usage sands words right down to their essential grain. *The Oxford Dictionary of Word Histories* makes the nuanced point that the word came to stand in for the mechanical devices that helped the common laborer, such as the *jackscrew, jackhammer, bootjack,* and *single-jacking,* one logger working a tree. The common thread is commonality itself, even in describing animals such as the *jackass, jackrabbit,* and *jackdaw,* and the expression *kookaburra jackeroo,* a greenhorn on a sheep ranch in Australia. By the time hipsters arrived on the scene, in the 1950s, *Jack* had evolved into "an all-purpose term of address by hipsters," as Max Décharné writes in his **cool** dictionary of hipster **slang**, *Straight from the Fridge, Dad.* Companion words and phrases include *jackaleg, jackalog, jackattack, flap-jack; jactitation,* a harmful boast or an "involuntary tossing and twitching of the body and limbs"; *balling the Jack* from Appalachia train lore, moving fast; and *blackjack,* both a card game and, as Francis Grosse writes in 1611, "a jug to drink out of, made of black leather." One for the curiosity cabinet is *jackanapes,* a conceited fellow, after the real-life *Jack of Naples,* who had the habit of going in public with a monkey, hence *jack of Naples with his ape.* We can't leave this entry without mentioning the perennial favorite *jack-in-the-box,* a 16th-century word for a cheat, swindler, or "sharp," one who "deceived tradesmen by substituting empty boxes for others full of money," recorded in 1702. Finally, my favorite, a *skipjack,* an upstart.

## JEOPARDY

*Hazard, chance, gamesmanship.* A word such as this reminds me of the painter Mark Rothko's ferocious belief that real **color** reveals a deeper reality behind the canvas, which is why he encouraged viewers to gaze long and deep into his paintings. If we were to gaze into *jeopardy*, as we might look closely at one of Rothko's famous "Red" paintings, it too would glow. We might even see a chessboard, which is based on *jeu parti*, an early French phrase for an (evenly) "divided game" in which the chance of escaping a problematic position was viewed as evenly balanced. As Skeat explains, "the chances were equal, hence, a risk, a hazard." By the late 14th century, the playful sense of the word had surrendered to the competitive aspect of the game, and then came to mean figuratively any situation (not just the position of the king on the board) viewed as perilous, such as the danger a defendant faces when on trial. All these senses are revealed in its Latin root *jocus*, game, **sport**, jest, which evolved into *joke*, a game of words, a sporting of wits. The poet Walt Whitman wrote, "Judging from the main portions of the history of the world so far, justice is always in *jeopardy.*" Historian Hannah Arendt said, "Power and violence are opposites; where the one rules absolutely, the other is absent. Violence appears where power is in *jeopardy*, but left to its own course it ends in power's disappearance." Companion words include the surprisingly crunchy *zugzwang* (German for "need to move"), the situation in chess where one is compelled to make a move even though it will weaken one's position.

## JOLIE LAIDE (FRENCH)

*Unconventionally beautifully; pretty-**ugly**.* A **gorgeously** unattractive loanword from France to describe something ineffable, usually in a woman, a quality that defies the straitjacket of supposedly ideal **beauty**. Not the pejorative "pretty ***ugly***" woman, but a *pretty-ugly* one possessing a "*fascinating* **quirkiness** implying charisma, a face you want to keep looking at, even if you can't decide whether it's beautiful or not." The writer J. J. Vadé's lovely line, "Nobody's sweetheart is ***ugly***," is a subtle suggestion of what *jolie laide* alludes to. The sultry actress Ellen Barkin comes to mind, with a face like a Lucien Freud portrait, soulful, disturbing, and bafflingly human. In November 2005 Daphne Merkin wrote in the *New York Times*, "Leave it to [the French] to introduce a concept of feminine beauty so pure in its abstraction as to defy all logic. I am referring to the term *jolie laide*, which translates literally into the clunking phrase 'pretty-***ugly***,' but which connotes something more lyrical, even transcendent … *jolie laide* aims to jog us out of our reflexive habits of looking and assessing by embracing the ***aesthetic*** pleasures of the visually off kilter: a bump on the nose, eyes that are set too closely together, a jagged smear of a mouth." E. M. Forster provides us with a dazzling distinction: "Beauty ought to look a little *surprised*: it is the emotion that best suits her face. The beauty who does not look surprised, who accepts her position as her due—she reminds us too much of a prima donna." Companion words include *comely,* as in come-hither, and *fair,* as in fair maiden, a scintilla of suggestion that the maiden is fairly beautiful.

## JOUISSANCE (FRENCH)

*A pleasure to rejoice in; sexual feelings; orgasm.* For such an ecstatic word comes the dullest possible definition from Webster's: "jollity, merriment." The true beauty and depths of the word are revealed by its earlier roots in the Latin *gaudere*, "to rejoice," and the verb *jouir*, "to have pleasure in, to enjoy, to appreciate, to savor." Currently it enjoys multiple meanings, describing *exquisite* pleasure, such as orgasm, but also the intense pleasure derived from philosophical pursuits. It also serves as a legal term signifying the right to use something, as in the phrase *"avoir la jouissance de quelque chose."* The consummate **flâneur** poet Charles Baudelaire captures in his poem *"Le Mauvais Vitrier,"* (The Bad Glazier) the sense of ecstatic timelessness of the word: *"Mais qu'importe l'éternité de la damnation à qui a trouvé dans une seconde l'infini de la jouissance?"* (What matters an eternity of damnation to someone who has found in one second the infinity of joy?) Companion words include the equally French *le petit mort*, the little death, a lethal euphemism for orgasm.

∽ა∽

## JUBILATION

*A celebration of joy, wild whooping.* One musty old dictionary merely provides a one-line mention that it is a late 14th-century word, from the Old French *jubilacion*, from the Latin *jubilationem*, Old Latin *iūbilātiō*, "a shouting for joy. "Much more colorful is William Anderson's riff, in his study *The Green Man*, that it derives from the singing of vineyard workers. "St. Augustine says that the word *jubilation* derives from *jubilus*, a perpetual humming song peasants and farmers used to sing while they tended and pruned their vines and olives. The leaves that issue from the Green Man's mouth are an answering song or incantation in which the spirits of trees speak to man." The Marvel Comic Book hero *Jubilation* Lee says, "Okay, I'll, like, bite. Who're the X-Men?" and just as memorably, "If you disappoint me, I'm going rogue." On *How I Met Your Mother*, Ted says, "I'm *jubilant* that my former paramour is *jubilant*." Companion words include *jubilee*, a twenty-fifth or fiftieth anniversary celebration, and also a flaming dessert.

## JUKEBOX

*An automatic, coin-operated, push-button equipped, music-playing machine.* Let's drop a nickel in the slot, push a button, and hear what we can hear—an old Doors song, "Roadhouse Blues," which riffs on the black English **slang** *jook joint*, first recorded in 1937. First spun, most scholars say, from **juke** or *joog*, wicked, disorderly, in African-

Gullah, possibly influenced by the "Creolized English of the coastlands of South Carolina, Georgia, and Florida, or from Wolof and Bambara *dzug*, unsavory, wicked." For instance, in Belizean Creole *jook* means "to poke or puncture," but also "copulate," an inside joke, so to speak, that "migrated" to the American South and inspired *jook house*, brothel, where music-playing boxes became *jook-boxes*, and eventually *jukeboxes*. One of America's most melodically **funky** words. In *American-Irish Slang*, David Cassidy drops a nickel into the slot and pushes the button for JUKE and up comes *Diug* [pronounced *jug*], a joint, drink, tipple, to the dregs. "*Juke* joints are wicked **fun**," writes Cassidy. Country-Western legend Willie Nelson spins it and hears its figurative sense: "Ninety-nine percent of the world's lovers are not with their first choice. That's what makes the *jukebox* play." PBS journalist Robert McNeil wrote in his memoir, *Wordstruck*, "Gradually, you become an unimaginably large *jukebox.*" But out of all the *juke-joint* quotes in all the world, my favorite is Frank Sinatra's. Here's one for the road: "A fella came up to me the other day in a bar with a nice story. He was in a bar somewhere and it was the quiet time of the night. Everybody's staring down at the sauce and one of my **saloon** songs comes on the *jukebox*, 'One for My Baby,' and after a while a drunk at the end of the bar looks up and says, jerking his thumb toward the *jukebox*, 'I wonder who he listens to?'"

# K

## KEEN

*Sharp, piercing, biting.* A word with an edge to it, a word that has been held up to the whetstone of common usage. I'm reminded of French poet and filmmaker Jean Cocteau's *keen* observation: "Take a commonplace, clean it and polish it, light it so that it produces the same effect of youth and freshness and originality and spontaneity as it did originally, and you have done a poet's job. The rest is literature." Our headword is so common we can scarcely see how uncommon and thus extraordinary is its backstory. Originating with a pugnacious 8th-century Old Norse word, *kænn*, skillful, wise, it moved through Middle Dutch *coene*, bold, was honed in the German *kühn*, bold and brave, and arrived sharp as a sword in the Old English *cene*, wise, daring, clever, where it is recognizable as our own *keen*. To the *keen-eyed* reader the metaphorical leap to our modern sense of "eager" may connote the desire to be brave or clever, but the element of being "sharp" is special to English, where it was tempered like a sword in the forge of time to describe, finally, blades, razors, and edges. *Keen* eyesight, as in sharp vision, was inevitable, arriving in the early 1700s. Later, the word was honed again to describe a *keen* wind, implying many of the above senses of sharp, biting, strong. For those who traveled in Ireland right up into modern times, *keening* is a distinctive *cri de coeur*, a lament as old as stone, first recorded in 1811, from Old Irish *caoinim,* "I weep, wail, lament," which led to the familiar *keen, keening.* By the early 1900s, in Irish American neighborhoods across the land, *keen* was **cool** before *cool.* The *keen*-minded Anne Frank wrote in her secret diary, stored in an old cupboard in Amsterdam, "I don't believe that the big men, the politicians and the capitalists alone are guilty of war. Oh, no, the little man is just as *keen*, otherwise the people of the world would have risen in revolt long ago!" Cutting to the sweet side of the word, e.e. cummings wrote, "who knows if the moon's / a balloon, coming out of a *keen* city / in the sky—filled with pretty people?" Companion words include **kenning**, the Old Norse technique of turning nouns into **metaphors**, such as *whale-road* for the sea; and *Keenan,* a male Irish name meaning "ancient, distant," originally O'Cianan, a tribe of old historians.

## KIT AND CABOODLE

*The whole lot, the complete package.* A humorous way to say
"all of them." The phrase breaks into three parts: *kit,* from
Middle Dutch *kitte*, a wooden tankard with hooped staves;
a container or basket, collection of articles in a soldier's
equipment, and the knapsack that held the *kit. Boodle*
may be from the Dutch *boedel*, estate, possession, stock.
Together, "the whole thing," a poetic attempt to describe
something ordinary. Its use today is *nugatory*, but we can
hope for better. When I played basketball in London in
the 1970s our coach was prone to bad puns such as "Don't
forget to bring your *kit and caboodle* to the game tomorrow
night," which was a riff on "kit," the English term for
duffle bag. Companion words and phrases include *the whole
kit, the whole caboodle, the whole works, the big picture,* and
more lately, *the full Monty.* "It's the whole **ball** of wax,"
snickered Lemony Snicket in *A Series of Unfortunate Events*,
"the entire *kit and caboodle*."

## KITSCH (YIDDISH)

*Gaudy, sentimental stuff.* A sonicky word to describe works
of art regarded as in terrible taste due their clinquant, or
gaudy, style, or their mawkish values, even while others
might appreciate them in a hipster or ironic way. Its roots
are in German dialect *kitschen*, to smear. Czech novelist
Milan Kundera insists that *kitsch* is the bane of modern
society. "No matter how much we scorn it, *kitsch* is an

integral part of the human condition." Companion words include the Russian *poshlost*, defined by Christopher J. Moore as an "acute awareness of the hollowness of false values and the need to deride and deflate them." For Vladimir Nabokov *poshlost* captured Russian life as "cheap, sham, common, pink-and-blue, **high falutin'**, in bad taste."

## KNUCKLE UNDER

*Give in, surrender; bear down.* The word *knuckle* refers of course to the joint in the finger, but it has long been used also as a verb to express the action of submitting, as in "knuckle down," and also to admit that one has been defeated and will surrender. Dr. Johnson speculates in his *Dictionary* that it means "To submit: I suppose from an odd custom of striking the underside of a table with the knuckles, in confession of an argumental defeat." Filmmaker Francis Ford Coppola once said, "You have to really be courageous about your instincts and your ideas. Otherwise you'll just *knuckle under*, and things that might have been memorable will be lost."

## KVETCH (YIDDISH)

*To whine or complain chronically.* We've all done it; we all know someone who's guilty of it. More than complaining, less than a psychotic breakdown, *kvetch* combines a **garrulous** grumble with an existential Sartrean sigh. The

Yiddish root word *kvetshn*, to squeeze or press, complain, paints a good word picture of its enduring power, pressing for sympathy. One of a yarmulke of Yiddish contributions to English, via the Jewish communities in the entertainment industry, **vaudeville**, the Borscht Belt, Hollywood, and literature. Companion words include *schlep*, shuffle along; *klutz*, clumsy person; *shnozz*, nose or bagel, round and doughy; and ***chutzpah***. A typical *kvetching* joke I heard from my friend Gary "Rhino" Rhine (who stored thousands of jokes in a file cabinet) after a hilarious visit with his parents: A Jewish man in a hospital tells the doctor he wants to be transferred to a different hospital. The doctor says, "What's wrong? Is it the food?" "No, the food is fine. I can't *kvetch*." "Is it the room?" "No, the room is fine. I can't *kvetch*." "Is it the staff?" "No, everyone on the staff is fine. I can't *kvetch*." "Then why do you want to be transferred?" "I can't *kvetch*!"

# L

## LAGOON

*A stretch of salt water separated from the sea by a low sand-bank or coral reef.* To utter the word *lagoon* is to evoke the lonely sailor's evocation of **paradise**. Merriam-Webster offers a secondary definition, "a *shallow sound*," which captures, however unwittingly, both the romance and a **pun**. The lexicographer responsible for the word played on its pondlike nature, and the *sound*, the long *oo's* that evoke the wind on the waves, which itself puns off the geographical term for a body of water. Its roots are more like tributaries, reaching back to both the French *lagune,* from Italian *laguna,* from Latin *lacuna* pit, pool, from *lacus* lake. First known use: 1673. "A ghost upon the sands of the sea," writes John Ruskin in *The Grand Canal,* "so weak—so quiet—so bereft of all but her loveliness, that we might well doubt, as we watched her faint reflection in the mirage of the *lagoon,* which was the City, and which the

Shadow." Companion words include *lacuna*, a gap, curiously close to *lagoon*, a gap in the land where water pools.

Lagoon

## LAMBENT

*Shining with soft light, playing lightly on the surface.* One of the most luminous words in our ever-flickering language. An *observant* word that arose naturally from centuries of closely watching the way that light doesn't just move, sometimes it dances. *The Concise Oxford Dictionary of English Etymology* states that the word was "born from the ancient and passionate comparison of flames to tongues," which is duly reflected in the Latin *lambere*, to lick, as flames lick at the air in the hearth. Figuratively, this notion led to the idea of a *lambent* style, brilliant, shining, nimble, as expressed in *a*

Lambent

*lambent* **wit** or a cinematographer's *lambent* shadows in film noir. Companion words include *lap* and *lampoon,* and the French **toast** *Lampons* ("Let's drink!") Alice MacGowan writes in *Judith of the Cumberlands*, "The thick dusky hair rose up around her brow in a massive, sculptural line; her dark eyes—the large, heavily fringed eyes of a dryad—glowed with the fires of youth, and with a certain *lambent* shining which was all their own; the stain on her cheeks was deep, answering to the ripe red of the full lips."

## LAVALIERE (FRENCH)

*A small pendant, generally tear-dropped; a small microphone, usually attached to the lapel.* Named after the Duchesse de la Vallière, King Louis XIV's mistress, her name echoing to this day as *lavaliere*. The fashion world shortened the word to *lavaliere*, which the world of recording kept as *lavalier*, due to the small microphone's resemblance to a pendant when it was clipped onto a lapel. But unlike visible or even ostentatious decoration, the minimicrophone is intended to be invisible, attached to a hidden wireless pack for broadcasting purposes. Thus, it is an inversion of the old scolding that children be seen and not heard: a *lavalier* should be heard and not seen. Companion words including *lavaliering*, the romantic gifting of a pendant to a lover.

## LEGO (DANISH)

*Plastic interlocking building blocks for kids.* An ingenious word story for an ingenious toy. The tale is told in the welcome pamphlets at the various *Legolands* around the world, and lauded in every one of its toy boxes. In 1932, Ole Kirk Christiansen started a company in Billund, Denmark, that produced an odd range of products from ironing boards and stepladders to wooden toys. He soon named the company *Lego*, Danish for "play well," from the expression *leg godt*. As often happens, a scholar called his attention to a curious fact about a word; in this case, that in Latin *Lego* means "I study," "I read," or "I put together." Undaunted, Christiansen kept the name anyway, pleased with the unwitting connection he had made between playing and learning. Since its founding *Lego* has sold over 200 billion plastic bricks (which it deems "elements") worldwide. On the Sunol Glen Lego Club website a *fan* named James Heald writes, "People should learn how to play *Lego* with their minds. Concepts are building bricks." Companion words include *legology*, the study of *Legos*, especially the role and function of building blocks.

## LEWD

*Coarse, vile, lustful.* This salacious adjective came from innocent beginnings. The Old English *laewede* was first recorded in 1225 as meaning "belonging to the laity," based on the Latin *laicus*, unlettered, uneducated, nonclerical. The implication was that someone not in a religious order couldn't possibly be educated. Within two hundred years *laewede* had devolved into the moralistic "coarse, vile, lustful," as if clergy never had a lustful thought. Presumably, the language needed more words for lusty behavior than it did for uncouth or **ugly** behavior, so the latter meanings dropped off like bad habits, leaving only lascivious associations. The actress Marilyn Monroe provided startling insight into the word when she said, "People had a habit of looking at me as if I were some kind of mirror instead of a person. They didn't see me, they saw their own *lewd* thoughts, then they white-masked themselves by calling me the *lewd* one." Companion words include *lewdster*, an indecent, obscene person, as recorded by Mackay, and the world-weary word *lasslorn*, to describe a man who has been dismissed by his mistress.

## LOOPHOLE

*Arrow slits, literally an opening, in law or an event.* Originally, a *loop* was a narrow slit or vertical **window** in a castle battlement large enough for an archer to release an arrow but too slim for an opposing arrow to find its way in. Figuratively, a *loophole* is a gap or exception that makes it possible to avoid or circumvent a law. Like medieval archers, modern people search for *loopholes* in tax laws, election rules, or political scrutiny. Seen this way, a legal *loophole* allows the law to be protected (like the medieval castle), but wards off any *illegal* attempts to break down the walls or the gate of our legal system. The ***zany*** English comic and actor Eddie Izzard noted, "There's a huge hole in the whole Flood drama because anything that could float or swim got away scot-free, and it was the idea to wipe out everything. He didn't say, 'I will kill everything except the floating ones and the swimming ones, who will get out of this due to a *loophole*.'" Companion words include the reverie-inducing *dream-hole*, a slit or hole in a tower or barn designed to let sound escape and let in light and air. ***Consider*** the marvelous **metaphor** here, the opening in a dreamer's dream that allows her to be "in a dream as awake."

## LUCUBRATION

*Thinking, studying, working by candlelight.* An ***owl*** of a word, a nocturnal hunter of language that refers to work done at night, but also nuanced enough to suggest work accomplished in the twilight of life through deep contemplation, such as late-life memoirs. The word has not lost its luster over time, now sometimes meaning simply illuminated study or meditation, but it is also occasionally misused to describe pedantic writing, which "smells of the lamp." Picasso said, "The idea of research has often made painting go astray, and made the artist lose himself in mental *lucubration*. All I have ever made is for the present." The Peruvian Spanish writer Mario Vargas Llosa writes in "Thugs Who Know Their Greek," in the *New York Times* in 1986, "Naturally, these fictions ran the risk of tumbling down the formalist hill and ending up at the bottom without readers—except the heroic students of Roland Barthes or Umberto Eco, professors whose *lucubrations* were much more interesting than the books about which they theorized." Companion words include *Lucubra*, the main character in *The Creature from Beyond Infinity,* by Henry Kuttner.

## LUDDITE

*A member of a 19th-century movement in England that protested against the encroachment of technology.* Originally, the movement was a response to the fear of unemployment, but the term is now used as an epithet for anyone expressing dissatisfaction with what society deems to be progress. A May 2011 letter to the editor of *Smithsonian* magazine retells an old chestnut about two men "watching the excavation of a building site in New York. As they observed steam shovels gouging the earth, one man, who had recently lost his job, commented that had it not been for the steam shovels there would have been work there for hundreds of men with picks and shovels. The other man nodded and added, 'Or for thousands with teaspoons.'" Companion words include *technophobia.*

## LUDICROUS

*Not to be believed; something that just does not play out.* No
mere play on words, *ludicrous* is a semiserious word, originally a sporting term going back to 1610, when its definition was "sportive, pertaining to play or *sport*." The Latin
root word is *ludicrum*, source of amusement, a joke, from
the earlier *ludere*, to play, and *ludus,* a game of play—which
may be, amusingly and playfully, one of the few Etruscan
words to enter into English. According to the OED, In
1782 we find the first attested use of it as *ridiculous*, an
unfortunate reflection of the contemporary disdain or
Puritanical attitude toward play itself. Companion words
abound: *interlude*, literally the time "between play"; *prelude*,
before the play; *allude*, refer to the play; *illusion*, deceptive
idea or appearance, and the arcane but eminently revivable
*illude*, to play with, as in make *fun* of.

## LULU (IRISH)

*A remarkable person, thing, or event.* Tracked down by word
detective Daniel Cassidy, in *American-Irish Slang*, this two-
syllable dandy derives from the Irish word *liu luigh*, "a
howl, a scream, a vigorous scream of joy," and more, "A
*lulu* can be spectacular or awful, but it's always a scream."
More surprisingly still, Cassidy's sleuthing tracked down
its earliest recorded mention, in the *New Orleans Lantern,*
on November 10, 1886, where it was used to describe the
shenanigans in a local baseball game: "Farrell's two baser

was a *lu-lu*." The citation would have delighted the late, great Ernie Harwell, Hall of Fame broadcaster and baseball historian, who was married to a *Lulu* of a wife for over sixty years. Companion words include *doozy*, from the Duesenberg car, as in "That's a *doozy!*"

# M

## MAELSTROM

*Strong whirlpool, violent upheaval; life gone haywire.* A roiling word that swirled around Scandinavia and arrived with the Viking ships that stormed the shores of Old England. The 16th-century English scholar and geographer Richard Hakluyt discovered the word on Dutch maps and discovered its roots in *Malestrand*, a "whirlpool off the northwest coast of Norway," which he derived from the Danish *malstrøm*, literally *grinding-stream*, from *malen*, to grind, and *stroom*, current. One theory credits Dutch cartographers such as Mercator with coining the word. By the 1840s, it had become popularized as a synonym for "whirlpool," possibly due to its sonicky effects, with that hard "a" and ominous "om" combining to echo that violent thing that whirls into the world without end. Figuratively, it is used to depict turbulence, as playwright Harold Pinter did in an interview: "One is and is not in the centre of the *maelstrom* of it all." Companion words include *mayhem*, Old French for "disorder."

## MALAPROP

*The fingernail-on-the-chalkboard, knickers-in-a-twist misuse of words.* Technically, this is called *catachresis*, the improper use of a word, which may be tautological, since the literary term sounds more like the misuse of *catechism* than a flouting of semantic rules. Perhaps that is why we have adopted such terms as this one, for it personifies the all-too-human foibles of speaking poorly, then being harangued by semanticists. Safe to say that it is the mistaken use of a word for one that sounds just like it, usually with humorous results, such as Yogi Berra's howler, "Texas has a lot of electrical votes." This nugget comes from a time when literary **characters** took on a life of their own, which is what happened with Mrs. Malaprop from Richard Brinsley Sheridan's play *The Rivals*. Sheridan simply borrowed the French *mal à propos*, ill-advised or inappropriate, for the name of a character who innocently mangles her sentences, who is "guilty of *ludicrous* use of words." Thusly introduced, Mrs. Malaprop uttered such lines as "She's as headstrong as an **allegory** on the banks of the Nile" and "She is the very pineapple of politeness." Companion words include *Bunkerisms* [Archie], *Yogisms* [Berra], and *Bushisms* [George].

## MAMMOTH

*A huge, hairy, ivory-tusked elephant (genus Mammuthus) that
flourished in the Pleistocene epoch.* The woolly *mammoth* lived
from the Pliocene Epoch, about 4.8 million years ago,
into the Holocene, only about 4,500 years ago, a staggering span of 4 million years. Thawing it out, we see
the petrified remains of the Russian *mamont*, possibly
derived from the Vogul (Mansi) *mang onti,* an earth horn,
a possible relic from the discovery of the animal's ivory
tusks. Wordpainter nonpareil Webb Garrison renders this
image: "Soon after the fall of the Roman Empire, traders
in northern Europe began to buy ivory from savage [!]
Tartar tribesmen. Questions about its source brought
little satisfaction; sellers would only mutter a native term
for an animal unfamiliar to civilized man [!]" Cartloads
full of tusks were bought in from the frozen wastes;
some ivory was exported to Chinese markets. Merchants
eventually learned that the tusks came from huge beasts
whose bodies were caught in centuries-old ice. Sometimes a lucky hunter would find an entire herd preserved
in nature's deep freeze. By 1700, European hunters and
scientists had come to appreciate how the ivory-bearing
animal was not just extinct, it was distinct—resembling no
known living animal; the word was first recorded a few
years later. By 1802, the term had become an adjective and
grown into a synonym for "large" or "gigantic." Traders in
Asia discovered the huge ivory tusks in far-flung *caravan-
saries* and inquired where the ivory came from. According

to legend, the word they heard sounded like "maamaa." This universally maternal sound possibly derived from a Finno-Ugric language known as Ostyak, from northern Russia, reminiscent of Finnish *maa*, for "earth." When their remains were removed from their icy tombs they were believed to be ginormous moles that used their tusks to root underground. In the 1983 movie *Mammoth*, Deputy Bud, hunting down a *mammoth* on the rampage in dark woods, asks his cohort, Deputy Dino: "Hey, d'ya think there's any spiders out here?" Deputy Dino: "You're afraid of spiders?" From the Curiosity Cabinet of Word History comes this: Thomas Jefferson is credited in the OED as the first written source for *mammoth*—along with the recording of 379 others, plus the coining of at least 106 other words, including *cross-street, neologize*, and *shag*. Companion words include *elephantine, behemoth, leviathan*.

### MANUSCRIPT

*A book, document, or work of music written by hand; a text as yet unpublished*. Out of the great **scriptorium** in the sky we find the Medieval Latin *manuscriptus*, from *manu scriptus*, written by hand, which lends the image of a quill and **parchment** paper. For centuries a *manuscript* was a piece of writing or music that was written out by hand and unpublished rather than being typed, printed, or spoken on tape. Fran Lebowitz is always there with a quip on hand: "Children ask better questions than adults: 'May I have a cookie?'

‿◠‿◠‿

Manuscript: *Wim Wenders/Sunset Boulevard*

'Why is the sky blue?' and 'What does a cow say?' are far more likely to elicit a cheerful response than 'Where's your *manuscript*?' 'Why haven't you called?' and 'Who's your lawyer?'" Two centuries earlier, Dr. Johnson wrote one of the most devastating reviews since the printing press was unveiled: "Your *manuscript* is both good and original, but the part that is good is not original, and the part that is

original is not good." Ring Lardner writes: "A good many
young writers make the mistake of enclosing a stamped,
self-addressed envelope, big enough for the *manuscript* to
come back in. This is too much of a temptation to the
editor." Companion words include *manuscriptors*, those
who write *manuscripts*, and *miniators*, scribes who specialized in painting miniatures and also the first, red, initial in
illuminated *manuscripts*, from the Latin *minium*, red lead.

## MAROON

*Abandon, leave behind, stultify.* You won't be stranded if
you stay on board for this word. Just don't abandon ship
when we suggest a connection here between the loneliest
of verbs and the boldest of colors. In the 1620s the French
*maron*, feral, was a fugitive black slave, abandoned sailor, or
escaped prisoner living wild in the jungles and mountains
of the West Indies, Suriname, or Dutch Guiana. The word
is possibly a truncation of Spanish *cimmarón*, a romantically
untamed word rooted in the Old Spanish *cimarra,* thicket,
probably from Spanish *cima*, summit, the top of a mountain. In the 1969 sci-fi flick *Marooned* the word is never
used but is on everyone's mind when three astronauts
on a spacecraft that is losing oxygen need to decide who
will stay and who will go. One of them must volunteer
to abandon ship and be *marooned* in outer space. Charles
Keith: "Is there sufficient oxygen for two men? For one?"
Flight Surgeon: [*long pause*] "Two might just make it."

Companion words include *maroon*, from the French word for chestnut, *marron,* a purplish to dark red shade, rooted in an earlier pre-Roman word from Liguria; or from Greek *maraon*, sweet chestnut.

## MAUNDER

*Move or act listlessly; talk in a dreamy or boring manner.* Another **rambling** word dating back to the 18th century, first in the sense of mumbling or grumbling, and then from French *mendier*, to beg, from the Latin *mendicare*, which gave us *mendicant*. The modern *maunder* comes from the observation of listless monks, or pesky nudniks. Plausibly, *maunder* is a **rhapsody** on the theme of *meander*. In *Timequake*, Kurt Vonnegut Jr. writes, "Now I find myself *maundering* about parts of plays hardly anybody knows or cares about anymore, such as the graveyard scene in *Our Town*, or the poker game in Tennessee Williams's *A Streetcar Named Desire*, or what Willy Loman's wife said after that tragically ordinary clumsily gallant American committed suicide in Arthur Miller's *Death of a Salesman*." *Maunder* is a word that shouldn't molder. Companion words include *maund*, a unit of weight in India and other Asian countries varying between 25 and 160 pounds, and *Maundy Thursday*, Holy Thursday, the Thursday of the Last Supper.

## MAUVE

*Light bluish to reddish violet-purple* **color**. So named around 1859 from the Old French *mauve*, mallow, and Latin *malva*, mallow, to describe the color of that plant. In the fall of 1906 the *New York Herald* brashly announced: "Coal Tar Wizard, Just Arrived in Country, Transmuted Liquid Gross to Gold." Say no more, as those other English wizards, Monty Python, used to joke. The English chemist William Perkin had just arrived in the docks of New York, a "scientific saint," as his biographer Simon Garfield writes, exactly fifty years after he pioneered the industrial applications of chemistry with his discovery of a new and "strangely beautiful **color**," a pale lavender-lilac, which he created by heating coal until it surrendered its color, which he called *mauve*. He fulfilled the dream of his grandfather, an early alchemist, who attempted to "transmute lead into gold." The discovery has led to at least 2,000 other artificial colors, all derived from his work. Garfield adds, "His great invention occurred purely by chance, for he was looking for something else [a cure for malaria] and what he found was the color that changed the world." Perkin's discovery of making dye from coal tar was seen as a kind of "magician's secret," which transformed both biochemistry and medicine. Eventually his dyes were also used as artist's pigments, and led to a host of brand-new colors, such a vermilionette, Post Office red, and emerald-tint green. In 1994, the *St. Louis Post-Dispatch* wrote, "For those who don't know, *mauve* is a delicate shade of purple."

Companion words include *magenta*, allegedly named after the Battle of Magenta, Italy, in 1859, which was fought, eerily, just before the blood-red dye was discovered.


## MELLIFLUOUS

*Sweet as honey; flowing with sweetness.* If you say it slowly enough, you can taste it, the honey, that is, in the old Greek word *mel*, and if you dwell on it you can appreciate the second half of the word, *fluere*, to flow. Together they offer up an image of yoghurt served with flowing honey in a taverna in the Greek islands. Surprisingly, it didn't enter English until the late 15th century. One of my top ten favorite words, but one that needs to be used sparingly, like Greek honey over Greek yoghurt. "Thus the shriek," wrote the music critic Lester Bangs, "the caterwaul, the chainsaw gnarlgnashing, the yowl and the whiz that decapitates may be reheard by the adventurous or emotionally damaged as *mellifluous* bursts of unarguable affirmation." We can say that Coleman Barks's **translations** of the mystic poet Rumi are "*mellifluous* versions." Companion words include *mellisonant*, sweet-sounding, pleasing to the ear, and *mellifluent*, also flowing like honey.


## MELODY

*A sequence of notes that create a musically satisfying phrase.* One of the loveliest words in the language; a Top Ten word on the list of perennial favorites. It harkens back to the late 13th-century Old French *melodie*, which was a slight refrain from Greek *melōidia*, "singing, chanting, a tune for lyric poetry," from *melos*, song, and even further back to *limb* and *oide*, song, ode. Commenting on "A Moorish Melody," from his groundbreaking album *Sketches in Spain*, Miles Davis remarked, "That *melody* is so strong that the softer you play it, the stronger it gets, and the stronger

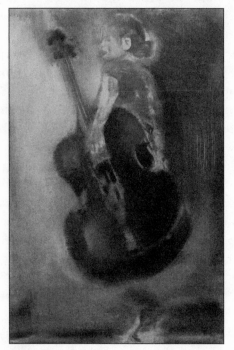

Melody: *Brecht's Song*

you play it, the weaker it gets." Thoreau said, "Friends do not live, merely in harmony, as they say, but in *melody.*" Violinist Yehudi Menuhin chimes in, "Music creates order out of chaos: for rhythm imposes unanimity upon the divergent, *melody* imposes continuity upon the disjointed, and harmony imposes compatibility upon the incongruous." Companion melodies: *raga,* from the Sanskrit for harmony, meaning *melody,* but literally **color** or mood; *air,* a *melody,* from the Italian *aria.*

## MERETRICIOUS

*Cheap, showy, pretentious, tawdry, appealing in an **embarrassing** fashion.* Think of terrible souvenirs at an amusement park, or a sorry prostitute with dripping purple eyeliner in a B movie, which is exactly its **bawdy** origins, from the early 17th-century Latin *meretrix,* prostitute, and the even earlier *mereri,* hired, or *merere,* to earn money. Its secondary meanings allude to a lack of value or integrity, evoking the insincerity of sex as a commercial transaction. When I was Writer in Residence at George Whitman's Shakespeare & Company Bookstore, in Paris, in 1989, I was reading *The Great Gatsby* late one night when I bumped up against the word in the following passage: "His parents were shiftless and unsuccessful farm people," F. Scott Fitzgerald writes. "His imagination had never really accepted them as his parents at all. The truth was that Jay Gatsby of West Egg, Long Island, sprang from his Platonic conception of himself. He was a son of God, and he must be about His Father's business, the service of a vast, vulgar, and *meretricious* beauty. So he invented Jay Gatsby ... and to this conception he was faithful to the end." Puzzled, I reached for one of George's oldest dictionaries, a 1929 edition of the OED, and was amazed to read its archaic meaning, "relating to or characteristic of a prostitute." In other words, Gatsby prostituted himself. Companion words include *brazen*, as in *hussy*, and *vulgar,* as in cheap.

## MESHUGGAH (YIDDISH)

**Crazy**, *eccentric, foolish.* Not to be confused with "Michigan," as I learned from the kibbutzniks at Ashdot Yaakov, in Israel, where I worked in the palm groves during the 1970s. "Where are you from?" "Michigan." "No, not what are you, where are you from?" The battle-hardened workers invariably cracked up when I said, "Detroit. Michigan," not realizing how close it sounded to their word for *cracked up, meshuggah,* which would have made me a *meshuggener*, a maniac from Michigan. I felt like a *nebbish* (from *nebekh*, poor, unfortunate), timid and misunderstood, just another dumb *putz* (Yiddish for "fool") because I couldn't explain where I was from. Suddenly I remembered the old Michigan semaphore for the Winter Wonderland and raised my hand in the familiar "mitt position" to illustrate the shape of my home state on a map. "*Gaon!*" cried Yehudi, one of my fellow workers in the groves. "He's a genius!" The *Stiletto Gang* website posted a response to a 2008 story in the *New York Times* in which Mathew Prichard, Dame Agatha Christie's grandson, was reported to have discovered twenty-seven hours of her audiotapes on which she bewailed the stream of letters urging her to bring together her most famous detectives in one story. The poster on the website responds: "First, I agree with Dame Agatha. The concept of Jane Marple and Hercule Poirot working on a case together is, as undoubtedly my grandmother would have answered, just plain *meshuggah*." Companion words? *Gott im Himmel,* God in heaven!

## MILLIHELEN

*A humorous measure of* **beauty** *purportedly based on the pulchritudinous qualities of Helen of Troy.* The Canadian novelist Robertson Davies writes in his novel *The Rebel Angels* that this too-clever-by-half measurement was invented by Cambridge mathematician W. A. Rushton. Others, naturally, disagree, fighting for the origin story as the Greeks and Trojans fought over the famously beautiful queen. Still, many scholars allot the attribution to that polymath Isaac Asimov, he of the 447 books. However you measure it, this playful unit of beauty was inspired by Christopher Marlowe's famous lines about the mythic beauty of Helen of Troy in Homer's *Iliad*: "Was this the face that launched a thousand ships? / And burnt the topless towers

Millihelen: *Where the Sky Opens*

of Ilium [Troy]?" The measurement is based on an ingenious idea: One *milliHelen* (mH) is a unit of pulchritude we
could think of as one glimpse of the immortal beauty of
Helen of Sparta, the most beautiful woman in the world,
beautiful enough to launch a thousand ships. The term
refers to one of the great myths of antiquity, the Judg-
ment of Paris, which centers on the power and magic of
beauty, and a challenge to decide who would win the first
beauty contest: Hera, Athene, or Aphrodite? Paris, prince

of Troy, chose the goddess of desire, **love,** and beauty, and she chose Helen as his reward, which in turn "launched a thousand ships." The power of her love and beauty is the engine behind this cavortingly clever neologism. Curiously, there is also a Chinese expression to describe a beautiful woman, "lovely enough to cause the fall of a city." Companion words include *Beauty Meter*, a new portable phone app, which allows people to score how beautiful others are.

## MITAKUYE OYASIN (LAKOTA SIOUX)

*All my relations; all my relatives.* This traditional Lakota invocation of the great web of life is used in prayers, songs, dances, rites, including peyote and pipe ceremonies and sweat lodges. Essentially, it expresses the native belief in the essential oneness of existence, the utter conviction that everything is connected. Joseph Epes Brown wrote the definite study of this primal understanding of the "underlying connection" of all life, which in turn inspired the animal rights movement, women's rights movement, gay rights movement, and especially the ecology movement. Mary Black Bonnet, of the Sicangu Lakota Nation, writes: "For Lakotas one of our common mantras is *Mitakuye Oyasin*—we are all related. All of us, no matter who you are (person), or what you are (grass, trees, rocks), are the same. No one is better than anyone else. Our lives really are circular, and yes, everything *really* is related to everything else. Some say related—I like to say enmeshed, because it really is."

## MOCCASIN

*A soft leather shoe worn by American Indian tribes.* One of hundreds of words from our American Indian hosts that were absorbed into English when Europeans first landed in the Americas, this one deriving from the Narragansett/Algonquian of Virginia *mocussin,* Massachusett *mokhisson*, and Powhatan *makasin*, shoe, Algonquian *mawcahsun*, Ojibwa *makisin,* and Micmac *m'kusun*. First recorded in 1612. Its homonym meaning the poisonous snake is considered to have different origins. My friend Vincent Parker, great-grandson of Comanche Chief Quanah Parker, was fond of using it figuratively: "Don't judge anyone until you have walked two moons in his *moccasins*." Companion words include the comfy *slipper*.

## MOJO (FULA)

*A charmed life; the quality that allows you to be in sync.* Today we call it "flow," or being in "the zone"; in the 1960s it was "the groove." You can hear it in Muddy Waters's bluesy cry, "*I got my mojo workin',* which is **juke-joint** code for feeling seductive and sexy. In Fula, the language of Cameroon, *mojo* is a magical charm kept in a charm bag, and the Fula word *mocc'o* means medicine man or woman.

This folk word came to the Deep South and was absorbed into Creole, transmuted into a *funky*, **untranslatable** word for that indefinable "it" that makes for great rhythm and blues music and the animal magnetism that makes for sexual attraction. In *No One Here Gets Out Alive*, his biography of Jim Morrison, my old buddy Danny Sugerman tells of how Jim wrote a song called "Mr. Mojo Risin'," which he proudly revealed later was an anagram for his own name, Jim Morrison. In *Austin Powers: International Man of Mystery*, Mike Meyers pleads with his love interest, "Wait, Vanessa, I can explain. You see, I was looking for Dr. Evil when the fembots came out and smoke started coming out of their jomblies. So I started to work my *mojo*, to counter their *mojo*; we got cross-*mojulation*, and their heads started exploding." Companion words include *charm, fetish, good luck.*

## MONIKER

*A nickname, pseudonym, assumed name.* Throughout history people have wanted to laminate their given names or hide behind another, for untold reasons, sometimes artistic, but also in the underground world of criminals or the realm of exiles such as the Roma, gypsy, or traveler's cultures, and now increasingly on the Internet. *Moniker* is such a word, dubious in its origins, but most scholars now agree that it arose from the Gaelic *ainm*, which developed into *munik* in Shelta, the secret language of the Irish "travelers," formerly called the Tinkers. By the early 1850s, it had crossed the sea to England with Irish immigrants, where it worked its way into English as a synonym or alternative for "name." The OED cites a mention in the November 11, 1895, edition of the *New York Times*: "The van is alright; I have had the '*monnick*' (**slang** word for name) taken of it." Companion words include *Bearlagar na Saor*, the secret language of Irish stonemasons, and Bog Latin, a derisive term for Shelta.

## MONKEY-PICKED (CHINESE)

*The finest tea of the house.* According to one of the greatest living tea scholars, James Norwood Pratt, the term is a misnomer, a myth in the pejorative sense of that word, based on an *apocryphal* story by a wandering English tea merchant. In the 19th century Aeneas A. was prowling China in search of her rarest teas and heard an old folktale about a certain *yancha* that was so rare and remote that "only monkeys" could reach the bushes high on the faces of cliffs. Thus, the legend of "*monkey-picked*" teas was born and an eager English public slurped up the colorful story. "Nowhere is tea plucked by monkeys," chides the polymathic Mr. Pratt, "and it never has been." However, he agrees that it is good practice to ask for the "*monkey-picked*" when ensconced in a world-class tea house because it will be the one that "the merchant or tea-maker takes most pride in." Companion words include *top-of-the-line, blue-ribbon, prime.*

## MONOGASHI (JAPANESE)

*The sigh or sadness of things.* The old chestnut by William Wordsworth about poetry being "the spontaneous over-flow of powerful emotion recollected in tranquility" helps us understand the nuanced beauty of this word. My friend and colleague Pico Iyer wrote to me recently about the serene melancholy of one of his favorite words: "*Monogashi* is akin to *lacrimae rerum* in the classical world. But really it's something much more mingled, akin to the blazing blue skies that surround the dying reds and golds and yellows of Japanese hills and trees in the autumn. It refers to the **beauty** of things that are dying, the sweetness of sadness, the mingled quality of life, and the way that dusk can be evocative and haunting precisely because it speaks for the end of things, the coming of the dark. Joy comes out of suffering, Zen teachers say, and suffering out of joy; nothing lasts or can be held to and life, some Buddhists claim, means joyful participation in a world of sorrows. I get all of this out of the word *monogashi*, which I have heard applied to Jackson Browne's early love songs (but never to the much deeper darkness of Leonard Cohen), to twilight but not to night, to maple leaves but not to cherry blossoms (which catch the other side of the equa-tion, a bright refulgence that ends within days). When first I moved to Japan, I realized that this word, which captures something more elusive than just Keats's odes to autumn or to **melancholy**, showed exactly where I had landed: in a realm that was consecrated not to the 'pursuit of happiness'

Monogashi : *Theatre of Memory*

but to the quieter Buddhist truth of the reality of suffering. In which reality we must find our joy." With that poetic evocation, the **peripatetic** Pico provides us with a lovely example of what Charles Mackay described in his masterpiece *Lost Beauties* as "a much-wanted word." Companion words include *wabi-sabi*, an aesthetic that evokes the transience of things, of imperfect beauty.

## MOOT

*Unresolved, therefore indisputable.* A relic word from the Old Norsemen who set up dispute courts called *mot*. The influence of their justice system was carried aboard the long ships to England and became part of the teaching of law at Cambridge and Oxford as early as the 15th century. An essential part of the **curriculum** in those colleges was the *moots*, or hypothetical courts. Webb Garrison explains the transition to modern times: "Cases tried in a *moot* court were seldom settled with any satisfaction, so any perplexing problem came to be termed a *moot question*." The national council or parliament of Anglo-Saxon England was called the Assembly of Wise Men, the *Witenagemot*. For the last few centuries, trying imaginary cases in "*moot* courts" has been a well-regarded practice, echoing the verb form of the word, which means to raise questions for discussion. The producer of the Beatles, George Martin, once remarked, "When the film [*A Hard Day's Night*] was *mooted*, the Beatles didn't like the idea at all. In fact, they wouldn't have any part of it." Companion words include Christopher "moot" Poole, the founder of 4chan, the phenomenally successful uncensored online imageboard.

## MORPHINE

*An analgesic; a strong sleep-inducing drug to stave off pain.* Chemistry books define it as a narcotic derivative of opium, often used to treat severe pain. The usually reliable Charles

Morphine: *The House of Dreams*

E. Funk suggests that Ovid conjured Morpheus out of his own imagination, to flesh out a story line in *Metamorphosis*, but a riffle of the pages of Hesiod and Cicero reveals two earlier versions of the myth. Hesiod claims that Morpheus is the shaper of dreams, son of Nyx (Night), who gave birth to him parthenogenetically. Cicero agrees about Morpheus's mother, but adds a father figure, Erebus, the personification of darkness. Ovid's adaptation in *Metamorphosis* claims that the god dreams he is the son of Somnos, god of sleep, ruler of The Kingdom of Hypnos, and the twin brother of Thanatos, god of death. The incestuously close relationship between sleep and death is an ancient one: sleep is a nightly little death, death is the long sleep. In the *Aeneid* Virgil writes, *Sunt geminae somni portae*, "there are two gates of sleep." As Alexander Eliot explains in his zetetic essay *Zen*, "The first gate, built of gleaming ivory, stands wide open to falsity. That gate, of course, commands a busy thoroughfare. But elsewhere stands a second gate of a secret and narrow kind, made of two curving horns, and it permits passage to true spirits alone." Virgil describes the House of Dreams as being flanked by two gates, one of ivory, through which "false, flattering dreams entered," and one of transparent horn, through which "good dreams proceeded." Carl Jung said, "Every form of addiction is bad, no matter whether the narcotic be alcohol or *morphine* or idealism." Film director Derek Jarman writes, "Pain can be alleviated by *morphine* but the pain of social **ostracism** cannot be taken away." In the iconic *To Kill a Mockingbird,* Atticus Finch says, "Mrs. Dubose was a *morphine* addict. She took it as a pain-killer for years. The doctor put her on it. She'd have spent the rest of her life on it and died without so much **agony**, but she was too contrary." Companion words and phrases include *belanterned*, led by a lantern or illuminants, and *fuddled*, led by the light of the planet Venus, the Shepherd's Lamp.

## MUDLARK

*A scavenger mired in river mud, searching for items to resell.*
During the 18th and 19th centuries *mudlarking* was a
common practice along the Thames at low tide for the
London poor, who usually earned a pittance, and often
took ill due to the fetid and festering conditions. In 1851,
in *London Labour and the London Poor*, Henry Mahew
wrote, "They generally consist of boys and girls, varying
in age from eight to fourteen or fifteen; with some persons
of more advanced years … Their practice is to get between
the barges, and one of them lifting the other up will knock
lumps of coal into the mud, which they pick up afterwards;
or if a barge is ladened with iron, one will get into it and
throw iron out to the other, and watch an **opportunity**
to carry away the plunder in bags to the nearest marine-
storeshop." *Mudlarking* has been revived in modern times
and is open to everyone, although there is the Society of
Thames *Mudlarks*, formed in 1980, which issues official
permits with wording such as "on behalf of the Queen's
Most Excellent Majesty," allowing the holder to "search
the bed and shore as a recreational pursuit." Treasures of
value are required to be sent to the Museum of London.
Companion words include *scavenging, beachcombing, foraging.*

Mystagogue: *Palmistry*

## MYSTAGOGUE

*A propounder of mystic knowledge; a guide through the under-
world.* One who teaches mystical doctrines, or instructs
or guides in initiation into the mystery cults, such as the
Eleusinian mysteries in ancient Greece or the Isis cult in
Egypt. The *mystagogue* led initiates into realms of secret
knowledge in rites that were absorbed into the early Christian church and recounted in theological books such as
the *Mystagogical Homilies* of St. Cyril of Jerusalem. German

sociologist Max Weber explained the *mystagogue* as one who performs magical acts and makes prophetic utterings which held "the boons of salvation." The word is initiated into English during the 16th century, from the Greek *mystagōgos,* from *mystēs,* initiate, and *myein,* with eyes or lips closed, and *agein,* to lead. Karl Kerenyi describes the role of the secret rites at Eleusis in his Eranos Foundation paper "The Mysteries of the Kabeiroi": "The Mysteria begin for the mystes when, as sufferer of the event (*muoú-menos*), he closes his eyes, falls back as it were into his own darkness, enters into the darkness … A festival of entering into the darkness, regardless of what issue and ascent this initiation may lead to: that is what the Mysteria were, in the original sense of the word." Companion words include *mysticism, mystery,* and *mist.*

# N

## NARCISSISM

*Self-love to the point of obsession with oneself or one's own reflection.* A psychological condition inspired by the Greek myth of the young and beautiful boy Narcissus, who fell in love with his own reflection in a pond and drowned when he tried to kiss himself. At heart, *narcissism* is exactly that, being smitten with yourself, or to paraphrase comedian Eddie Izzard, the **wanton** result of "personal nepotism." The Roman poet Ovid immortalized the doomed love affair in *Metamorphoses*: "When as glass again the rippling waters smoothed, and when / such beauty in the stream the youth observed, / no more could he endure. As in the flame / the yellow wax, or as the hoar-frost melts / in early morning 'neath the genial sun; / so did he pine away, by love consumed, / and slowly wasted by a hidden flame." In *The Culture of Narcissism*, Christopher Lasch mirrors the image: "*Narcissism* in this sense is the longing to be free from longing. ... Its scorn for the body's demands distinguishes narcissism from ordinary egoism or from the survival instinct. ... Since [primary] *narcissism* does not acknowledge the separate existence of the self, it has no fear of death. *Narcissus* drowns in his own reflection, never understanding that it is a reflection." The seafaring novelist Herman Melville wrote, "And still deeper the meaning of that story of *Narcissus*, who because he could not grasp the tormenting, mild image he saw in the fountain, plunged into it and was drowned. But that same image, we ourselves see in all rivers and oceans. It is the image of the ungraspable phantom of life; and this is the key to it all." Companion words include *solipsism*, the philosophy that nothing exists outside the self. Let's reflect on that.

### NEPENTHE

*The mythic potion imbibed to forget or dull one's sorrows or assuage one's grief.* According to Homer, *nepenthe* (from Greek *ne*, not, and *pathos*, pain) was a drug from Egypt that banished any trouble from the mind and soothed the sorrowful heart. The river of that name appears in Roman histories, in the works of Pliny, and then later, in the 1570s, in the poetry of Edmund Spenser. When Orson Welles and Rita Hayworth lived in Big Sur, they named their home *Nepenthe,* presumably so they might forget Hollywood for a while; the name was kept by the new owners, who turned their cliffside house into a fabled restaurant. Figuratively, the word is now used to describe anything that can banish

Nepenthe: *Orson Welles in Big Sur*

grief or bring **oblivion** to sorrow. Revived in modern times
by Edgar Allen Poe ("Quaff, oh quaff this kind *nepenthe*,
and forget this lost Lenore!") as well as in the mystery
writing of H. P. Lovecraft: "For although *nepenthe* has
calmed me, I know always that I am an outsider; a stranger
in this century and among those who are still men."

## NERD

*A 21st-century square; a computer geek.* For half a century there has raged—well, spitballs have been fired in—a twerpy debate over the true origins of this word. First recorded in 1950 in Dr. Seuss's *If I Ran the Zoo*, *nerd* became student **slang** for "stupid or **crazy** person," possibly an alteration of *nut*, as in "He's a nutcase!" Dr. Seuss's clever uses may have contributed to its popularity: "And then, just to show them, / I'll sail to Ka-Troo / And bring back an It-Kutch a Preep and a Proo/ a Nerkle a *Nerd* and a Seersucker too!" A mere seven years later the word appeared in a Glasgow newspaper, but not again until the 1960s, when it was used by the younger siblings of the kids who first read or heard it in Dr. Seuss. Recently, legendary *Jeopardy* record-winner Ken Jennings said, "Being a *nerd* really pays off sometimes." Companion words include *geek, dweeb,* and the ever-popular *dork*.

## NEWFANGLED

*Modern, innovative, fashionable.* A perennial favorite word of many writers and poets, advertising writers and popular speakers—but what about *oldfangled*? Is it even a word? And what is *fangled*, anyway? So glad you asked. According to Mackay, a *fangle* was originally a "toy, trifle, or other article, laid hold of by the fashion." Hence, *newfangled* is *newly fashionable*. Out of this sense of newness came a 14th-century definition that means "addicted to novelty," which should remind us that novelty isn't always new. It is rooted in Old English *fon*, to capture, which led to *fang*, and then to the adjective *newefangel*. Taken together, *The Oxford Book of Word Histories* suggests that newfangled was *new,* an Old English adjective meaning "liking what is new," linked up with the obsolete Old English *fang*, to take, grasp, hold, seize. Together, *new* and *fangle* referred to a liking for novel things, ideas, or fashions. **Rhapsodies** on the theme, though, go all the way back to Plato, who is reputed to have said, "They do certainly give very ***strange***, and *newfangled*, names to disease." I wonder what the original Greek word was! Centuries later, Chaucer wrote, in a quainter sense, "By nature, men love *newfangledness*." What about *oldfangled?* Curiously, the word can be tracked back to 1842, when it meant that something could be characterized by being out of fashion or old-fashioned. In a poem about a fellow poet, Canadian poet George Johnston writes, "*Newfangled*, oldfangled, / in, either way." Companion words include *oldfangled,* old-fashioned, *yesterfang*, anything taken the day before, and, surprisingly, the Old Norse–influenced *spick-and-span*, from *span-nyr,* brand-new.

## NIP, NIPPER

*Cut, snip; a small child; name of a famous dog.* In the argot of the 16th century, a *nip* was a *cutpurse*, a word coined by one who would know, a certain alehouse owner, Wotton, who

Nipper

ran a school for street thieves around 1585. Wotton trained his little *nips* by hanging a purse and a pocket stuffed with silver but trimmed with bells. The boys who could "nip" or cut them could keep the silver and earned their way onto the street. A *foyster* was someone who *foisted* things, a pickpocket; a *nipper* was a pick or pickpocket or cutpurse, from the German *nipen*, to nip, and Dutch *nijpen*. From around 1393 onward both personified the ability "to pinch sharply, to bite." By 1551, those who could *nip* were turned into nouns and eventually into any small boy, hence a "little *nipper*," by 1859. In 1894, RCA Victor chose a cute Dalmatian as its mascot to represent a series of children's programs titled "Little *Nipper.*" Companion words and phrases include the figurative *to nip (something) in the bud*,

1606; *nip and tuck*, a close call, 1832, possibly associated with the nautical or garment worlds; *nippy*, referring to a chill wind that bites, dating back to 1896. A *nipperkin* is a half pint of booze.

## NORMAL

*Average, usual, typical.* A right-angled carpenter's square called a *norma* was used to establish straightness in ancient Greece: standing at the correct angle. The Latin *normalis* was like a straight edge, from *norma*, rule, pattern. The modern meaning of conforming to common standards, not deviating from the *norm*, is a 19th-century notion from 1828. *Normal*, Illinois, was named for the *normal* school, an institution for teacher training, established there in 1857. *Normal* as in "free from mental disorder" occurs in the late 19th century with the advent of psychiatric practice, which prompted Carl Jung to warn, "To be *normal* is the ideal aim of the unsuccessful. *Norm* (Cash) was a powerful slugger for the Detroit Tigers who hit. 361 to lead the American League in batting *average* in 1961, and *Norm* Peterson was an above-*average* beer drinker on *Cheers*. Dorothy Parker reminded us, "Heterosexuality is not *normal*; it's just common." Companion words include *enormous*, from Latin *enorma*, *not* normal, out of line with a mason's square or pattern; a deviance from a plan.

# O

## OBLIVION

*The state or condition of being forgotten or being unaware.* When the first railroad tracks were laid down in Egypt the engineers ran out of wood to burn for fuel, so they *obliviously* burned mummies in the locomotives. Now that fact has been consigned to *oblivion*. Etymologically, from the Latin *oblivio*, forgetfulness, and *oblivisci*, from *ob*, over, and *levis*, smooth, combining for an unforgettable word meaning the smoothing over or evening out of memory. Thus outlined, it is easy to paint a picture of *oblivion* as meaning sanded down by the attrition of time, out of memory until we're unmindful. By the mid-19th century, *oblivion* had been sanded down so much it came to imply being "unaware," and eventually the sense of being banished and utterly forgotten. Think of Ovid's banishment to Constanta, Romania, the furthest reaches of the Roman empire, or Alexander Solzhenitsyn's imprisonment in Siberia—classic examples of *oblivion*. The poet John Dryden observed, "Among our crimes *oblivion* must be noted." He added that *oblivion* "reflects lack of a divine poet because most **heroes** arise from friends who sing praises or poets who delay *oblivion* with the beauty of poetry." For the sublime Emily Dickinson there is hope ("the thing with feathers") on the other side: "Above *Oblivion's* Tide there is a Pier / And an effaceless 'Few' are lifted there—" Companion words include *oblivious*, a mid–15th-century adaptation that personifies *oblivion* so it means "forgetful," applied to someone whose awareness has been so exiled that he or she is, well, *obtuse*, really blunt or dull.

## OK, OKAY

*Good, acceptable, fine, agreed.* Widely regarded now as the most understood word around the world, though it varies widely in its shades of meaning, from "great" to "mediocre." According to the OED, the word "swept into popular use in the US during the mid-19th century." *OK* seems all right with everyone except word scholars. A fistful of etymologies have been propounded, but virtually none are agreed upon. Most of them are pure speculation, if not downright anachronistic. It does not seem at all likely, from the linguistic and historical evidence, that *OK* comes from the Greek *ola kala* ("it is good"), the French *aux Cayes* ("to Les Cayes," a port in Haiti with a reputation for good rum), *au quai* ("to the quay," supposedly said by French-speaking dockers), or the initials of a railway freight agent named Obadiah Kelly, who is said to have written them on documents he had checked. The most recent theory places the earliest recorded mention of the word in 1790, in court papers found in 1859 by Albigence Waldo Putnam, a local historian from Sumner County, Tennessee. There, it is claimed, Andrew Jackson said he "proved a bill of sale from Hugh McGary to Gasper Mansker, for an uncalled good, which was *O.K.*" Beyond this startling claim, there are plenty of other candidates for the honor of earliest written record. They include the phrase "we arrived *ok*" in William Richardson's handwritten diary after traveling safely from Boston to New Orleans in 1815. Among the competing theories is the tantalizing one that the initials O.K. stand for *Oll Korrect*, a "facetious alteration" of *all correct*," or the initials of "Old Kinderhook," a nickname for President Martin Van Buren, an oblique reference to his birthplace, Kinderhook, New York. Other candidates include the Choctaw words *okeh* ("It is so") and *hoke* ("No other way"); the Wolof and Bantu *waw-kay*; and the Scottish phrase "*Och aye*" ("Oh, yes").

## OMPHALOSKEPSIS

*Navel-gazing; to look deeply into yourself.* A colorful mythological alternative to the academic **narcissism**. Coined only in 1925, it leans on the word *omphalos*, which harkens back to Delphi, Greece, home of the oracle, which featured a large stone with carvings of serpents called the *omphalos,* Greek for "navel," and was believed to mark the center of the world. The second part of *omphaloskepsis* is *skepsis,* thinking, which led to *skeptic* and *skeptesthai,* to reflect or view; this led to *scope,* to see through, as with a *telescope* or *microscope.* Originally, the word suggested a practice of mystical self-examination, "scoping out" one's inward life. Companion words include *omphalopsychic,* a clutch/gathering of mystics who practiced self-hypnosis in search of reverie; *omphalomancy,* a very old form of "divination in which the number of children a woman would bear was determined from counting the knots in her umbilical cord at birth"; *omphalotomy,* the cutting of the umbilical cord; and *umbilicus urbis Roma,* the center of Rome from which all distances were measured across the empire and marked by milestones.

## ONOMATOPOEIA

*The imitation of a sound in a word.* A word dating from the 1570s, from Greek *onomatopoiia,* the making of a name or word in imitation of a sound associated with the thing being named, from *onomatopoios,* from *onoma,* word, name, and a derivative of *poiein,* compose, make. The sublimely **strange** British novelist Meryvn Peake wrote in *Titus Groaned,* "Life is too fleet for *onomatopoeia.*" A deft example of *onomatopoeia* can be found in Lewis Carroll's "Jabberwocky" (italicized here): "One, two! One, two and through and through / The vorpal bland went *snicker-snack*! He left it dead, and with its head he went *galumphing* back." *Wordstruck* author Robert MacNeil recounts the impact that Robert Louis Stevenson's language had on him: "Stevenson chooses words that sound like the thing he describes, they are *onomatopoeic*. The *shishing* and *hissing* sounds of *'and ships are tossed at sea'* is one example." Companion words include *sonicky*, Roy Blount Jr.'s term for great-sounding words.

## OPALESCENCE

*Reflecting* **iridescent** *colors, as milky opals do.* This shimmering word reflects the French *opalle*, from Latin *opalus* and Greek *opallios*. The lustrous gem of a word shimmers and plays with rainbow colors. The poet Wallace Stevens wrote, "The wind / Of green blooms turning crisped the motley hue / To clearing *opalescence*. Then the sea / And heaven rolled as one and from the two / Came fresh transfigurings of freshest blue." Companion words include *pearlescent, nacreous,* **iridescent***.*

## OPPORTUNITY

*A favorable chance for movement, circumstances for progress, a* **window** *for advancement.* When the time is fit, the time is favorable, dating back to the late-14th-century Old French *opportunité*, from the Latin *opportunitatem*, favorable time:

*ob*, toward, and *Portunas*, Roman god of keys, doors, locks, and harbors, from *portus*, harbor. An *opportunity* is an opening for **happy** and safe landings, versus an *importunate* moment, from Latin *importunes*, unfit, but originally "having no harbor." An importunate moment is an unsafe time to seek harbor. The Roman philosopher Seneca wrote, "Luck is what happens when preparation meets *opportunity*." *Opportunity* only knocks once, as the proverb has it. The *opportunistic* existential philosopher Ayn Rand preached, "The ladder of success is best climbed by stepping on the rungs of *opportunity*." Novelist Maya Angelou wrote **smirkily**: "Most plain girls are virtuous because of the scarcity of *opportunity* to be otherwise." Companion words include *opportunism*, amoral exploitation.

## ORDEAL

*Struggle, obstacle, trial.* In the time of the ancient Vikings justice was meted out by a mysterious system of dealing out physical tests called *aedaelan*, old Norse for "deal out," which evolved into our *ordeal*. These *ordeals* involved torturous methods to try an accused person, such as plunging his hand into boiling oil to see if his skin burned. If he was burned, he was guilty; if not, innocent. So unpopular was the *ordeal* method it was finally abolished in 1215. "Come tell me of thine *ordeal*," Homer has "wise Penelope" whisper to "myriad-minded" Odysseus when he returns home after twenty years, "for methinks the day will come when I must learn it, and timely knowledge is no hurt." Danish American actor Viggo Mortensen, Aragorn/Strider in the movie *The Lord of the Rings*, has said, "Any *ordeal* that you can survive as a human being is an improvement in your **character**, and usually an improvement in your life." Companion words include *trial, crucible, affliction*.

## OSCILLATE

*To waver, move back and forth.* An imaginative word that is rooted in the Latin *oscillum*, a little mouth, most visually imagined in Virgil's *Georgics* when he describes a small mask of open-mouthed Bacchus swinging to and fro from a tree in a vineyard. The swaying verb swings one way, into French in the 1650s as *oscillation*, and soon afterward the other way, into English in 1726. Leave it to the pawky H. L. Mencken, whose sly sense of humor swung wildly between acerbic and compassionate, to capture its momentum in this epigram: "Life is a constant *oscillation* between the sharp horns of dilemmas." Companion words include *vacillate,* to waver, evocative of waves of *oscillation*.

## OSTRACIZE

*Exclude from a group, shun from society.* The practice of *ostracism* was a decidedly undemocratic practice under Greek democracy that was designed to rid ancient Athens of unwanted, unpopular, or dangerously powerful politicians for five to ten years. In effect, it was a self-balancing act to "neutralize someone considered a threat to the system." Curiously (and tantalizingly), the Athenian citizens were asked every year if they had any candidates to nominate for *ostracism*. If any were nominated, a vote was held in the agora, where the names of those to be expelled were etched on potsherds or pottery fragments called *ostraka* and handed to those who were forced into exile as a consequence of the practice of *ostrakizein*, which was then formalized by a declaration of banishment by the Senate. A trove of *ostraka* with their inscriptions intact was discovered in the agora of Athens in 1932, during digs for the subway. Berkeley poet Adrienne Rich uses the sharp-edged word powerfully: "Yet everywhere women have resisted [heterosexuality], often at the cost of physical torture, imprisonment, psychosurgery, social *ostracism*, and extreme poverty." Companion words include the Greek *pharmakos,* the ultimate source for our phrase "a shred of truth," which was originally "a shard of truth," from the very shards of pottery, the *ostraka*, that were used to cast votes of exile in ancient Athens.

## OUBLIETTE

*Dungeon; a deep or narrow well in which to imprison and thus to forget a person.* On the rue Galandes, in Paris, the Le caveau des *oubliettes* now specializes in hot **chocolate** and crepes, but boasts a grisly past as a 12th-century prison that specialized in a particularly grim form of dungeon, dank one-man holes in the ground with the only door placed in the ceiling, where the world would *oublier*, forget, the prisoners forever. In the movie *First Knight*, the character Malignant says, "This is called an *oubliette*. That's French for 'a place of forgetting.' Your quarters, my **lady**. No gates, no bars, no locks. Just walls of air." Companion words include *forgettery*, Robert Frost's inspired name for the place in the brain where we store forgotten memories.

## OWL / OL' (IRISH)

*An old Irish expression for something regarded as beloved, intimate, or simply comfortable.* Serendipity lives. In the fall of 2011 I was co-leading a literary tour around the West of Ireland and had a free evening, which I used to review the present *manuscript*. Being there on the Old Sod, it seemed logical to find a local bookstore in the *town* where we were staying, Balleybofey, Donegal, and ask for a book of Irish words. Whereupon I tripped over the winsomely titled *I Have Been Busy with Words,* by the journalist John D. Sheridan. When I cracked the thin *volume*, it opened its wings like the gulls over the Irish Sea, revealing a chapter titled "Just One Little Word." If only I knew the Irish for "Eureka!" By chance that lilting three-page essay provided me with the *one little word* I needed to bridge one of the odder gaps in English. To wit: a word to describe a long-

time, affectionate, even intimate relationship—whether
with an old friend or a car whose odometer you've seen
roll over 100,000 miles. If we want to say, "I'd like you
to meet my *old* friend, Jaz," we're in danger of suggesting
that he is *old* in years. If we want to say, "Let me take you
for a drive in my *old* '65 Mustang," we risk suggesting it
might be old, meaning *dangerous*, when we really want to
express our abiding affection, our oddly tender feelings
for it. Fortunately, Sheridan points out that the ambiguous
and bland English "old" is drawn out and tenderized in
Irish to become *owl*, as intimate as an *owl sweater*. Sheridan
describes hearing an old fellah at a pub talking about cures
for the common cold, who concluded, "There's nothing
to beat *th'owl* malt." Compressed into that sentence is more
than a description of a glass of whiskey. It is closer to say
it is a shot of a beloved drink, which Sheridan defines as
**untranslatable**. Similarly, the phrase "It's time to don the
*owl* overcoat" doesn't suggest that the coat is chronologi-
cally old, but infers untold or untellable things, such as
comfort and tradition, time and death. "*Owl* can be full
of tenderness or sentiment. It can tell a love story or a life
story," Sheridan concludes. "We have one little word that
sees us through all our emotional difficulties and it is a fine
standby when it fails, when the *owl* tongue lets us down."
Companion words include *venerable, honest-to-goodness,
genuine*—none as *auld* as *owl*.

## OXYMORON

A *self-contradiction*. Examples abound. Groucho Marx cites "military intelligence"; one particularly nasty French writer offers "American literature." Its roots dig down into the Greek *oxys*, sharp, and *moros*, foolish. Hence, sharply foolish. Companion words include *sophomore*, a student in his tenth year of school, but also one who straddles two worlds, ignorance and **wisdom**, the sweet and sorrow, bittersweet years of high school or college; *morosoph*, a learned fool, and *sophomania*, one who pretends to be intellectual.

# P

## PAL (ROMANY, GYPSY)

*Friend.* One of the few words that has wandered into English from the wandering people themselves, the Romany, and furtively at that, through their secret language. According to Metcalf, it was first recorded in 1678 in a legal deposition in Hertfordshire, England: "Where have you been all this day, *pal*? What would you have me doing, *pal*?" This term of affectionate friendship suggesting "brother or comrade" derived from the Romany *pral, plal, phral*, arriving in Europe after a long linguistic journey with the gypsies from India, scholars say, around 3,000 years ago from the borderlands between India and Persia. Its origin in Sanskrit is *bhrata*, brother. The common phrase "Better late than never, *pal*," can be traced back to the poet Lord Byron. "I never did *pal* around with actresses," sighed actress Bette Davis. "Their talk usually bored me to tears." Companion words include Paltalk, a

Pal: *When Slow October*

free service providing video chat and instant messaging; a pastiche of friendly terms not excluding *companion* itself, and the chummy *buddy*, possibly derived from *brother*.

## PALAVER

*Small talk; parley; misleading speech.* A loanword from Portuguese sailor's **slang** and a trader's term, *palavra*, word, speech, adopted from West African traders. Also related to Late Latin *parabola*, proverb, parable, speech, comparison, originally from Greek *parabolein*, to compare, *para*, beside, and *ballein*, to **throw**. Its first use in the sense of "empty talk" was registered in 1748. "He is glad to *palaver* of his many adventures, as a boy will **whistle** after sundown in a wood," wrote O. Henry in his short story "The Man Higher Up." Companion words include *lalophobia*, fear of speaking, presumably referring to someone who prefers as little talk as possible.

## PALINDROME

*A word, phrase, or sequence of words that reads the same forward and backward.* 1620s, from Greek *palindromos*, a recurrence, literally running backward, from *palin*, again, back, and *dromos*, running. Some entire poems are *palindromes*, and in genetics a *palindrome* is a stretch of DNA where a sequence of nucleotides on one strand mirrors the adjacent one. Classic examples abound: "Able was I ere I saw Elba," "Nate bit a Tibetan," "Sex at noon taxes," "Zeus sees Suez," "Oh, **cameras** are macho," "Eros saw I was sore." Single word *palindromes* include *mom, dad, level, madam, kayak,* and *racecar.* While sitting in front of a turf fire in a pub in Ballyvaughan, Ireland, in 2002, my late great friend the Irish poet-mystic John O'Donohue asked me, "I wonder why *palindrome* isn't spelled the same backwards and forwards?"

## PALTRY

*Pitifully small, ragged, meager, petty,* **trivial**. Let's sift through the trashy remains of the 16th-century Low German *paltrig*, ragged, *pelt*, trash, rags, and see what we can see. As I was standing outside Yeats Tower, near Ennis in the West of Ireland, in the fall of 2010, a retired poetry teacher approached the group I was leading and offered to recite some of the old poet's verse. How could we resist? With little nudging he recited by heart "When I am Old and Grey" ( "… and lying by the fire / take down this book …") and then a few lines from "Sailing to Byzantium," "An aged man is but a *paltry* thing, a tattered coat upon a stick, unless soul clap its hands and sing, and louder sing for every tatter in its mortal dress." The journalist P. J. O'Rourke trenchantly observed: "Politics are for foreigners with their endless wrongs and *paltry* rights. Politics are a lousy way to get things done. Politics are, like God's infinite mercy, a last resort."

## PANACEA / HYGIENE

*A cure-all; health, cleanliness.* The Greek myths are infinitely **ramifying**, branching out into psychologically insightful stories and words that still speak to us today. Take the etymology of these healthy terms. Asclepius, god of medicine, healing, and the personification of the "healthful art" (*hygieine techne*), is the father of *Panacea*, all-curing, and *Hygieia*, the very personification of health, as used by Aristotle. As Michael Madrone writes, "she personified one of her father's powers: the ability to heal with plants." The Romans later applied *Panacea*'s name to a particular genus of herbs they fancied could "heal all" diseases, exactly as her name implies: cure all, from *pan*, all, and *cea*, cure. Her symbol was an echo of her healer father's, a serpent drinking from a cup that she held in her hand. Ancient Greeks credited her with providing clean air and the power to fend off disease. Compare comedian George Carlin's riff on cleanliness: "When I got out of high school they retired my jersey, but it was for *hygiene* and sanitary reasons." Companion words include *salutary,* healthful, stemming from *Salus*, the Roman equivalent of *Hygieia.* Furthermore, a *salutation* is what we offer when we express interest in someone else's well-being, in their health: "How are you?" If our interest is formal enough we may actually *salute* them.

## PANDEMONIUM

*Madcap confusion; what happens when all hell breaks loose.* Coined in 1667 by John Milton in *Paradise Lost,* Pandemonium was the name he gave to "the palace built in the middle of Hell … the high capital of Satan and all his peers." Milton created the word by combining the Greek *pan*, all, and *daemon*, evil spirit or inferior divine power. Its familiar modern usage, "a wild and raucous confusion," dates to 1865. Frank Sinatra's favorite female singer, Jo

Stafford, described her band's wild and crazy music as if all heaven broke loose: "The *pandemonium* was in full swing."

## PARADISE

*A place of* **happiness***; a world of harmony; the abode of bliss.* The story line, as they say in Hollywood, is strong and clear here. This dreamy word embodies the human dream of contentment, the utopian vision of peace and perfection, the ultimate abode, it is said, of the kind and just. But its origins are more *aesthetic* than philosophical. Our earliest citing is in the 4th-century scholar Xenophon's *Anabasis*, where he describes a *páradeisos* as an "animal park." Later, Herodotus wrote in his *Histories* about the walled-in parks where the nobility used to walk and even hunt. The word derives from Avestan/Old Persian *pairidaeza*, a walled-in park or orchard, from *pairi*, around, and *daēza,* wall. The notion of a Garden of Eden is reflected in the Late Hebrew *pardes*, the royal forest of King Artaxerxes, who provided Nehemiah with timber "to make beams for the gates of the palace." This early urban improvement was inspired by the Zoroastrian's fondness for planting arbors and gardens, eventually leading to the construction of the Hanging Gardens of Babylon, one of the Seven Wonders of the Ancient World. Wordsmiths have forged a word, *amelioration*, which means a kind of improvement on the original. If you peer over the wall of this dulcet word, you see that it was picked like fruit and replanted in the Septuagint

**translation** of Genesis, in the Old **Testament**, which grew into our now familiar Garden of Eden. There is a relevant Arab proverb: "*Paradise* can be found on the backs of horses, in books and between the breasts of women." On the front of a menu in Tahiti I once read a reference to the island's beautiful lagoons by Henri Matisse, who asked, "Aren't you the seven wonders of the *Paradise* of painters?" Companion words include *the Elysian Fields*, the Greek afterworld of eternal delights, namesake of the *Champs-Élysées*, in Paris, and the earliest known baseball field, in Hoboken, New Jersey.


## PARAPHERNALIA

*Miscellaneous things, essential items for a specific task, but also, curiously, devolving into unessential things, trappings, distractions.* Originally, the Greek *parapherna* referred to the property that was set apart or not intended for a woman's dowry, from *para*, beyond, and *pherna* (from *pherne*), dowry. It's not a leap to suspect that the word started with a literal and legal meaning but resentment soon crept in that husbands were not inheriting everything from their wife's family, and so the *paraphernalia* began to be referred to in a disdainful manner. The Indian spiritual leader Sri Sathva Sai Baba gives a succinct modern usage: "There will also be some people who concentrate their attention on the rituals of worship and the offerings being made, such as the breaking of coconuts, the waving of lamps and incense, and the devotion expressed through these rituals. The number of people with this kind of vision and interest will be much smaller than those who concentrate on the decorations, the dances and dramas and all the external *paraphernalia* associated with the festival." The rock star Peter Gabriel, solo artist and former member of Genesis, used it pejoratively to describe the extraneous things in life that just get in the way: "In the digital world, it is so much easier to put stuff out without a great deal of *paraphernalia* and fanfare." Companion words include *paraphernal* or "extra-dotal" property, a legal term to describe items excluded from a woman's dowry.

## PARCHMENT

*In ancient and medieval times, sheepskin or goatskin prepared for writing on; strong, tough, translucent paper. Parchment* is the bridge material for writing between ancient Egyptian papyrus and the Greek tablet and modern paper. Around 200 BCE, it arose as a clever, timely innovation by a young scribe in Pergamon, in western Asia Minor, now Turkey. His was a creative response to the sudden shortage of papyrus after its export was banned by Ptolemy V in Egypt. No doubt after much experimentation, the scribe discovered that if he split the skin of a kid goat or sheep and then bleached, battered, and burnished it, the surface was smooth enough to write on and strong enough to hold ink, and also pliable enough to roll up like a scroll. So successful was this substitute for papyrus that around

1300 BCE it came to be known after the Greek city where it was first extensively used, *Pergamenon*, or Pergamon. The Colombian writer Gabriel García Márquez writes: "Between the covers of the books that no one had ever read again, in the old *parchments* damaged by dampness, a livid flower had prospered, and in the air that had been the purest and brightest in the house an unbearable smell of rotten tomatoes floated." Companion words include the color ***parchment***, a light tan or off-white.

## PARIAH (TAMIL)

*A social outcast; a member of an indigenous people of a low caste in Hindu southern India.* Irony of ironies, the very people who personify the indignity of living as outcasts on the fringes of society have been immortalized because of the one important function they filled in Tamil society. *Pariahs* were *paraiyan,* which literally means "(hereditary) drummer," derived from the word *parai,* the name of a festival drum. Curiously, that long lone hard *"i"* sound in *pariah* perfectly captures the sense of banishment of those whose "I," their very identity, is too much for their family or tribe or community to tolerate. Consequently, they are "drummed out of ***town***." Over time, as the 2009 edition of *The American Heritage Dictionary* says, the word came be used "for anyone who is a social outcast, independent of social position; recalls a much more rigid social system, which made only certain people *pariahs*." First recorded in English in 1613, the word's widespread use is likely the result of the colonial period in India. *Pariah* was banished as an exclusive term for festival drummers by 1819, when it was recorded in the modern sense of "social outcast." Citations include a passage I remember coming across while reading *The Adventures of Huckleberry Finn* with my father when I was a boy: "Shortly Tom [Sawyer] came upon the juvenile *pariah* of the village, Huckleberry Finn, son of the **town** drunkard." Mystery writer Ken Follett writes, "There was a very serious communist strain among American intellectuals before the war. America was a more tolerant place in those days, and Communists were not treated as *pariahs*. That ended with the McCarthy era." Companion words include *castaway, leper, untouchable*.

## PECULIAR

*Strange, odd,* **weird**. No more so than its backstory. During Roman times the medium of exchange was cattle, *pecu*, which led to the notion of private property, *peculiarus*. To be *impecunious* meant you had no cattle, no sheep, nothing to your name worth bartering. To be *peculiar* meant that all the cattle, all the animals worth trading, were owned by just one man, which made it odd for anyone who wanted to make any money, or *pecunia*. Thus, an early version of Catch-22. If you wanted money, you needed cattle, which were nearly the same thing (*pecu*); but to get cattle you needed money. This strange paradox evolved into the modern sense of the word *peculiar* by around 1600. Charles Kennedy writes, "Courage is a *peculiar* kind of fear." Thomas Wolfe wrote, "The whole conviction of my life now rests upon the belief that loneliness, far from being a rare and curious phenomenon, *peculiar* to myself and to a few other solitary men, is the central and inevitable fact of human existence." Companion words include *penury,* the state of being destitute, and *peculiarity,* oddity.


## PENGUIN

*An aquatic, flightless bird (order Sphenisciformes) that lives in the southern hemisphere, mostly in Antarctica, but got its name from the Welsh.* In dramatic contrast to our emphasis on colorful or polychromatic words, this one is in glorious black and white. These lovable birds, described as "countershaded" in dark and white plumage, live on krill, fish, squid, and other delectable seafood, and like their half-and-half coloring, spend half their life on land and half in the ocean. Their accompanying word story is likewise half-and-half, half recorded, half anecdotal. The word *penguin* is of uncertain origin, but of certain shambling speculation. The OED, AHD, and MW all suggest a derivation from the Welsh *pen*, head, and *gwyn*, white (think: Gwendolyn). Their argument centers on an earlier version of *penguin* that had been used for the great auk of Newfoundland (now extinct) which featured great white spots around its eyes, set off against a jet-black head. The later French and Breton word *pinguoin*, auk, swam across the Channel from England. In the 1990s, cartoonist Gary Larson began to play off the stereotype that all *penguins* look alike because they live in large groups; one cartoon featured a huddle of *penguins* crowded together as one in the middle sings the old Sammy Davis Jr. song, "I just gotta to be me!" Companion terms include *Penguin Books*, the revolutionary publishing firm founded in England in 1935 by Sir Allen Lane and V. K. Krishna Menon, featuring high-quality, low-cost editions; its motto was "Because what you read matters."

## PEREGRINATION

*Pilgrimage; travel on foot; walking tour.* One of a passel of picaresque terms for a sacred journey. Our English word *pilgrim* derives from the Provençal *pelegrin,* from the Latin *perigrinus*, abroad, to describe one who has walked a long distance across **strange** lands, stemming from the earlier *peregre* (*per ager*), literally "through the fields." Since the long walks to Rome and Jerusalem crossed all borders in Europe, derivative words are closely related, such as the French *pèlerin,* Italian *pellegrino,* Spanish and Portuguese *peregrino*, German *Pilger*, and Icelandic *pilagrimur.* Companion words include **saunter**, from *Sainte Terre*, Holy Land, to walk to the Holy Land; *canter*, to walk or ride a horse to Canterbury; *peregrine* falcon, one that travels great distances; *trek*, the Afrikaans word for the arduous

Peregrination

journey into the interior of South Africa; and *journey* itself, from the French *journée*, a day's **travel**.


## PHARMACY

*The administration of medicinal drugs.* The word and the practice date back to ancient Greece: *pharmakeia,* the druggist's practice, and *pharmakon,* drug, one of the most versatile words in Greek, which can mean remedy, poison, medicine, philter, charm, spell, enchantment, even paint. The earliest use for the place where drugs are prepared and dispensed is recorded in 1833. Your friendly author was inspired to write this entry after visiting, in the summer of 2011, the Old Pharmacy, in the Franciscan monastery in Dubrovnik, Croatia. This still thriving business opened it its doors and vials in 1317, making it the third-oldest and longest-operating *pharmacy* in the world. A wonderful citation comes from the *Familiar Letters on Chemistry*, by Justus von Liebig, from 1851: "Only about seventy years ago was chemistry, like a grain of seed from a ripe fruit, separated from the other physical sciences. With Black, Cavendish and Priestley, its new era began. Medicine, *pharmacy*, and the useful arts had prepared the soil upon which this seed was to germinate and to flourish." The French emperor Napoleon Bonaparte wrote, "Water, air, and cleanliness are chief articles in my *pharmacy*." Companion words include *Big Pharma*, a euphemism for major pharmaceutical companies, and *pharmacopeia*, a book or publication that contains a list of medicinal drugs, accompanied by directions for their safe use.

## PHILOMATH

*Someone who loves to learn.* The origins are a good place to start—to learn from—going back to the Greek *philo*, to **love**, and *mathein*, to learn. So, a lover of learning. The psychotropic, literally soul-turning, response to ineptitude, the desire to teach ourselves what we don't know but feel we need to learn. A *philomath* is distinguished from a *philosopher* by the love of knowledge in contrast to the love of wisdom. The great *Time* magazine art critic Alexander Eliot once told me, "Oh, he was a *philomath*," in reference to his great-grandfather, Charles W. Eliot, president of Harvard University. Companion words include *chrestomathy*, useful learning based on carefully chosen passages, and *Philomath*, Oregon, a town founded, it would be lovely to think, on the love of learning.

## PHLUG

*Belly-button lint.* Now tell me you've *never* wondered what to call it. File this one under **whatchamacallits**, that vast category of indescribables, *unmentionables*, or just plain word gaps in the language—all those words waiting, like long-buried treasure, to be rediscovered, or at least to help us with our stammering. Comparably icky names would be *snot*, from the old word capturing the similarity between hardened mucus in the nostrils and a burnt wick. And **consider** this more vivid than you may like: *snotterclout*, an unfortunately vivid word for a hanky. *Phlug* is a sterling example of a word that sounds and even looks like the thing it means, although we may never actually want to use it. "Hey, honey, can you pluck that *phlug* out of your belly button?" may be technically correct but is certainly romantically incorrect. Companion words include *snot*, mucus from the nose, from the old Middle English *snotte*, which is intimately related to *snout*. Also, a word that has bedeviled me for years, the very snotty word *booger*, possibly from the French *bouger*, to move.

## PHOBIA

*Irrational fear, the offspring of war and violence.* I fear the list is long, then wonder, is there a word for a fear of long lists? The Greek *phobos*, fear, was inspired by Phobos, the very personification of fear, with his brother Deimos, god of terror. Both were sons of Ares, god of violence and war, one who reveled in striking fear in the hearts of others. The psychological condition of *phobia* is more nuanced, referring to any abnormal or irrational fear. Hence we have a raft of fearsome words, including *logophobia*, fear of words; *pogonophobia*, fear of beards; *dystychiphobia*, fear of accidents; *felinophobia*, fear of cats; *scotophobia*, fear of darkness; *koniophobia*, fear of dust; *batrachophobia*, fear of frogs; *apeirophobia*, fear of infinity; *catapedaphobia*, fear of jumping; *gelotophobia*, fear of being laughed at; *brontophobia*, fear of thunder; *metrophobia*, fear of poetry. When asked, I often cite my favorite, *arachibutyrophobia*, the fear of peanut butter sticking to the roof of your mouth, or alternately, *abibliophobia*, the fear of running out of reading material. If it exists, somebody is trembling with fear about it. *Staurophobia* is a morbid fear of crosses, like Bela Lugosi's in *Dracula*. If I were worried that the number of *phobias* listed above totals thirteen, I would be *triskaidekaphobic*, rooted, in case you're wondering, in the story of the betrayal of Jesus by Judas at the Last Supper. I'm afraid of listing more because it might task the patience of the reader, a reluctance that could be diagnosed as *kakorrhaphiophobia,* the fear of failure itself.

## PHOSPHORUS

*A glowing element found in rocks.* Elementary, my dear Watson, right? Sounds straightforward enough, but one online dictionary strains credulity as well as readability by offering this definition: "a multivalent nonmetallic element of the nitrogen family that occurs commonly in inorganic phosphate rocks and as organic phosphates in all living cells; is highly reactive and occurs in several allotropic forms." In contrast, ancient Greek astronomers nicknamed Venus, the rising morning star, *Phosphoros*, the light bringer, from *phos*, light, and *pheinen*, carry, to bring light. The glowing word elements within the core of *phosphorus* were ferried across into English from the Romans as *phosphorus*. Not until 1602 do we hear of the word again, when, Webb Garrison writes, "a shoemaker from Bologna, Italy, was exploring near Mount Paterno, where he discovered a **strange** mineral that glowed in the dark." When scholars/geologist came to name it, they recalled the old Roman word because it suited the stone, which was duly a "light-bringer." *Phosphorus* was a favorite of the alchemists, as evidenced by their description of it as a mysterious "substance or organism that shines of itself," attested from the 1640s. Recently, brain researchers detected the presence of *phosphorus* in the brain and in human nutrition. French novelist Stendahl asked, "Who knows whether it is not true that *phosphorus* and mind are not the same thing?" Companion words include *phosphate*, a soda jerk's carbonative concoction, and *phosphenes*, those optical shapes we see when we see "stars" after hitting our head.


## PIE

*A pastry consisting of a crust with various contents, from fruit to meat, dropped inside.* An observational word, dating back to the unknown and unknowable moment when someone decided to encrust a stew, then dropped in a little of this and that to keep it together. Then they needed to name it. Perhaps that person was staring out the kitchen **window** and happened to notice a *pie*, the earliest known name for *magpie*, perched on a nearby branch while constructing a nest by dropping in an assortment of twigs, feathers, and dirt. The association of the bird's nest and the nest for food stuck in the throat of language. Actress Lynn Redgrave once said, "God always has another custard *pie* up his sleeve." Companion words include *pi*, the mathematical constant, a tasty slice denoting the ratio of a circle's circumference to its diameter.

**PLUCKY**

*Courageous, sly, or cunning in risky circumstances; knowing how to pull the strings of life; in art, clear in outline or detail.* Of obscure origins, but probably related to the act of plucking, as in the old English idiom "plucking up one's courage," which means to "pick up or bolster one's confidence," as one would *pluck* or pick a chicken's feathers or *pluck* the strings of a musical instrument. The word has a surprising use as a collective noun, as in a *pluck* of *shawmers*, those who play the *shawm*, a medieval woodwind instrument. "The *plucky* Brits were shaken but not stirred by the Superdome **ordeal**," said James Murray. Former Presidential Press Secretary Pierre Salinger quipped: "I may be *plucky* but I'm not stupid." Companion words include The Cluster *Pluckers*, a quartet of singer-songwriters and country-music instrumentalists.

**PODUNK**

*A small **town** of legend, the middle of nowhere.* An American **slang** word dating back to 1846, sometimes in the form *Podunk Hollow,* but always spoken in a dismissive or condescending tone. This sonicky word is another contribution of the Algonquin Indians, referring to an actual tribe, the *Podunk*, which thrived in a marsh around the Podunk River in Connecticut. First recorded in colonial records from 1656, as Potunck or Potunk, a possible evolution of *ptukohke*, a neck of the woods, or a boggy place. The earliest citation in its modern form occurs in Samuel Griswold Goodrich's 1840 *Dictionary of American Regional English*; the entry "The Politician of Podunk" reads: "Solomon Waxtend was a shoemaker of Podunk, a small village of New York some forty years ago." The United States Board of Geographic Names provides the names of five different *Podunks*, one in Connecticut, another in New York, and three in Michigan, plus several other locations such as the ghost town of Shattuck, Oklahoma. Its popularity as the name of a typical (if mythical) US small ***town*** dates from a series of witty "Letters from Podunk" which ran in the *Buffalo Daily National Pilot* beginning on January 5, 1846. Companion words include *Hicksville;* a Beat poets favorite term, *Squaresville;* and **boondocks**.

## PRECOCIOUS

*Possessing unusual talent or ability at an early age.* Usually said of children who are too smart for their own good; its Latin roots *pre*, before, and *coquere*, to cook, provide a startling picture of *precociousness*, like a steak broiled too early for dinner. Speaking of raw meat, I recall my Uncle Cy once telling me how he befriended Jackie Coogan, the Hollywood child star, during World War II, referring to him as "still a *precocious* kid." Picasso said, "What might be taken for a *precocious* genius is the genius of childhood. When the child grows up, it disappears without a trace. It may happen that this boy will become a real painter some day, or even a great painter. But then he will have to begin everything again, from zero." Einstein massaged the point by saying, "When I was still a rather *precocious* young man, I already realized most vividly the futility of the hopes and aspirations that most men pursue throughout their lives." Companion words include *Precocious*, a webcomic penned by Christopher J. Paulsen, whose motto is "Because Knowledge is a Weapon!"


**PRESTIGE**

*Reputation.* Another case of verbal amelioration. The word began life around the 1650s meaning "illusion, deceit, imposture, juggling tricks," from Latin *prestigiae*, and then took on the figurative sense of blindfolding or dazzling somebody, before becoming associated with the illusionist or the conjurer. The name became the fame, the thing illusionists did and became famous for, creating illusion, and by which they earned *prestige*. Margaret Ernst defined *prestige's* cousin, *prestidigitation,* as a sleight of hand signaled by **quick** fingering. *Prestige*, then, is the **glamour** that arises from a genuine ***achievement***, and the reputation that comes with it. In the 2006 movie *The Prestige*, Cutter says, "Every great magic trick consists of three parts or acts. The first part is called 'the Pledge.' The magician shows you something ordinary: a deck of cards, a bird or a man. He shows you this object. Perhaps he asks you to inspect it to see if it is indeed real, unaltered, ***normal***.

But of course—it probably isn't. The second act is called 'the Turn.' The magician takes the ordinary something and makes it do something extraordinary. Now you're looking for the secret—but you won't find it, because of course you're not really looking. You don't really want to know. You want to be fooled. But you wouldn't clap yet. Because making something disappear isn't enough; you have to bring it back. That's why every magic trick has a third act, the hardest part, the part we call 'the Prestige.'" Companion words include *prestidigitator*, a conjurer by reputation, one whose fame and influence comes from sleight of hand.

## PREVARICATE

*To lie, evade, stray from the truth*. Its Latin roots ground us in its deeper, more fertile meanings, from *praevaricare*, to spread apart; its roots in the plowman's work give us "to make crooked ridges and furrows," straying from the straight line—figuratively, straying from the truth. The figurative sense originates in slick handling card shufflers, which in turn suggests someone who walks crookedly, deviating from the true path—or the path of truth. Companion words include *boustrophedonic*, plowing back and forth in a field, and the ultimate wandering word, *meander*, from the name of a winding river in present-day Turkey.

## PUNGENT

*Acrid, penetrating, biting, caustic; said of a taste or smell, acidic or spicy substances.* Its derivation delivers a pointed origin story dating back to the 1590s: Latin *pungentum*, sharp, poignant, causing grief, from the earlier *pungere*, to prick, pierce, sting. If you picture the pain caused by an angry fist (*pugnus*), you've got the *pugnacious* idea. If you can imagine the horrific conditions during "The Big Stink" in London in 1858, you might appreciate odors so strong they *sting the nose.* An ancient Chinese proverb says, "Sour, sweet, bitter, *pungent*, all must be tasted." In *The Journal of Eugène Delacroix* we find this droll entry: "Monday, 1 March. The man who brings our coal and wood is a bit of a wag—great chatterbox. When he asked for a tip the other day saying he had a great many children to feed, Jenny said, 'Well why did you have so many?' and he answered: 'It was my wife who had them.' A perfect example of Gallic humor. He said something equally *pungent* a year ago, but I forget what it was." Companion words include *punctum*, a point, especially a sharp point; and *puncture*, to perforate.

## PUPIL

*Student; center of the eye.* A doublet word, both of whose meanings are rooted in the Latin *pupa*, girl or doll, and *pupilla*, a small girl doll. Conjured up by particularly attentive people who look directly into other people's eyes, enabling them to see tiny images of themselves reflected there. Possible older influence from the Greek *kore*, girl, but likewise referring to both *doll* and the *pupil* of the eye. The useful *Online Dictionary* cites Plato's *Alcibiades*: "Self-knowledge can be obtained only by looking into the mind and virtue of the soul, which is the diviner part of a man, as we see our own image in another's eye." The transition to the contemporary meaning of "student" dates back to the late 14th century, when it meant "orphan child, ward," from the same Old French *pupille* and Latin *pupillus*, orphan, ward, eventually graduating to mean "disciple or student" by 1560. In the spirit of the title *The Painted Word* we are happy to cite painter Paul Cézanne: "I am a *pupil* of Pissaro." Opera singer Maria Callas is recorded as saying, "That is the difference between good teachers and great teachers: good teachers make the best of a *pupil's* means; great teachers foresee a *pupil's* ends." Companion words include the optometrist's *pupilometer*, the instrument that gauges the distance between a patient's *pupils*.

# Q

## QUANDARY

*A perplexity, a puzzle, often requiring a choice between two bad options.* Some say it dates back to the late 16th century, possibly deriving from the Latin *quando*, simply "When?" asked in a ***stymied*** tone of voice. Still, its etymology is a tautology; figuring out a *quandary* is a *quandary*. *Quandary* may also derive from Old Norse *vandraedi*, "difficulty, trouble, evil plight," and Icelandic *wandreth*, "plight, peril, adversity." Skeat believed it derived from the French "*Qu'en dirai je?*" ("What shall I say of it?"), and cites Gilbert Blackhall's 17th-century phrase "*Condarye* for *hypo-condarye*" as his source for the clearly dark psychological origins of the word: "great *hypo-condarye*, i. e., a morbid state of mind." For Skeat to be in a *quandary* was a situation from which derived the figurative and general sense of "extrication [that] is difficult, especially an unpleasant or trying one." An old English proverb suggests a typical *quandary*: "One is so over-gorged as to be doubtful which he should do first, shit or spew." Companion words include *Quandary Peak,* in the Mosquito Range of Colorado, the state's fourteenth highest, and also commonly regarded as a "fourteener," a mountain peak that reaches at least 14,000 feet.

## QUICKEN

*Hurry; revive; come to life.* This invigorating verb comes from the Old Icelandic *wprdd kykna,* come into being. There is an echo here of the ancient theological belief in the "moment of *quickening,*" when the soul enters the fetus, which gives us the notion of *animating,* ensouling, bringing life to the inanimate. In Ireland, Share reminds us, to *quicken* also means to "bring up a smoldering fire," or to bring life to the party by being "*quickened* with drink." Frank O'Connor, in *Irish Miles,* writes, "'Sure, man,' said the poet, 'don't you see 'tis the way I'm so *quickened* with drink.'" Companion words include the *quickening,* the first stirrings of a fetus in the womb, the first signs of life, or in medieval theology, the first evidence of the soul, as felt by a pregnant woman.

## QUINTESSENTIAL

*The fifth essence, the highest element (after the main four: earth, air, fire, water), therefore the purest.* It was deemed "the fifth element" by Aristotle, the "ether," to complement the traditional four elements of the Greeks: earth, water, fire, and air. Literally, *quinta essentia*, from Latin *essentia*, quality or being: the fifth essence. The philosopher wrote that the moon, sun, and stars were composed of this ether, later transposed as the quinta essentia, which now means, essentially, the highest quality. Companion words include *quintet*, a five-member group, usually musical, and *Quintet,* a 1979 post-apocalypse science fiction film by Robert Altman.

# R

## RAMBLE

*To stray, rove, **roam**; incoherent talk.* An emotion-in-motion word. *The Concise Oxford Dictionary* (1996) provides a tantalizing possible connection between the Latin *romen* and the Middle Dutch *rammelen* and German *rammeln*, said of cats and rabbits that are "excited by sexual desire and wandering" around in heat, or as philologist Ernest Weekley put it, "the night wanderings of the amorous cat." With the imprimatur of no less than the OED, we can say that *ramble* derives from *rammen*, to copulate. So to *ramble* means "to go catting around." Around the 1630s, *ramble* was personified to describe wandering with words, talking or writing without direction, incoherently. Irish poet William Butler Yeats wrote, "The last stroke of midnight dies. / All day in the one chair / From dream to dream and rhyme to rhyme I have ranged / In *rambling* talk with an image of air: Vague moments, nothing but memories." For modern usage, look and listen no further than Detroit's own Bob Seger's first big hit, *"Ramblin', Gamblin' Man,"* or Nat King Cole's *"Ramblin' Rose."* And let's not forget the hipster **slang** expression "If you crack the whip, I'll take the trip," as I heard one **cool** *cat* say at Baker's Keyboard Lounge one night in the early 1970s while we were listening to Thelonious Monk. Companion words include *ramblin' man*, a guy who wanders from *town* to town doin' what comes naturally.

Ramble: *Cadillac Desert*

Ramify: *Spring Departure*

## RAMIFY

*To branch out; to imply.* From the Old French *ramifier,* to make
branches, from Latin *ramus,* branch, and *facere,* to make.
The figurative meaning is to branch or spread out, but also
to have complicated consequences, reminiscent of the way
that branches sometimes get twisted and outgrowths are
growing pains. John Updike writes in his heartbreaking
last book of poems, *Endgame,* "An eternally *ramifying*
moment." Gregory Bateson, a philosopher whose ideas

branched out and bore fruit in every imaginable direction, said, "If a man achieves or suffers change in premises which are deeply embedded in his mind, he will surely find that the results of that change will *ramify* throughout his whole universe." Companion words include *rambunctious*, a boisterous way of branching out.


## RECIPE

*A medical prescription; a formula for preparing food.* Literally, it is exhortative advice from your doctor to you and your local **pharmacist**: "Take it!" The imperious tone is rooted in the imperative Latin form *recipe*—meaning both *"*Receive!*"* and *"*Take!*"* From such commanding origins came the compassionate advice delivered today by doctors who are allowed to prescribe medication. If, that is, the **pharmacist** can read his or her instructions, since the historical sense survives in the cryptic Rx, which is an adaption of ℞, the symbol written at the beginning of doctor's prescriptions, itself an abbreviation for Latin *recipe*. Margaret Ernst defined the symbol as a way to make medicine more magical, adding that the earliest known record comes in 1926, "by some unknown **pharmacist** trying to save some time." In *My Life in France*, Julia Child dispenses this sage advice: "This is my invariable advice to people: Learn how to cook—try new *recipes*, learn from your mistakes, be fearless, and above all have *fun*!" The culinary aspect of *recipe*, a softer command closer to a recommendation for preparing meals, doesn't come into the kitchen of English until 1743. Companion words include *receipt, conceive, deceive.*

Recipe: *I Canti (The Cantos)*

## REJECT

*A person or thing dismissed as unacceptable or inappropriate; to throw something away.* To describe *rejecting* something by saying we are ***throwing*** it away would be redundant. Here's why. This deceptively simple word is another in the surprisingly talented bullpen of "***throw*** words." Startlingly, *reject* means "to throw *back*," from the Latin *re*, back, *jacere*, throw, which is what we are really saying when we get rid of bad fruit, jilt a lover, or throw the visiting team's home run ***ball*** into the stands. The Buddha said, "The whole secret of existence is to have no fear. Never fear what will become of you, depend on no one. Only the moment you *reject* all help are you freed." Mary Baker Eddy advised, "*Reject* hatred without hating." Companion words include *inject*, to throw in, and *project*, to throw ahead. The adjective *rejected* is a descriptive word you throw at a noun: the *rejected* lover was *dejected*, the latter meaning "thrown down," or cast away.

## REPUGNANT

*Extremely distasteful, unacceptable, inciting the urge to fight back.* If you look too closely at the word, you better duck. A fist is coming at you, from the Latin *pugnus*. The word picture here is that of our conscience putting up its fist and trying to fend off something that is in conflict with it, or is incompatible. Disposed to fight against; hostile; at war with; being at variance; contrary; inconsistent;

refractory; disobedient; also, distasteful in a high degree; offensive. Repugnant is usually followed by *to*, rarely and less properly by *with*; as, all rudeness was *repugnant* to her nature." Considering the **metaphors** of illness, philosopher Susan Sontag wrote, "Cancer patients are lied to, not just because the disease is (or is thought to be) a death sentence, but because it is felt to be obscure—in the original sense of the word: ill-omened, abominable, *repugnant* to the senses." Companion words include *pugnacious,* having a fighting spirit.

**RIFFRAFF**

*The poor regarded as the dregs by the privileged.* Here is an example of contentiousness in tracing words back in time. Melvyn Bragg chooses the painted word route, which Winslow Homer would have been the perfect painter to illustrate because of his genius for river scenes. According to Bragg *riff* was originally a word for poor people, because they were forced by circumstances to travel by simple *rafts*, which they propelled by oars commonly called *riffs*. Hence, the *riff raff* were ordinary people traveling in an extraordinary way. Bragg contrasts the simple raft with the fancy steamboats floating often on the same rivers, a sight which gave us the word **hifalutin** from the "high fluted smokestacks that carried the soot and cinders well away from the passengers." Far more conventionally, Webster's attributes the word to the Middle English *ryffe raffe*, from *rif* and *raf*, "every single one." Companion words include *riff*, a brief rhythmic phrase in musical improvisation or brief improvisational remarks in speech; clever rhythmic talk.

## ROAM

*Wander.* A restless verb long thought to be inspired by the pilgrims who meandered to Rome over the centuries. Although there is still no recorded evidence for this in English, there are tantalizing footprints left behind in other languages. "The tradition is strengthened," writes linguist Charles Funk, "… by the fact that other countries, from which pilgrimages were also made to Rome, had similar words." They include such word gems such as *romeo*, in Italian, *romero*, in Spanish, *romier*, in French. Companion pilgrim words include *divagation,* the act of wandering; *vagus nerve*; and *vagary.* Most *roamin'* of all recent **ramblin'** words may be *far-flungery*, distant lands, a word coined by the intrepid Irish traveler Dervla Murphy, although it could very well be an archaic Irishism. The theme song for the 1950s television show *Rawhide* had this infectious refrain: "*Roamin', roamin', roamin'* … rawhide." And finally, there is *paseo,* a leisurely stroll, or the path where that leisure is strolled. Speaking of travel, if you've ever been a little self-indulgent in your travels, let's say staying in *exorbitant* hotels, or paying exorbitant prices for meals or souvenirs, you have gotten "off track" in terms of your **budget** in an effort to have an experience that was "out of this world."

Or let's say you've taken your eye off the **ball**, which is to feel the soul of the place. These are attributes of the Late Latin *exorbita*, from *ex,* out of, *orbita*, orbit. Figuratively, it means off track, out of this world, out of sync. Companion words include *eccentric*, out of the center, out of orbit, from *orb*, world, sphere, planet, **ball**, eye.

Roam: *New Amsterdam*

## ROBOT (CZECH)

*A humanlike machine.* More exciting, or terrifying, it is a machine that is designed to act independently of human beings. Twice-coined by the collaborating Czech brothers Josef and Karel Capek, first by Josef in a 1917 short story, then by Karel in his stage play *R.U.R.,* which was an acronym for *Rossum's Universal Robots,* in 1921. Long after, Karel remembered suggesting to his brother Josef that he combine the Czech word *roboti,* forced labor or drudgery, with the Old Church Slavonic *robota,* servitude, from *rabu,* slave. His reason was poetic; he wanted to use their own mother tongues instead of a Latin term. The play and the word are prophetic, a double vision of the world to come, in automation and in slavery, sterile labor. "Runaround," a 1942 short story by Isaac Asimov, provided the future with the three immutable laws for *robots:* "1. A *robot* may not harm a human, or allow a human to come to harm through action. 2. A *robot* must obey a human's orders unless they conflict with the first law. 3. A *robot* must protect itself unless this conflicts with the first or second law." Companion words include *android,* which dates back to 1727, according to the OED, meaning "an automaton resembling a human being"; *RoboCop,* a 1987 cult movie; *robo-calls;* and *bots,* competitions in building *robots.*

## ROUÉ

*A debauched or lecherous person; a man devoted to sensual plea-sures.* A dissipated self-portrait of a word, the French *roué* is a rake, with its roots in *rouer*, a medieval torture meant to break a victim's spirit and bones "on the wheel." Think of it as torture roulette. Legend has it that this was the fate of the debauched friends of the Duke of Orleans, regent of France, around 1715–23, "to suggest the punishment they deserved." The remark, though glib, gave rise to *roué* in the sense we know today. Companion words include Abel Gance's 1923 movie *La Roue*, and *La Roue de Paris*, the mighty Ferris Wheel erected in the Place de la Concorde for the millennium celebrations.

## RUMOR

*An unverified story, a circulating doubtful account, often spread maliciously; a tall tale disseminated with no known source.* The word *rumor* has spread since its first recorded usage in 1858, from the French *rumeur*, clamor, gossip, noise, via the Latin *rumorem*, clamor, common talk, and significantly, *ravus*, hoarse, the price paid for the shouting of a *rumor-monger*. Skeat simply defines a *rumor* as a *noise*, a whisper, a spread report. Other sources trace the word back to the Old English *reon*, lament, or Sanskrit *rauti*, roar, again a reference to *rumors* being noisy and bothersome stories. Long before any of these senses was the story of winged Ossa, the Greek goddess of *rumor* (Roman Fama), the personification of nasty news, a messenger of Zeus, like Isis and Hermes, but one usually bearing bad tidings. Ossa was the daughter of Elpis, the goddess of Hope, signifying the naive side of hopefulness or optimism, a vulnerability to hopeful stories. She was depicted as "a swift-footed and feathered demon goddess who delivered messages— not always truthfully, and even had her own altar in the agora of Athens." The Roman historian Tacitus wrote, "*Rumor* is not always wrong." The devilish dictionary writer Ambrose Bierce defined it thusly: "RUMOR, n. A favorite weapon of the **assassins** of character." That old quipster Will Rogers remarked, "*Rumor* travels faster, but it don't stay put as long as truth." Companion words include *rumor mill*.

### RUN

*To move in a hurried manner.* On May 28, 2011, journalist and author Simon Winchester wrote in the *New York Times* that this deceptively simple three-letter word had won the race for earning the most entries in the OED. Going even further, Winchester asked if it has become "the most lustrously complex word" in the English language. Our *simplexified* word, he reports, has recently passed *set* and *put* as the word with the most meanings and entries in the OED. This development, he adds, "may well say something about the current state of English-speaking humankind." The "victor" of the 1928 edition of the

Run: *Chicanismo (for Gilbert "Magu" Lujan)*

OED was *set*, with seventy-five columns of type and some
two hundred senses, while the word for "today's rather
more frantic and uncongenial world is, without a doubt,
the three-letter word *run*." Thus, *run* can have multiple
meanings. In his *Times* article, Winchester playfully wrote:
"HER birthday: must set plans in motion, *Run* a bath, put
on cologne, set the table. High anxiety. Run down list:
set watch again, put water in glasses, set flowers. Run to
the **window**—phew! Watch her put a finger to the door-
bell. Such joy! What timing! And just as the sun sets,
too!" *Run* emerged as the victor of the word race after
the OED's lexicographer Peter Gilliver spent nine months
*running* down 645 different meanings for it. "For while *set*
stood for stability and sturdy conservatism," Winchester

concludes, "so the **newfangled**, richest-of-all-today's-words *run* is all about ambition and optimism and the possibilities of the future. *Set* is England, old and fusty. *Run* is America, new and **cool**. *Set* is yesterday; *run* is tomorrow. In short: to set is human, but to run—divine." Onondagan Chief Oren Lyons declares himself a "runner" for the five hundred nations. Companion words and phrases include "along the riverrun," from *Finnegans Wake*, by James Joyce; *run* aground, *run* in her stocking, an also-*ran*, a home *run*. Companion information about our word includes the writer who has been "run" the most often in the OED, Shakespeare, 33,303 times, followed a distant second by Walter Scott with a mere 1,700.

## RUNT

*A stump, the smallest critter of the litter.* We can thank loggers for inventing this word. For this wordsmith, *runt* is the literary equivalent of *luce di sotto* in painting, "the luminosity of an undercolor that may be seen through an underglaze," in Levy's terms, such as the bright and seemingly burning light of a flame in early Flemish painting. Originally, around 1600, a *runt* was a tree stump, an "old and decayed remnant of a fallen tree. By our old literary friend, metaphorical extension, within a hundred years or so *runt* came to be used to describe smaller than usual cows, then oxen. According to the Concise OED, around that time *runt* was *rudely* used to describe "uncouth, ill-conditioned, or dwarfish persons." As unsettling as it may appear, the latter illustrates how noticing similarities between two different things can result in the transfer of a word from one to the other, in this case the grooved lines of bark of an old tree to the lines grooved into the face of an elderly person. By the mid-19th century, the meaning had shrunk to describe the smallest and most helpless creature in any animal litter, and finally small children. To illustrate the effect certain words can have on us, ***consider*** actor Don ("Nash Bridges") Johnson's comment, "I was a skinny little *runt* kid, and I decided that bowling was what I was going to do in life." Companion words include *stumpy*, short and squat.

# S

## SABOTAGE

*A subversive or malicious action meant to weaken, undermine, or obstruct.* Sabotage is an incendiary word, a monkey wrench thrown into the works of etymology in hopes of disrupting it. As *The Oxford Dictionary of Word Histories* says, "An English use of a French word, *saboter*, to kick with a shoe, willfully destroy." One legend goes that workers in 15th-century Holland threw their sabots, or wooden shoes, into the wooden gears of the textile looms to break the cogs, fearing the automated machines would render the human workers obsolete. Another has it that *sabot* is late 19th-century French **slang** to describe an unskilled worker, so called for their wooden clogs. Hence, *sabotage* was used to describe intentionally poor quality work produced by dissatisfied workers. Today its figurative sense is as powerful as ever, as when publisher Katharine Graham of the *Washington Post* wrote about the Watergate scandal in 1974, "If we had failed to pursue the facts as far as they led, we would have denied the public any knowledge of an unprecedented scheme of political surveillance and *sabotage*." Companion words include *sabotage radio*, a two-way radio used by the resistance movement in World War II, and *saboteur,* from 1921.

## SACKBUT

*A wind instrument; the forerunner of the trombone.* Every word book deserves at least one grin-and-bear-it, hilarious-sounding word, and this is that entry. This quizzical word **baffles** the experts, which is oddly rewarding. It possibly derives from an incorrect **translation** of *Aramaic sabecha*, a stringed instrument similar to the lyre. Skeat traces its roots back to the French *saquebute,* from the earlier *saquer,* to draw out hastily, as from a sack. The word helps us see the effort to draw out the breath necessary to make the instrument sound, but also the effort to draw out or pull the *slide* of the trombone, not unlike a knight pulling on the reins of a horse. Hence, a *sackbut* is also a hooked lance for jousting on horseback. Viewed or heard in this spirit, musicologists *consider* it to be a forerunner of the trombone, an example of how often visual correspondence informs language. Imagine, if you will, how the shape of the trombone's slide recalls the *oldfangled* hook used to pull a man off a horse, and an *Aha!* might be pulled out of you. "Therefore at that time," it is written in Daniel 2:3, "when all the people heard the sound of the cornet, flute, harp, *sackbut*, psaltery, and all kinds of musick, all the people, the nations, and the languages, fell down and worshipped the golden image that Nebuchadnezzar the king had set up." Companion words include *clarinet*, for which the website violinist.com gives this cockamamie Country and Western definition: "The name used on your second daughter if you've already used Betty Jo."

## SALOON

*A drinking establishment; a tavern or large room or hall for entertainment; a Wild West term for a bar.* Curiously, the word pushes through the *saloon* doors from the Italian *salone*, simply a large hall; the French redecorated the *salon* as a room for social and literary events, a practice founded by the legendary Madame de Sévigné in Paris in the 17th century and continued by Gertrude Stein in the 20th. The first recorded appearance of *saloon* in English was in 1728, as an Anglicized form of *salon*, referring to a large hall in a public place, especially of a passenger boat. Around 1835, it began to describe the plushly furnished drawing rooms in railway cars. The American English *saloon* as a name for a public bar was first recorded in 1841. Companion words include *saloon car*, an early name for a *sedan car*; *saloon lounge*, a plush railway carriage.

Saloon: *The Transparent Life*

## SANDLOT

*An unused or abandoned piece of land used by children or amateurs for casual games played for the **fun** of it.* According to baseball historian Kevin Nelsen, in *The Golden Game*, the term was inspired by the sudden profusion of empty lots in downtown San Francisco after the 1906 earthquake, which local players cleared of rubble so they could finally play **ball** again and help bring the city back to life. Paul Dickson writes in *Baseball*, "It is said that college **ball**, American Legion, and Little League have all but made *sandlot* baseball obsolete." Milwaukee Brewers outfielder Rickie Weeks says, "It's just *sandlot* baseball. You have some **fun** sometimes, just playing around with your boys." Companion phrases include *The Sandlot Kid*, a bronze sculpture outside the Baseball Hall of Fame, in Cooperstown, New York; and *The Sandlot,* a perennial favorite flick from 1993 that preserves in amber neighborhood baseball and friendship.

## SANDWICH

*A serving of food consisting of two pieces of bread enclosing a filling of some kind, usually meat or cheese.* The notorious Fourth Earl of Sandwich, born John Montagu, was one of the most intrepid travelers of the 18th century and also an avid card player who once played for twenty-four straight hours, "subsisting" only on hefty slices of meat wrapped around slices of **toast** delivered to him at the gaming table. Thus was born the *sandwich*. For those who have sailed the South Seas the name of the Sandwich Islands will be a cause of great wonder—which came first? Indeed, they were named after Montagu, who "at one time was made First Lord of the Admiralty, by Captain James Cook." Companion words include the main course, *Sandwich*, a **town** in Kent, and for dessert, an *ice cream sandwich*, that felicitous invention that brought together ice cream and **biscuits** or slices of cake, created around 1945 by Jerry Newcombe at Forbes Field, Pittsburgh.


## SARCASM

*Harsh, bitter derision; an ironic taunt; a biting putdown.* This word practically **sneers** on the page, coming as it does from vivid Greek *sarx,* flesh, and *sarkazein,* to speak bitterly, but literally to strip off the flesh—which is what *sarcasm* can feel like to the one who is suffering the cutting, caustic remarks. Stripped clean, cut down, burned. A 1570s word from Latin *sarcasmos*, from Greek *sarkasmos,* "a sneer, jest, taunt, mockery." Curiously, there is an equivalent in the art world, where the etching process by which acid is used is called *mordant*, Mervyn Levy writes, "for the purpose of biting the lines drawn by the etching needle." Nineteenth-century novelist Samuel Butler argued, "Neither irony or *sarcasm* is argument." During the Golden Era of movies, legendary producer Samuel Goldwyn said, "This music won't do. There's not enough *sarcasm* in it." The word works in reverse, as well, as poet Marianne Moore observed: "We are suffering from too much *sarcasm*." Companion words include *sarcophagus*, a "body-eating" stone casket, and *snarky*, mean-spirited.


## SCHMEAR (YIDDISH)

*Bribery; the whole thing; the entire matter.* A funny, useful, greasy word dating back to 1961, from Yiddish *shmir*, to spread or grease, from German *smirwen*, to smear. To *schmear* inevitably came to mean smearing cream cheese on a bagel. The term also has several metaphorical senses. In English we have "grease his palm" (to bribe) and "butter her up" (to flatter); also *smear*, as in "to smear someone's reputation." The cult movie *Caddyshack* features a **flamboyant** performance by Rodney Dangerfield as a character named Al Czervik, a nouveau-riche real estate tycoon, who says, "Give me half a dozen of the Vulcan D-tens and set my friend up with the whole *schmear*. You know, clubs, bags, shoes, gloves, shirt, pants. Hey, orange balls!" Companion phrase: *the whole shebang*, the Irish version of *schmear*.


## SCRIPTORIUM

*A building or small room in medieval monasteries and abbeys devoted to the copying and illumination of ancient texts.* Not unlike a stonemason, we can set the two old Latin parts of this word next to each other: *script*, a written document, *orium*, a room. The painted word reveals "a place for writing," which was most commonly executed in the private cells of monks. If a monastery was blessed to receive a large arrival of new **manuscripts**, separate buildings or rooms were built alongside the library and more monks employed. This was due to the paucity of **manuscripts** or books during the so-called Dark Ages, a time in Europe that Thomas Cahill, in *How the Irish Saved Civilization*, describes as having virtually no libraries. All had been razed or burned to the ground. Other scholars suggest that *scriptoria* referred to the collective effort of all the monks in a particular monastery instead of a separate room, as depicted in movies like *The Name of the Rose*. By the start of the 13th century, secular copy shops developed; professional scribes may have had special rooms set aside for writing, but in most cases they simply had a writing desk next to a **window** in their own house. The illuminators of **manuscripts** worked in collaboration with scribes in an intricate variety of interaction that precluded any simple pattern of monastic manuscript production. A 10th-century prior left behind a poetic complaint about his life in the *scriptorium*: "Only try to do it yourself and you will learn how arduous is the writer's task. It dims your eyes, makes your back ache, and knits your chest and belly together. It is a terrible **ordeal** for the whole body." Companion words include *scripture*, from Latin *scriptura*, studies pertaining to the Christian Bible.

## SCRUPLE

*Moral reservations; the little stone in the sandal of your conscience.*
The word has taken a bumpy ride from the Latin *scruple*,
pebble, that annoying little thing that bothers you when
you walk. Cicero was the first to see its figurative poten-
tial, using it as a term for conscience, writing that it was
"the cause of unease or anxiety." *Scruple* became synonymous with the doubt or hesitation that troubles one's
conscience, or that comes from the difficulty of determining whether something is right. We feel the pebble
of guilt in our sandals when we violate our own principles. To feel *scrupled* is to hesitate, to feel qualms. "There's
nothing to winning, really," **sneered** Alfred Hitchcock.
"That is, if you happen to be blessed with a **keen** eye, an
agile mind, and no *scruples* whatsoever." The **protean**
writer John Updike hones the line: "I would rather chance
my personal vision of truth striking home here and there
in the chaos of publication that exists than attempt to filter
it through a few sets of official, honorably public-spirited
*scruples*." Companion words include *scrupulosity,* obsessive
concern with one's own sins and compulsive performance
of religious devotion.

## SESQUIPEDALIAN

*A word that measures a foot and a half long.* Coined by the
Roman poet Horace, my grandfather's namesake, in his
*Ars Poetica*, to describe a very, very long word, from *sesqui,*

one and a half, and *pedalis*, from *pes*, foot. An esoteric but effective example would be the German *Gesamtkunstwerk*, a universal work of art; also *kakistocracy*, government by the worst people, and *schmaltzed*, the longest monosyllabic word in the OED. Here is an example of what the Greeks called *amaxiaia remata*, "words large enough for a wagon." Companion words include *sesquip*, a word-grubber, someone who digs around for and uses long, unusual words, and *hippopotomonstrosesquipedalian*, presumably a word as long as a monster and as wide as a hippo's mouth.

## SHERBET (TURKISH/PERSIAN)

*A flavored ice dessert made from fruit juice, sugar, water, milk, egg, and gelatin.* The ancient Persians created a delicious and cooling concoction called *sharbat*, a word derived from Arabic *arba*, which consisted of diluted, sweetened fruit juice cooled with snow. By the time it left the deserts of Persia for the cities of Europe it had been transformed into an "Orientalized" dessert called *sorbetto* in Italian and *sorbet* in French. This fruit-flavored ice was served between courses, and eventually became the frozen dessert we now know as *sherbet*, first recorded in English in 1891. One of the outtakes from the psychedelic spy movie *Austin Powers* featured our hero (Mike Meyers) hypnotizing a security guard (Christian Slater) and ordering him to buy him some orange *sherbet*. Companion words include

the French *sorbet*, a similar dessert but without milk, and
Italian *sorbetto*, both featuring a softer consistency than its
frozen cousin.

Sherbet

## SIDEKICK

*Close companion, **pal**, co-conspirator.* Occasionally, secret languages don't remain secret; they become absorbed into the larger language. This handy term was stolen from the den of thieves operating in olde England, along with *pratt,* for back pocket, *jerve,* for breast pocket, *pit,* for vest pocket, and *kick,* for the "side-breeches" pocket, which was the toughest for pickpockets to pick. Later, the image slipped like a stealthy hand into the side pocket, which was as close to your skin as you could get, and the term became synonymous with "close friend." In fall 2010 the *Los Angeles Times* reported, "Entertainer Ed McMahon, best known for his nearly 30-year stint as *sidekick* to Johnny Carson on *The Tonight Show*, died today at age 86." Companion words include *sidecar,* a cocktail made with cognac, orange liqueur, and lemon juice, and *sidecar,* a small vehicle attached to a motorcycle to hold an extra passenger.

## SILHOUETTE

*A profile or shadow in a dark **color**, usually black, imposed on a white background.* An **adumbrated** word from the *ancien régime*, a shadow of its former self. The backstory is lit from behind, like a shadow puppet of a word, dating back to an 18th-century French Controller General of Finance, Etienne de *Silhouette*. His short time in office was ridiculed for its "parsimony and some *capricious* reforms," such as reducing the pensions and benefits of the nobility. So

Silhouette

despised was he that his name inspired the mordant phrase
à la Silhouette, meaning "plain" and "cheap." There the
story splits apart, some scholars saying the word arises from
the brevity of Monsieur Silhouette's tenure in office, while
others credit him with the inventing the hobby of shadow-
graphy, claiming that his posh château at Bry-sur-Marne
was festooned with the ancient art. Even though this word
can be reliably traced to an actual person, there is still a
*fascinating* backstory. The scuttlebutt behind this perenni-
ally favorite word is that it became popular because cutting
out a paper *silhouette* was simply a cheap way to create a
likeness of someone; the term would have been spoken in

the spirit of fashionable ridicule of the time, a swipe at what the nobility believed to be the Finance Minister's miserly financing of the Seven Years' War. The modernist architect Le Corbusier left this stunning and concise observation of New York: "... vehement *silhouettes* of Manhattan—that vertical city with unimaginable diamonds." Companion words include *stencil*, a copy in outline, from Middle French *estenceler*, to cover with sparkles or stars, from estencèle, spark, spangle, from Latin *scintilla*, spark; *skiagraph*, an image produced by shadow photography; and *sciamachy*, shadowboxing, fighting against a shadowy enemy.

### SILLY

*Goofy, humorous, simple.* A *giddy* example of the way that words often reverse course, inverting their meaning over time, from one end of the linguistic spectrum to the other. Originally, the Old English *gesælig* simply meant "**happy**," the Old Norse *sæll*, happy, Gothic *sels*, kindhearted, the German *selig*, blessed, blissful, back, back, back to the Indo-European base word *\*sel-* happy. The Greek *hilaros* (as in *hilarious*) cheerful, Latin *solari*, comfort, and *salvus*, safe, are all related. The long train of linked words is necessary to understand the associations that went behind its U-turn, linguistically speaking. Around the turn of the 1200s, the image of a *silly* person was someone "blessed" by God, but then devolved into a word of suspicion, "pious," then "innocent," on to "harmless," and finally "pitiable," or deserving of compassion and sympathy. By the late 1500s, *silly* had been enfeebled to mean merely foolish, and then was stunned into linguistic submission, as if dazed in a boxing match, a vivid image echoed in the expression "knocked *silly*." The journalism **slang** *silly season*, for the slow news months of August and September when "**trivial** stories" take over the papers, dates from 1861. The trademark *Silly Putty* claims use from July 1949. Companion words and phrases include *silly late*, as in "She was up *silly late* last Saturday night," an expression sent to me by friends in London.

## SISU (FINNISH)

*Tenacity, guts, determination, inner strength, sustained courage.* A concept word widely regarded by the Finns as defying direct **translation**, only describable in proper context—for example, perseverance in the face of adversity, such as the Nazi presence in World War II—and so indispensable to understanding that culture. So *sisu* commands respect as an **untranslatable** from the far north, the closest translation in English being "gutsy." *Sisu* is that rare word that defines an entire culture, its self-reflection of persistence, obstinacy, willpower. The Finnish *sisa*, inner, and Greenlandic Inupik *sisu*, to roll or slide, paint the picture. Peer closely and you'll see someone who possesses the knowledge and the willpower to move with the prevailing winds, to be flexible, to slide with the times, revealing a doggedness (dog sled?), or tenacity. Arguably, its first appearance in English occurred on January 8, 1940, when *Time* magazine reported: "The Finns have something they call *sisu*. It is a compound of bravado and bravery, of ferocity and tenacity, of the ability to keep fighting after most people would have quit, and to fight with the will to win. The Finns translate *sisu* as 'the Finnish spirit' but it is a much more gutful word than that. Last week the Finns gave the world a good example of *sisu* by carrying the war into Russian territory on one front while on another they withstood merciless attacks by a reinforced Russian Army. In the wilderness that forms most of the Russo-Finnish frontier between Lake Laatokka and the Arctic Ocean, the Finns definitely gained the upper hand." A northern Michigan newspaper reported in early 2010 that Joe Paquette Jr., a 63-year-old resident of Munising, walked the length of the state, 425 miles, to bring to the training camp of the Detroit Lions, a perennial doormat team, what he called "the spirit of *sisu*" to his favorite club. Companion words include **chutzpah**, a Yiddish term for courage; *cojones*, in Spanish, literally testicles, but connoting courage; and élan, French for verve, strength, ardor to the point of revolutionary action.

## SKIRL

*To shriek, wail, cry out; the sound of a bagpipe.* The word screams across the sky to us from the 14th-century Norwegian *skyrla, skrella*, to make a shrill sound. Three centuries later, in the 1660s, we can hear the first reference to the inimitable cry of bagpipes. The English philologist Skeat described the sound: "This word is never used to express the shriek or scream of pain, but is suggestive either of anger or glee. In *Tam O'Shanter,* the 'deil' on the window-ledge of Alloway Kirk [church], screwed up the bagpipes, and made them *'skirl'* so loudly that the vibration shook the rafters." Scottish poet Robert Burns writes in *Scotch Drink*, "When *skirling* weanies see the light, / Thou makes the gossips clatter bright." Companion words, for the sheer sound, include *scoon,* a scintillating Scottish verb to describe skipping a stone across the water.

## SKULDUGGERY

*Underhanded acts of thievery or treachery.* Not the descriptor for the famous skull-diggers or body snatchers of 19th-century England, with an even more devilish origin story dating back to 1856. Instead, it may originate with the Scottish *sculduderie,* jocular **slang** for **fornication** or adultery. Eventually the old Highlands term developed into *sculduddery*, **bawdy**, obscene behavior. Now picture a **rival** etymologist with arms akimbo, hands on hips, saying the opposite, that body snatching was common in 18th-century England. To combat the practice, an ingenious innovation was developed called the "mortsafe," a protective iron cage that enveloped the coffin and made abduction impossible. By the 20th century, *skulduggery* was used to describe any kind of "underhanded" (underground) dealings, or clandestine activities. In 1980, the *London Times* wrote, "Watergate was a sensational piece of *skulduggery*." Companion words include *Skulduggery Pleasant*, a series of novels by the rumbustious Irish playwright Derek Landy; and *Skuld*, one of a trio of Norns or Valkyries in Norse mythology, with the possible double meaning of "debt" and "future."

## SLÁINTE (GAELIC)

*Cheers, health, a **toast**.* Pronounced "SLAAN-sha" this typical Irish toast translates literally as "health." If you need to know one word for your travels around the Celtic world, this is the one, a shot glass version of a long Irish **toast**: *"Sláinte chuig na fir, agus go mairfidh na mna go deo."* ("Health to the men, and may the women live forever!") The short version, *sláinte,* simply means "I drink to your health!" *Sian* is Irish for "soft and sorrowful music full of enchantment, which can be heard coming from a fairy knoll." Together, the meaning is "healthy" or "safe," but this form (pronounced "slaan") is used to wish a safe journey and healthy return. The extended *slán abhaile* (*"slaan aval"*) is used by the host and means "safe homewards." Other forms are *slan agat* and *slan leat*, both meaning "goodbye." Companion expressions include "So long," which derives from *slán,* goodbye, and other memorable **toasts**, such as the Swahili *"Oogie-wa-wa!"* And a toast, of course, may precede a smirt. Since anti-smoking laws went into effect in Ireland's pubs smokers now gather outside for a quick drag, which often results in *smirting*—smoking and flirting.

Smirk: *Smoke and Flirt*

## SMIRK

*An expression in that emotional no-man's-land between a smile and a simper.* Scornful, smug, conceitful, contemptuous, affected, crooked—the word currently reflects an attitude of superior or **insolent** behavior, but that is after a sea change in meaning. Originally, the Old English *smearcian* meant a smile and ended up as a frown, like the face of a person listening to a "good news, bad news" scenario. No exact cognates exist in other languages, but it might be related to *smerian*, to laugh at. As a noun, it was first recorded by the 1560s, to describe the kind of smiling expression one uses when something unfortunate has happened to someone else that provides the *smirker* with an advantage. The Earl of Chesterfield wrote in a letter to his son, "A constant *smirk* upon the face, and a whifling activity of the body, are strong indications of futility." Companion words include *smirkish,* which the anti-urbane Urban Dictionary defines as "shaky, bad feeling, or **sneaky**."

### SNEER

*A contemptuous or mocking expression or remark.* Imagine a **smirk** without even a hint of a smile. The contorted facial expression can send a chill through anyone it is directed to, so primal is the contempt or condescension. With the signature flare of nostrils and the pulled-back lips, the *sneer* reveals scorn and disdain. If the painted word appears animalistic, there's good reason: its origins are the Latin *nares*, nostrils, echoic of the flaring of a snorting horse, and the Old English *fnæran*, to snort, gnash one's teeth. Similarly, the Danish *snærre* means to grin like a dog, with the sense of smiling contemptuously from 1680. The sense of a *sneer* as the curling of the upper lip in scorn, as a kind of Evil Elvis, is attested from 1775. Companion words include *snivel* and *scorn*.

## SNOB

*A pretentious twit.* There are competing theories for the word history here. *Snob* is either the Old Norse word for *dolt*, a Cambridge chestnut, or **slang** for a peasant trying to pass as an Oxbridge-educated student. A *snob* was originally a shoemaker or cobbler but by 1796 it had become a slang term at Cambridge University for any townsman or merchant. By 1843, the upper classes must have thought that the lower classes were getting uppity, that they "didn't know their place," as the old saying goes, because *snob* came to express their resentment over "a person who vulgarly apes his social superiors." Finally, the word was inverted again in William Thackeray's highbrow *The Book of Snobs*, where he writes, "You, who are ashamed of your poverty, and blush for your calling, are a *snob*; as are you who boast of your wealth." Salvador Dalí paints a priggishly surreal picture: "In order to acquire a growing and lasting respect in society, it is a good thing, if you possess a great talent, early in your youth, to give a very hard kick to the right shin of the society you love. After that, be a *snob*."

The meaning later broadened to include those who insist on their gentility in addition to those who merely aspire to it, and by 1911 the word had acquired its main modern sense of "one who despises those considered inferior in rank, attainment, or taste." Companion words include San Francisco's *Snob Theater,* ironically described locally as "the only place where it's **cool** to be stuck-up," a play on words of the *snobbery theaters* of culture vultures.

## SNOLLYGOSTER

*A shrewd but corrupt politician, one who ruins the spirit of the day.* A raffish 19th-century Americanism for an unprincipled politician, otherwise known as a con man or *panjandrum.* Something *strange* this way comes in its derivation, the legend of a *peculiar* species of Maryland monster, half reptile, half bird, that preyed upon barnyard animals and children: a *snallygaster*—possibly deriving from the Old German or Pennsylvania Dutch *schnelle Geister,* a **quick**-moving, *schnell,* spirit, *geist.* First popularized by President Harry Truman in the early 1950s, delivering a train-platform speech in Parkersburg, West Virginia, "full of fine indignation," as the papers said at the time, and castigating his Republican opponents as "*snollygosters*" because they cast *aspersions* on his foreign policy. It was also duly noted that his tone of voice suggested that the dreaded *snollygoster* was a terrible monster, but few, if any, in the audience had ever heard of it. According to one austere authority, the word is "a lower grade of colloquialism." A classic definition was published in the *Columbus* (Ohio) *Dispatch,* 1895:

"A Georgia editor kindly explains that 'a *snollygoster* is a fellow who wants office regardless of party, platform or principles and who, whenever he wins, gets there by the sheer force of monumental talknothical assumnacy.'" How serious a charge "talknothical assumnacy" was, no one seems equipped to explain. Companion words include the hipster term *fraudster*.

Sough: *A Secret Blue*

## SOUGH

*To moan,* **murmur**. One of the loveliest illustrations of the way sound works on us in subterranean ways. Listen for the whisper of the Old English *swoga*, Old Saxon *swogan*, to rustle, and Gothic *gaswogjan*, to sigh. "This venerable piece of **onomatopoeia**," Robert Haas calls it. In his book on Walt Whitman, Haas writes, "the OED, more evocatively than usual, defines sough as 'a murmuring of wind, water, or the like, esp. one of a gentle or soothing nature.'" Emily Bronte: "The evening **calm** betrayed alike the tinkle of the nearest stream and the sough of the most remote." Companion words include *susurrus*, a soft whisper, from the Latin for a whispering or humming sound.

## SOUPÇON (FRENCH)

*A small amount, a touch, a tincture.* A word of many wendings, many spellings in French, but originally from Latin *suspicio*, suspicion. Linked together, they provide a subtle layer of meaning that a *soupçon* is an amount so miniscule its very existence is in suspicion. The French roots meant "to suspect," and also "a little bit"—as in, *Je sens juste un soupçon d'estragon* (I taste just a hint of tarragon). Generally, it now refers to a very small portion, but with a tincture of suspicion, a mere speck. On the FruitGuys Almanac website Heidi Lewis writes, "Love that word, *soupçon*. It sounds like the kind of word a French cartoon chef might use—eyes closed, spoon to his nose." Companion words include *hint, mite, jot.*

## SPHINX

*An inscrutable Egyptian goddess, part woman, part lion, with wings.* A word dug out of the sands of Giza around the 15th century, based on the Greek *sphingein*, to squeeze, bind, which of course is what the monster did to those who failed to her answer her riddles. With her lion's winged body and sporting a woman's head, she guarded the cross-road outside Thebes. Those who failed to answer correctly she squeezed to death, then summarily ate them for supper. No one until Oedipus solved her riddle, which humiliated the proud monster so much she killed herself. The correspondence between the unbearable tightness of being and holding secrets eventually led to the figurative sense of a mysterious person or thing by the early 1600s, around the same time that travelers tales and engravings from Egypt made Europe aware of the *Sphinx* near the Giza pyramids. The French explorer Pierre Loti, he of the hothouse imagination, wrote, "The pyramid once passed, there was still a short way to go before we confronted the *Sphinx*, in the middle of what our contemporaries have left him of his desert." Ex–San Francisco '49ers guard and center Randy Cross uses the word to explain the cold silence of many football players after a game: "They all come off as the Great *Sphinx* because they have marching orders about not talking to the media." Novelist Rebecca West said: "Humanity is never more *sphinxlike* than when it is expressing itself."

## SPINDRIFT

*Spray blown from the crests of waves by the wind.* Occasionally also used to describe "driving snow or sand," *spindrift* spins off the old word *spume*, via Latin *spuma*, foam. The Scottish formation, from around 1600, combines *spene*, to spin, sail before the wind, and *drift*, slowly carried by a current or wind. In 1886, a certain Robert Brown wrote *Spunyard & Spindrift*, a book of life at sea. He writes, "Then, the names of all the other things on board a ship! I don't know half of them yet, even the sailors forget at times, and if the exact name of anything they want happens to slip from their memory, they call it a chicken-fixing, or a *gadjet*, or a gill-guy, or a timmey-noggy, or a wim-wam—just *pro tem,* you know." A word that **soughs** across the page, this one holds the minor distinction of being the only word I believe I ever taught my old friend mythologist Joseph Campbell. One day we were walking together down the beach in La Jolla, California, watching the waves explode upon the rocks, throwing great gobs of spray, and I said something like, "Wonderful *spindrift* today, Joe." He smiled and said, "Hmmm, *spindrift.* I didn't know that. Sounds like a word Robinson Jeffers would have used. I think I'll use it in my next lecture." Companions include such frothy words as *spume,* old Latin *spuma*, froth.

## SPORT

*A physical activity or game or pastime involving exertion and skill in which individuals or teams compete against each other; to wear or display.* A chance to be playful, since it is a word close to my heart since I was a boy and it has reappeared time and time again in ways that link all my work. Not unlike a versatile **athlete**, *sport* itself is a flexible word, one that can play several positions on the linguistic field. Primarily, it refers to competitive play, but as a verb it also means "to wear or display" or "to mock or jest." According to the great Skeat, *sport* simply means *mirth*, underscoring its playful aspect. What makes it such a valuable word is how *transportive* it is, which is a **sneaky** piece of tautology. *Sport* derives from the Latin *deportare,* to carry across, which gave us *transport.* To play and often to watch a *sport* is transportive; it carries us from the everyday world into a special and heightened realm. This we generally find enjoyable, as reflected in the way it came into Old French as *desport*, pastime, recreation, pleasure, via the Middle French *desporter,* to divert, amuse, please, play, and Middle English *disporten,* to **amuse**, take pleasure in. Thus, *sport* is an activity that is transportive, playful, mirthful, amusing, uplifting, pleasureful; a stage for the *display* (dis-play) of talent or skill. *Consider* now, if you will, the complete version of the famous maxim of the philosopher Horace from 2,000 years ago: "Seize the day; let us *sport* while we may." Companion words and phrases include *good sport*, meaning "good fellow," first recorded in 1881. *Sportswear* was first seen in 1912; *sports* car in 1928; *sportscast* in 1938; *sportsman* first recorded in 1706.


## SPREZZATURA (ITALIAN)

*Effortless grace, an ease of living.* The sweet and easy way of living, *la dolce vita*, also expressed in *sapere vivere*, knowing *how* to live, especially how to be diplomatic with other people; the art of living well. The French call it *savoir-faire*, which is a kind of art of living, or *sangfroid*, just cold-blooded enough to be **cool** under pressure. Too cool for school, as my steelworker friends in Detroit used to joke. According to Mervyn Levy, in *The Pocket Dictionary of Art Terms*, the Italian *sprezzatura* has an earlier meaning of a rapid sketch or drawing that may be fine enough to be a completed work. Companion words include *brio*, élan, **panache**.

Sprezzatura: *Tokyo Western*

## STEAMPUNK

*An amalgam of science fiction, high camp, and speculative history.* The game is afoot, Sherlock, in tracking down the story behind this relatively new word. Imagine, if you will, a word and genre built like the time travel machine in the H. G. Wells novel, made up of bits and pieces of every gizmo known to the late 19th century. *Steampunk* resembles that machine, but in a retro sense, cobbling together such genres as "science fiction, alternate history, and speculative fiction that came into prominence during the 1980s and early 1990s." One of the hallmarks of *steampunk* is **nostalgia**. It is redolent of Victorian locations and an era when steam power still held sway, and it celebrates other forms of "anachronistic technology," such as dirigibles or mechanical computers or futuristic innovations, at least as Victorians such as Wells and Verne may have envisioned them. The *steampunk* sensibility can be enshrined in the following anecdote: "When Professor John Henry Pepper was demonstrating certain pieces of chemistry [equipment] before an audience that happened to include Queen Victoria, he is reported to have calmly introduced one demonstration with: 'The oxygen and hydrogen will now have the honor of combining before Your Majesty.'" Companion words include K. W. Jeter's *gonzo-historical*, and *cyberpunk*.

## STRANGE, MAKING STRANGE

*Odd, foreign, distant,* **weird**. All of the above and *stranger* yet. In the fall of 2011, in the ***town*** of Donegal, Ireland, I overheard a shopkeeper whisper to a friend, "Aye, herself has been *making strange* lately." This is an enormously useful phrase that could contribute to common American English: not just to say that someone is *strange*, which is sire to **cliché**, but *making strange*, conveys a deliberateness, whether defensive or offensive. Bernard Share cites John Banville's *The Untouchable*: "The Irish say, when a child turns from his parents, that it is *making strange*; it comes from the belief that fairy folk, a jealous tribe, would steal a too-fair human babe and leave a changeling in its place." Companion words include **ostranenie**, Russian for *making strange*, the familiar unfamiliar.

## STYMIE

*To thwart, frustrate, discombobulate.* Have you ever felt *stymied* on the golf course when you hit the green and your ***ball*** lay only a few feet from the pin—only to have another player, perhaps deliberately, land his or her ball between yours and the hole? Then you've felt the particular golf-club-snapped-over-the-knee frustration that the old Scottish word *stymie* has meant for lo on two hundred years, first recorded on the scorecard of word history in 1834. So frustrating is this potentially dicey situation that it was outlawed as a strategy in 1952, replaced by a ***keener*** system of coins placed where golfers' balls land. Etymologists are likewise *stymied*, as there is little consensus about where the word came from. However, we might find a connection if we peer through the smirr of time to the 14th-century Scottish *stymie*, someone who sees poorly, from *stime*, which may be predated by the Icelandic *skima*. By metaphorical extension it now has the broader meaning "to block, hinder, thwart." In the 1994 remake of *Little Rascals* little *Stymie* says, "Wood doesn't grow on trees!" Remarkably, golf legend Bobby Jones uses the word in its original sense in this interview: "I particularly regretted winning at the nineteenth hole by the aid of a *stymie*, which was almost impossible to negotiate." Actress and model Morgan Fairchild once said, "I've seen several attempts to move into the future and adapt to our changing business models *stymied* at every turn. I think we all need to sit down and start working together." Companion verbs include *block, impede, obstruct, hinder,* and *stump*.

## SUB ROSA

*Under the rose, confidential, secret.* The fairly furtive story unfolds like a Japanese fan. The god of love, Eros (Cupid), presented a rose to Harpocrates, the god of silence (visualize: Harpo Marx) with the instruction that he not reveal the love affairs of his mother, Aphrodite (Venus), the concupiscent goddess of love and lust. The power of myth is revealed in how the story evolved into the custom of

Sub Rosa: *Venetian Secrets*

ancient counsels that date back to the 5th century BCE:
"a rose hanging from the ceiling enjoined all present to
observe secrecy on matters discussed." Later, the rose
appeared on the ceilings of dining rooms as rosettes, to
suggest privacy. Companion words include *surreptitious*
(Latin *surrepticius*), secret, clandestine; and *cupidity*, inordi-
nate or excessive desire—and the desire to keep it secret.
In other words, "What happens in Vegas stays in Vegas."

## SUPERCALIFRAGILISTICEXPIALIDOCIOUS

*Extraordinary, amazing, too* **cool** *for words, except this one, for those of a certain age.* Surprisingly, this fourteen–syllable jawbreaker is an actual word, according to *Mrs. Byrne's Dictionary.* One of the most recognizable long words in the language, rescued from anonymity by the Sherman brothers songwriting team for the movie *Mary Poppins.* The word actually dates back to 1926. Broken down, it looks like this: *super,* over, *cali,* beautiful, *fragilistic*, delicate, *expiali,* to atone for, *docious,* educatable. In plain English, it means "atoning for the mistake that a well–educated person can make by overrelying on their physical **beauty**." The implication being, some people drop out of school to spend their youth entering beauty pageants or weight lifting competitions. Two beauties come immediately to mind: the mythical Helen of Troy, who returned to the bed of her husband, Menelaus, in Sparta after the tragic Trojan War and tried to lead a righteous life; and in another aspect of the word, Marilyn Monroe, reading *Ulysses* on the beach, marrying the great playwright Arthur Miller, and even writing her own poetry. The song says, "*Supercalifragilisticexpialidocious* … it's really quite atrocious," but the effort the word points to is bittersweetly touching.

## SUPERSTITIOUS

*Susceptible to folk belief, magical thinking, chance; unreasonable, irrational.* Someone who is *superstitious* reveals a certain ignorance—an unknowing—of the laws of nature. From the Latin *superstitionem*, referring to a jaded look at prophecy, soothsaying, or an irrational fear of the gods, and *superstitis,* standing over or above itself, similar to ecstasy, the state of exaltation. However, I recently learned a new interpretation from a guide named Colette at the megalithic site of Knowth, in Ireland, when she peeled back the palimpsest that had long covered the word: "The local people never destroyed the site because of the old *superstitions* that it was sacred." Later, she told me that the old folk beliefs may have been prescientific, but they were still worthy of respect. The painted word that emerges is a person or force "standing or dwelling above us" that has power over us, but which can be discerned through certain rituals of prophecy. Hypatia, the 1st-century female librarian at Alexandria, said: "In fact men will fight for a *superstition* quite as quickly as for a living truth—often more so, since a *superstition* is so intangible you cannot get at it to refute it, but truth is a point of view, and so is changeable." Two thousand years later, George Bernard Shaw expressed his disdain for magical thinking: "A fool's brain digests philosophy into folly, science into *superstition*, and art into pedantry. Hence University education."

## SUPRASTERNAL NOTCH / UCIPITAL MAPILARY

*The subtle but sensuous dimple or declivity in a person's throat.* An unfortunately fancy word for the fortunately **gorgeous** part of the throat. How else to describe the casually dipped area where the breastbone and shoulder blades meet to form a beautiful wishbone. One of the least appreciated and understated erotic zones or beauty parts of the human anatomy. Long considered a sign of **beauty**, it was highlighted by the ancient Egyptians, as seen in depictions of Cleopatra, but hidden in other eras by high collars, which at least inspired the word **gorgeous** in medieval France. This eye-catching, swoon-inducing indentation on a woman's neck happens to be a perfect resting place for a pendant or a kiss. Anatomically known as the *fossa jugularis sternalis*, or *jugular notch*, in Latin it is the *lacuna suprasternalis*. Culturally, it's known as the *ucipital mapilary,* a mouthful of a term invented by screenwriter Samson Raphaelson, in Hitchcock's *Suspicion*, and uttered with sexy urbanity by Cary Grant to Joan Fontaine. Likewise, Ralph Fiennes purred to Kristin Scott Thomas in *The English Patient*, "I claim this shoulder blade … I love this place, what's it called? I'm going to ask the king to call it the 'Omar's Bosphorus.'" In 1998, Mel Brooks revived the word in his spoof *Dracula*. Leslie Nielsen eyes the tasty throat of his first victim and tells her, "Your *ucipital mapilary* is quite beautiful." Companion words for uncommonly named body parts include *philtrum*, the vertical groove in the upper lip, *purlicue*, the crescent-moon shaped area between the thumb and forefinger, and *glabella*, the flat area between the eyebrows and just above the nose.

## SWASHBUCKLER

*A dashing pirate.* So dashing is this **moniker** that it covers both swaggering soldiers and bon vivants. In the 1550s it referred to a harmless or inept swordfighter, as evident in its components. A *swash* was the swing of a sword that missed its target, and soon stood for the blustering fighter himself, and *buckler* referred to the embossed shield of an opponent. Together, the piquantly painted word provides a dashing image of a harmless swordsman who is more frightening by his boasting than by the caliber of his swordplay. Think of a cross between Errol Flynn, Bluebeard, and Johnny Depp in his recent pirate chest of movies. The biographical film about actor Errol Flynn was subtitled *Portrait of a Swashbuckler.* Comic Jack Handy quipped, "If they ever come up with a *swashbuckling* school, I think one of the courses should be Laughing, Then Jumping Off Something." Companion words include *buccaneer, gasconade, swordplayer.*

## SYMPOSIUM

*A scholarly seminar; a drinking party.* One of the most surprising words in the language. A venerable old Greek word used most famously by Plato, and that is where we find its etymology and story. From the Greek *sym*, together, *posis*, drinking, hence "drinking together," as in a party, and more, as in *symposion*, "a convivial gathering of the educated." The modern sense of bringing learned people together to celebrate or explore a subject dates back to 1784, a practice that reflects the Greek admiration for mixing wine and **conversation**. A *symposium* was also the third element in the triad of disciplines of the ideal or well-lived life, the pursuit of excellence in mind, body, and soul. Aristotle deemed this the life of excellence: a visit to a temple in the morning, wrestling or running in the **gymnasium** in the afternoon, and drinking, talking, and carousing at an evening *symposium*, literally a drinking party or celebration. Companion words include *symposiarch*, the host or leader of such a Dionysian gathering, and *merryfeast,* a festive gathering.

## SYNDROME

*A number of symptoms occurring together, or a condition marked by associated symptoms.* A *syndrome* is characterized by a running together of medical signs, or opinions, emotions, behavior. One of the great surprises of the English language is the frequency of words rooted in *sporting* terms, such as words ending in the suffix *–drome. Syndrome* is a mid-16th-century word from Latin that runs back to the Greek *syndromos*, literally "running together," from *syn*, with, and *dromos*, a running course. Companion words include *hippodrome*, a horse-racing course in ancient times, and *velodrome*, a bicycle race track. The psychological use of *syndrome* dates from 1955. Comedienne Roseanne Barr jokes, "Women complain about premenstrual *syndrome*, but I think of it as the only time of the month that I can be myself." Tennis great Arthur Ashe once said, "There is a *syndrome* in **sports** called "paralysis by analysis."

## SYNESTHESIA

*The phenomenon of experiencing sensation or perception in one of the five senses that is produced by a stimulus in another.* In other words, what happens when the senses are cross-wired. Together, the stems of this relatively new word (1881), from the Greek *syn*, together, and *aisthe*, feel or perceive, give us some *in*-sight into *synesthetes* like the poet Charles Baudelaire, who had the ability to smell colors and see tastes. In the masterly *The Art of Writing,* a Qing Dynasty commentator, Sun Lian-kui, cites a couplet by his friend Yuanhai: "Where the moon doesn't reach / The sound of the spring is darker." Translators Tony Barnstone and Chou Ping comment: "The *synesthesia* of this moment comes directly from nature, not from overthinking." Perhaps the most famous modern-day *synesthete* was Vladimir Nabokov. The Russian novelist associated the number five with the **color** red, and in *Speak Memory* writes, "The long 'a' of the English **alphabet** ... has for me the tint of weathered wood, but a French 'a' evokes polished ebony. This black group also includes hard 'g' (vulcanized rubber) and 'r' (a sooty rag being ripped). Oatmeal 'n', noodle-limp 'l' and the ivory-backed hand-mirror of 'o' take care of the white. ... Passing on to the blue group, there is steely 'x', thundercloud 'z' and huckleberry 'h.' Since a subtle interaction exists between sound and shape, I see 'q' as browner than 'k', while 's' is not the light blue of 'c' but a curious mixture of *azure* and mother-of-pearl." The blind war hero and world traveler James Holman attributed his success to *synesthesia:* "In fact, every portion of the brain devoted to a particular sense can experience the phenomenon of *synesthesia*, a sort of neurological cross-wiring that floods it with nonsensory stimuli."

# T

## TALE TELLER

*Professional storyteller of olde.* Today we call them *fabulists*, science-fiction writers, or filmmakers, but those who could carry a tale, **saunter** with a story, have always been at the heart of culture. Storytellers are the DNA of culture, the conveyor belt of values. My informant in Ballyvaughan, Ireland, P. J. Curtis, tells me that *tale tellers* were itinerant storytellers who were paid to weave a spell with their tales about the wild Celtic heroes, frisky fairies, and Tir na Nog, the Land of Eternal Youth. According to the reliable reports *tale bearers* were mischief makers, incendiaries in families—more proof of the perennial suspicion about the function of storytellers. However, some of our greatest and most stouthearted thinkers believe otherwise, such as philosopher Eric Hoffer: "Man is eminently a *storyteller*. His search for a purpose, a cause, an ideal, a mission and the like is largely a search for a plot and a pattern in the development of his life story—a story that is basically without meaning or pattern." Companion words include *talesman*, the author of a story or report, and the venerable Hawaiian *talk story*, described as an effort to "rekindle old times" by way of the simple but profound social interaction of the act of storytelling itself. The *seanachie* or *shenachie*, from Gaelic *sean*, old, and *achie*, speaker, is a *tale teller* of age-old Gaelic stories, poems, riddles, chants, and more. A term of Scottish Gaelic background that went on to flourish in Ireland up to the present, this was "a member of the clan chief's household whose duty was to record clan history and genealogy and to recite these when called upon to do so."

## THAUMATURGE, THAUMATURGY (GREEK)

*A miracle worker; wonderworking.* A marvel of a word based on the Greek *thauma*, wonder, and *ergon*, work, *thaumaturge* describes a saint or magician. Nowadays one who practices magic is called a magician, but in ancient times was called by the venerable word *thaumaturgist*. Padua's Saint Anthony would be a Christian *thaumaturge*. It first entered into English via the occultist John Dee, in his magisterial work *Mathematicall Praeface to Euclid's Elements* (1570), where he describes math as an art and mathematicians as those who practice *thaumaturgy*, "which giveth certain order to make **strange** works, of the sense to be perceived and of men greatly to be wondered at." While researching a lecture on "The Seven Wonders of the Ancient World," I discovered one of the great "happy accidents" of classical history. When the 2nd-century BCE writer Antipater compiled his first list of fantastic sites he used the Greek word *theamata*, which really refers to "sights to be seen," echoed centuries later in the word *sightseers*. Countless travelers in antiquity used Antipater's list like an early travel guide, and over time their praises slurred and blurred with the similar-sounding Greek word *thaumata*, which was and still is a "wonder." Now you know how we arrived at the Seven Wonders and not the Seven Super Sites of the Ancient World. Jacques Derrida, in *The Gift of Death*, famously described philosophy as *thaumaturgy*, or, we might as well say, one of the wonders of the mind. In a 1998 essay in *Contemporary Review* titled "Devoted People: Belief and Religion in Early Modern Ireland," John McGurk wrote, "There was ever a cautious hesitancy on the part of the clergy to recognize evidence of *thaumaturgy*, and the **superstitious** use of relics."

## THIMBLE

*A small protective metal or plastic covering for the thumb of a seamstress or sewer.* A relic of sailing days when sailors had to repair torn sails but needed to protect their thumbs from the constant and painful pricks of the sewing needles. Gradually, a bell-shaped leather covering over the thumb, a *thumb bell,* became the most popular form of protection. In 17th-century London a metalworker named John Lofting devised a metal version of the sailor's *thumb bell*, which was an immediate hit among housewives, and slowly the word "slurred into *thimble*," in the inimitable phrasing of Webb B. Garrison. *The Hunting of the Snark* is a metaphysical hero's journey in the mythopoetics of Lewis Carroll, who wrote, "You may seek it with *thimbles*—and seek it with care; You may hunt it with forks and hope; You may threaten its life with a railway-share; You may charm it with smiles and soap." Legendary Beatles guitarist George Harrison once explained his own roots: "There was this big skiffle craze happening for a while in England … All you needed was an acoustic guitar, a washboard with *thimbles* for percussion, and a tea-chest, you know, the ones they used to ship tea from India—and you just put a broom handle on it and a bit of string, and you had a bass [guitar] … You only needed two chords: *Jing-jinga-jing jing-jinga-jing jing-jinga-jing jing-jinga-jing.* And I think that's basically where I've always been at. I'm just a skiffler, you know. Now I do posh skiffle. That's all it is." Companion words include *sea thimbles*, thumb-sized jellyfish that sting like a needle; *thimblerig*, a swindler's sleight-of-hand game; and *witch-thimble*, Northern English for *foxglove,* a corruption, Mackay informs us, of *folk's glove*, the glove worn by fairies.

## THROW

*To propel or cast something through the air by a sudden movement of the hand.* When I was researching this word for my book on the Olympics, I was *thrown* for a loop by the startling number of *throw* words in English. Recently, I heard the savvy travel writer Tim Cahill talk about a character he called "Atlatl Bob," after the Paleolithic spear, who told him that the ability to *throw* may be one of the great engines in human evolution. The sense evolution of *throw* is harder to **catch**, having been thrown to us from the early 14th-century Old English *þrawan*, to twist, **writhe**, Old Saxon *thraian*, and Welsh *taraw*, to strike, as in whirling a missile before releasing it. To be *thrown* into jail is first recorded 1560; to be *thrown off*, as in being confused, dates from 1844. To *throw* (one's) hat in the ring, meaning "to issue a challenge," especially to announce one's candidacy, was first recorded in 1917. To *throw up*, or "vomit," was first recorded in 1732. So versatile is the word, here are two imaginative uses. Maya Angelou once said, "I've learned that you shouldn't go through life with a catcher's mitt on both hands; you need to be able to *throw* something back." On a humorous note, Groucho Marx quipped, "In Hollywood, brides keep the **bouquets** and *throw* away the groom." Companion words include *throwster*, one who *throws* silk by reeling and twisting it into **yarn**.

## TIMSHEL (HEBREW)

*Thou mayest.* The King James translation makes a promise in the phrase "Thou shalt," meaning that men will surely triumph over sin. But the Hebrew word *timshel* carries a different weight. In John Steinbeck's *East of Eden*, young Cal says, "'Thou mayest'—that gives a choice. It might be the most important word in the world. That says the way is open. That **throws** it right back on a man. For if 'Thou mayest'—it is also true that 'Thou mayest not.' Don't you see? ... This is not theology. I have no bent toward gods. But I have a new love for that glittering instrument, the human soul. It is a lovely and unique thing in the universe. It is always attacked and never destroyed—because 'Thou mayest.'" In essence, *timshel*, or *timshol*, meaning "you will rule," allows you to make the choice to live a good life—you are not predestined. In *East of Eden*, it gives Adam the chance to accept his mother's choice of sins without letting it predetermine his own life. At the end of the novel, Lee begs Adam to give Cal his blessing. "Don't leave him alone with his guilt. Let him be free." And Adam, as he is dying, whispers one word: "*Timshel!*" He thus affirms that Cal has indeed, by accepting responsibility, demonstrated that he is capable of ruling over sin. After each day's writing on the book Steinbeck wrote a letter to his editor, Pasal Covici, about his progress; he made a wooden box for the **manuscript** and mailed it to Covici. On its cover he carved T I M S H E L, "the most important word in the world."

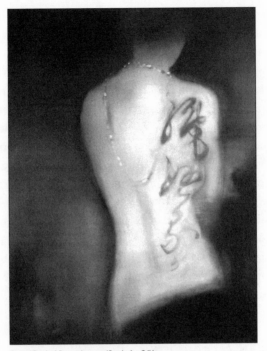

Toast: *Pool of Remembrance (Study for Silk)*

## TOAST

*A call to drink to someone's health; sliced bread browned by heat.*
First recorded in 1709 by Richard Steele, who described
the custom of *toasting* as a drink to the health and honor of
a beautiful or popular woman—the drink of choice being
a glass of wine with a wee bit of spiced *toast*, burned bread,

dropped in for flavor or to disguise the poor quality of the
wine back in the day. The allusion was a form of magical
thinking, or should we say, magical drinking? The subtle
suggestion was that the **lady** to be so honored was, figuratively speaking, a *spicy* gal, adding a certain piquancy
to the wine. The other familiar meaning of *toast*, bread
browned by heat, dates to the late 14th century, from
French *toster*, to *toast* or grill. Companion words and
phrases include *toast*, "a goner, person or thing already
doomed or destroyed," recorded by 1987. Favorite *toasts*
include "May you have the hindsight to know where
you've been, the foresight to know where you are going,
and the insight to know when you have gone too far."
Show business legend Frank Sinatra was fond of saying
that his favorite *toast* to close friends was "May the last
thing you hear be one of my songs."

### TOBOGGAN (ALGONQUIN)

*A long, flat-bottomed, usually wooden sled for carrying supplies—
or sliding down a steep hill white with snow.* A hill canoe, as my
relatives in northern Ontario called it when I was growing
up in Michigan. This is of the many vivacious contributions to English from our *voyageur* French Canadian neigh-
bors. Officially recorded only in 1829, *toboggan* comes
down river, or downhill, by way of *tabagane*, Algonquian-
Micmac, *tobakun*. By the Roaring Twenties, it took on the
meaning of a type of long woolen cap, presumably because

one wore such a cap while *tobogganing*. The Avid World website reports in a February 2011 article titled *Toboggan Love* that Camden, New Jersey, is the home of the *Toboggan* Championships. "For three days every February, frozen Hosmer Pond is home to *Tobogganville*, where teams with wild costumes and names like *That's What She Sled* pitch tents on the ice and drink free beer in the glow of their campfires." Companion words include *canoe*, or dugout boat, from the Spanish *canoa*, first recorded by Columbus as a word he learned from the Arawaks, in Haiti; *kayak*, from the Greenland Eskimo word *qayaq*, first recorded in 1757, referring to a small boat made of skins; and the Irish *curragh*, a tarred animal-hide canoe.

## TOMAHAWK (POWHATAN RENAPE INDIAN)

*A hand axe used by American Indians as a tool and weapon.* Captain John Smith, of Pocahontas fame, is credited with the first English rendering of this venerable dialect word from the Virginia Indians. The original Renape term was *tämähak*, an abbreviated form of *tämähakan*, a cutting tool, from *tamaham*, he who cuts, as recounted by Funk. The word is easily recognizable in several other Indian dialects, such as the Mahican *tomahick*, the Delaware *tummahegan*, and the Passamaquoddy *tumigen*. *Tomahawk* is a versatile word used in James Fenimore Cooper's *The Last of the Mohicans*: "It is prudent for every warrior to **consider** well before he strikes his *tomahawk* into the head of his prisoner." Tecumseh, leader of the Shawnees and organizer of a vital tribal confederacy, said, "As we intend to hold our council at our Huron village, this near the British, we may probably make them a visit. Should they offer us any presents of goods, we will not take them; but should they offer us [gun]powder and the *tomahawk*, we will take the powder and refuse the *tomahawk*." San Francisco Giants announcer Duane Kuiper described the Dodgers' Raul Ibanez hitting a fly ***ball*** off Brian "The Beard" Wilson in August 2011 by saying, "Boy, he *tomahawked* that thing." Companion words include the streamlined *Tomahawk motorcycle*, and the *tomahawk chop*, one of the racist ***sports*** gestures that inspired the eminent writer and lawyer Vine Deloria Jr. to launch his campaign against the racist appropriation of American Indian symbols.

## TOOTH-JUMPING

*Pulling teeth.* As Elizabeth Knowles writes in *How to Read a Word,* when a word is invented "we are essentially turning our thoughts into sounds." Here is one of the most wrenching examples of a sound-word or phrase, one that *yelps* off the page, or leaps like a jump cut in the movies by hurtling us to another time and place. In this case the word could describe a rollicking scene right out of a Looney Tunes cartoon, but it turns out to be an obsolete Appalachian practice of extracting a tooth with hammer and nail. As one wandering dentist put it, "A man who knows how

can *jump a tooth* without it hurtin' half as bad as pullin'."
Companions include *The Tooth Will Out*, the 1951 send-up
of teeth extraction by The Three Stooges, and *jump-start*,
sparking a car battery.


## TOUCHSTONE

*A smooth piece of black quartz or basalt used to test the purity
of gold and silver by the **color** streak left behind when rubbed
over the precious metal.* Figuratively, since the early 16th
century it has served as a grand trope for the criterion for
determining value or excellence. *Touché!* Originally an
alchemical term from the late 15th century, from *touch*
and *stone*. An elemental etymology, from the Old French
*touchepierre*, contemporary French *pierre de touche*, the
stone one touches to a gold object to determine its purity.
Today a *touchstone* remains the measure of authenticity,
genuineness, even soulfulness of an object, quality, or
person. The indefatigable diarist Anaïs Nin wrote, "I do
not want to be the leader. I refuse to be the leader. I want
to live darkly and richly in my femaleness. I want a man
lying over me, always over me. His will, his pleasure, his
desire, his life, his work, his sexuality the *touchstone*, the
command, my pivot." Companion words include *touch-
up,* a last minute improvement.

## TOUT

*To advertise, recommend, or push in an annoying manner; a person who advertises in such a manner.* Someone known throughout history, the pest in front of the hotel, restaurant, or bar luring the unsuspecting inside. A word right off the ship, the serpent-bowed Viking one to be precise, one of dozens of Old Norse words to survive the attacks on Old England. It derives from *tota*, which referred to both a teat, and the toe of a shoe, and in turn suggests a *tip*, which brings us full circle to the *tout*, who provides a *tip*, usually in an irksome way. According to Francis Grosse, in his decidedly *not* vulgar *Dictionary of the Vulgar Tongue* (1811), *tout* derives from *tueri*, to look about, and referred to "publicans forestalling guests or meeting them on the road, and begging their custom," with a secondary reference to thieves and smugglers "on the lookout," presumably for easy marks, travelers with money or jewelry. The connection between the two kinds of *touts* becomes more understandable: each is vying to take advantage of someone else. There are competing theories for the root meaning; some sources trace *tout* back to thieves' cant from the early 1700s for acting as a lookout or spying on someone, from Middle English *tuten*, to peep, peer. *Looking out* for someone— or yourself—invariably led to the sense, in the mid-18th century, of being on the lookout. To *tout* effectively, the *tout* had to know how to praise the person or the product to high heaven. By the 19th century, *touts* were such hard sells that they were pests, as we read in sources like Mark

Twain's volume of travel writing, *The Innocents Abroad.*
"I've never been one of those actors who has *touted* myself
as a ***fascinating*** human being," says Robert De Niro. "I
had to decide early on whether I was to be an actor or a
personality." Companion words include, since I have your
attention, *Le Souffleur,* a theater prompter, in the painting
by Jean Siméon Chardin, hired to look out for actors who
forgot their lines.

## TOWN

*An enclosed place for people to live together "firmly" in "fast-*
*ness," in safety.* To study this most ancient of English words
is the equivalent of gazing at what artists call the *offskip,*
"the far distance in a landscape painting." It derives from
the Middle English *toun,* Icelandic *tun,* Gaelic *dun,* a fort,
and the German *Zaun,* a hedge. According to the OED,
*priest* and *town* are the oldest words in English, *town* being
first recorded in *The Laws of Ethelbert* between 601 and
604. Until *town* was adopted, the standard term in English
was *burg,* which gave us *borough.* It's hard to imagine nowadays, but until modern times most settlements around the
world were surrounded by walls, towers, even hedges, as
suggested in the backstory of *town.* Nighttime itself was a
source of fear, as we know from ***curfew,*** from Old French
*couvre feu,* "to cover the fire," a regulation all over Europe,
so as not to attract wild animals, strangers, or thieves.
*Town* has the feeling of safety in numbers, people held fast,

together. When Sinatra sang "My Kind of *Town*," he was "rooting" for the love of place. Companion words and phrases include *town hall*; *townie*, a *townsman,* as opposed to university students or circus workers who were just passing through; *town **ball***, a forerunner of baseball, scored from 1852; *town car;* and *man about town,* surprisingly, attested from 1734.

## TSMESIS

*The intentional (clever) inclusion of a (descriptive) word, usually for (friggin') humorous emphasis; or the breaking up of one word into two for em phasis. Abso-blooming-lutely,* this rather stuck-up (pretentious) rhetorical scheme reflects two common practices or conversational habits, that of inserting a bold or even offensive word smack-dab in the middle of another word in an effort to be funny or hip (strong/upset/ obscene), as in "O-holy-bama." Late Latin, from Greek *tmēsis,* the act of cutting, from *temnein,* to cut. The Yogi Berra of Hollywood, Samuel Goldwyn, once wrote, "I have but two words to say to your request: *Im Possible.*" The Simpsons' neighbor Ned Flanders, the impossibly sunny character, chimes in with his "Wel-diddly-elcome." Companion words include *schizophraxia*, a wonderful word for *word splitting,* usually the insertion of a swear word between the first and last syllable of a common word, as in "abso*frigging*lutely.".

## TWITTERATI

*Those who belong to the instant-messaging, faster-than-the-speed-of-light reviewing and marketing world.* A so-called imitative word, from the sound of *twittering* birds, coupled with the familiar and slightly pejorative *-ati* suffix of such words as *literati, glitterati,* and *illuminati.* Originally, there were variations in lexical use: *all atwitter* meant busy with gossip, a condition of excitement, and *twittery* perhaps described a birdhouse or a gossipy teahouse. Michael Quinion writes in World Wide Words: "You're right to suggest that words ending in *-ati* do tend to be mildly pejorative, often with undertones of **triviality**." Companion words include *snarkerati*, the more-**sarcastic**-than-thou commentators; *glitterati*, those engaged in glamorous activity; *fasherati*, the set of people concerned with fashion; *soccerati*, those involved with soccer; *digerati*, digital wizards, people with expertise or professional involvement in information technology; and *cliterati*, woman journalists, a term coined by P. J. Mara in Dublin. And, of course, *illuminati*, so-called illuminated people, originally the name of a Bavarian secret society founded in 1776, used today by conspiracy theorists to describe the people who really run the world.

## TYPHOON

*A violent storm or whirlwind.* A storm-blown word launched from the shores of Greece as typhoon, personified as Tuphoesus, the hundred-headed father of the winds, also

❧

known as the father of the **Sphinx**. According to some linguists, the Greek *typhon* (to smoke) was borrowed from the Persian *Tufan*, their term for the violent cyclones in the Indian Ocean. The storm of language never stops blowing. From there it entered English around 1588 as *tuoffon* and *tufan*, and finally took on our modern spelling, *typhoon*, when it was transcribed in 1819 by the poet Percy Shelley, in *Prometheus Unbound*. The wordsmith Joseph Conrad writes in his novel of the same name, "The *typhoon* had got on Juke's nerves." *Typhoon* by any measure of weather is word-wrecked. Companion words include the turbinating *cyclone, hurricane,* and *twister.*

# U

## UBUNTU (BANTU/XHOSA)

*An invaluable African concept word for the interconnected-ness of all beings.* This word, from the Bantu languages of southern Africa, gained worldwide use through the influence of South African Archbishop Desmond Tutu and the country's ex-president Nelson Mandela, and thus it has acquired a powerful metaphorical application as an ethic or humanist philosophy focusing on people's allegiances and relations with each other. The most highly regarded definition is found in Tutu's 1999 book *No Future without Forgiveness:* "A person with *Ubuntu* is open and available to others, affirming of others, does not feel threatened that others are able and good, for he or she has a proper self-assurance that comes from knowing that he or she belongs in a greater whole and is diminished when others are humiliated or diminished, when others are tortured or oppressed." Companion words include the Hindu *Net of Gems* or *Indra's Net*, the notion that the universe is a net in which everything is connected and where it connects it shines like a jewel.

## UGLY

*Unattractive, unpleasant to look at, displeasing; repulsive in behavior or appearance; used to describe circumstances that have turned dangerous.* The unattractive Old Norse word *ugga* displays the very fear it describes, an ominous word even as an adjective, *ugsome*. *Ugly* is frightful, unpleasant, repulsive, often triggering a violent response either mentally or physically. **Consider** these contorted features, as revealed in early records: "morally offensive" is attested from around 1300, "ill-tempered" from the 1680s, and "ill-shaped," from the 17th century. Taken together, seen through the anamorphoscope of word study, these meanings suggest that *ugliness* appears dreadful because it suggests *illness*, bad health. Dr. Johnson's merciless pen dug this up from a certain Mr. Dier, who he says deduced *ugly* from *ouphlike*; that is, like an *ough*, *elf,* or **goblin**, which he traces back to the Saxon *oga*, terror, and the Gothic *oogan*, to fear. In this we get a compression of centuries of responses to what is deemed *ugly*, the quality that brings terror and fear. Johnson adds, "Deformed, offensive to the sight; contrary to beautiful." This is what John Cleese, host of the BBC series *Faces*, claims, that generally speaking **beauty** betokens or promises health, and *ugliness* is a kind of evolutionary

warning about illness, ill health, disease, and thus a poten-
tial end to the bloodline. Companion words and phrases
include *ugly duckling* (1877), from the story by Hans Christian Andersen, first translated into English from Danish in
1846; *ugly American*, "a U.S. citizen who behaves offen-
sively abroad," first recorded in 1958 as a book title. Emily
Brontë wrote, "A good heart will help you to a bonny face,
my lad, and a bad one will turn the bonniest into something worse than *ugly*." Redd Foxx joked, "Beauty may be
skin deep, but ugly goes clear to the bone." Companion
words include plug-*ugly*, American slang first recorded in
1856, *ugsome*, from Gaelic *oich*, which Mackay describes as
"an exclamation expressive of weariness and exhaustion
... such as when a man climbs a hill, and is compelled to
take a breath."

## UMBRAGE

*Resentment, annoyance, offense; a shadow cast by trees.* All told,
we take *umbrage* when we're ***thrown*** into the shade. Being
insulted, hurt, or slighted casts a pall over our mood, trig-
gers our resentment, and often our urge for revenge. The
various ways of being insulted or slighted are recognizable
in the French root word *ombrage*, shade or shadow, from
Latin *umbraticum*. The numerous figurative uses catch on in
the 17th century, such as the feeling or suspicion of having
one's feathers ruffled—another way of saying that someone
feels overshadowed, cast aside, thrown into the shade. *To*

*take umbrage*, then, means to be piqued or offended. *American Literary Anecdotes*, published in 1990, reported, "There is a story about the editor of a small newspaper who quickly read a wire service story during World War II stating that the Russians had taken *umbrage* at something, as they often did. Not knowing what the phrase meant, he headlined the story: "Russians Capture *Umbrage*."

## UNKEMPT

*Slovenly, sloppy, untended.* The word is a portrait of someone poorly dressed and poorly coiffed, from the root word *kempt*, which is basically our word for "combed." It derives from the 16th-century Old English *unkembed*, from *un*, not, and *kempt*, well-combed. Someone *unkempt* is not well combed, coiffed, brushed, or dressed. Is there a pattern in English that so often the negative form of a word survives and the positive one disappears? How come nobody says a well-groomed person is *kempt*? The Polish author and aphorist Stanislaw J. Lec writes in *Unkempt Thoughts*, "Advice to writers: Sometimes you have to stop writing. Even before you begin." Companion words include *ungroomed; well-kempt*, tidy.

## UNMENTIONABLES

*A Victorian euphemism for underwear and other delicate garments.* An untoward, or awkward, word to go along with **untranslatables**. Years of prudery took the upper hand in the English language during the Victorian era and elevated the art of euphemism, reflected in such *peculiarly* precise terms as *upper unmentionables* and *lower unmentionables*. By way of indirection, an array of suggestive phrases such as "privates," "behind," and "sleep together"—and notoriously, "trousers"—are attested to in an 1829 book, *Sailors and Saints, or Matrimonial Manoeuvres,* by the dubiously named William Glascock. Glascock records one of the earliest underwear euphemisms: "a blue coat … with a pair of blue *unmentionables* [breeches and trousers], white fleecy stockings, and short black gaiters." *Unmentionables* was an expression concocted with Victorian prissiness for underwear "too shocking to say." The word *cockroach* was even shortened to *roach* "for the sake of euphony." No surprise that the *bawdy* James Joyce writes in *Ulysses,* "His little man-o'-war top and *unmentionables* were all full of sand." Companion words include *inexpressibles, etceteras, unimaginables, unutterables, unprintables, never-mention-'ems,* and my favorite, *unwhisperables.*

## UP TO SCRATCH

*Worthy of consideration, adequate.* An old boxing term that comes from the custom of calling a pugilist out of his corner to the center of the ring to stand on a line scratched on the canvas. If he couldn't make it *up to the scratch* he was presumably done for; if he could walk or hobble to the scratch mark, he could continue to compete. The new rule was intended to end the gambling-induced pressure to fight, literally, to the bitter end, which often happened. Also reflective of the ancient Greek running custom in the ancient Olympics of drawing or *scratching* a line in the sand to mark the start of a race. (Remember: "On your mark, get set, go!") Satirist Dorothy Parker: "The sweeter the apple, the blacker the core. *Scratch* a lover and find a foe."

## UTANG NA LOOB (TAGALOG / FILIPINO)

*A debt of gratitude passed from generation to generation.* A mouthful to say, but a word worthy of wider acceptance since it describes a phenomenon detectable throughout human history. Pronounced *u-tang na lo-ob*, it literally translates as "an inner debt," from *utang*, debt, and *na loob*, from the inside. This concept word reveals a particular Filipino cultural trait that anthropologists explain as a kind of intense reciprocity. More than just economic debt, it is an obligation to repay anyone who has done you a favor. This is a debt of gratitude that is profoundly personal from individual to individual, family to family, and borders on the spiritual, as is echoed in the word *loob*, one's inner self. It is sometimes translated as a "debt of gratitude," but it is clearly more than owing someone a favor. My informant, ChiChing Herlihy, from Manila, tells me that it is "the be-all and end-all of Filipino life, and so reveals much more than gratitude. Actually, it is the poor man's version

of *noblesse oblige*." The word also reflects another fundamental aspect of Filipino character, *kapwa*, translated by
my friend Ernie Unson from Manila as "shared self," which
throbs at the heart of Filipino culture. "He wouldn't spend
Christmas," as Myles O'Reilly says of a certain legendary
reporter's cheapness, would be the opposite of *utang na
loob*. Companion words include *sitike*, an Apache word for
closely knit community, and Balinese *same*, which likewise
shares this spiritual sense of the essential oneness of the
tribe or community.


## UZZIE PIE

*A **pie** that tries to fly away.* Truly a **weird** *and* wonderful
word. The old English nursery rhyme (dating to 1549)
"Sing a Song of Sixpence" contains a startling image that
has long **baffled** me: "Four and twenty blackbirds / baked
in a pie. / When the **pie** was opened, / the birds began
to sing…" The crust was filled with dried fruit and beans
to weigh it down while the pie baked. Inside, the songbirds (larks, blackbirds, finches, and thrushes) waited until
the top crust was removed, and then began to sing for the
delight of the king. Many folklore commentators have
attempted to interpret this seemingly simple children's
rhyme. For instance, it was a 16th-century amusement to
place live birds in a **pie**, as revealed in an Italian cook-
book from 1549. Its **recipe** reads more like anthropological
tract: "to make pies so that birds may be alive in them and

flie out when it is cut up." An account of the banquet at the wedding of Marie de' Medici and Henry IV of France in 1600 contains this: "The first surprise, though, came shortly before the starter—when the guests sat down, unfolded their napkins and saw songbirds fly out. The highlight of the meal were **sherbets** of milk and honey, which were created by Buontalenti." Companion words include *maggot-pie*, a magpie to Shakespeare, and *printer's pie*, a jumble of type.

# V

## VARNISH

*A protective, clear, shiny surface coating made from resin.* It's a long way from your local hardware store where *varnish* is a popular product to ancient Egypt, but that's how far we have to travel to track down the roots of this brilliant word. Credit goes to the strong-willed Berenice of Egypt, daughter of Magas, King of Cyrenece, and sister-wife of Ptolemy III, who invaded Syria to avenge the death of his other sister. The story goes that Queen Berenice was so distraught over the disappearance of her beloved sister that she offered a sacrifice of her golden hair to the goddess Venus to ensure her sister's safe return home. Reverently, Berenice cut her hair and left it on the altar in Venus's temple at Zephyrium, along the Nile. For some reason long lost to history, her hair was stolen and Venus was much devastated. To appease her, Colon, sage of Samos, confabulated a poetic tale that the hair disappeared because

Venus herself carried it off to heaven so it might appear among the stars. Her roots have been showing ever since in the constellation of Coma Berenices, near the tail of Leo. Her name has been immortalized by time as *berenix*, and further burnished as *vernix,* varnish, which is to say to give something a golden glow. The mid-14th-century Old French word is *vernis*, varnish, from Middle English *vernix*, odorous resin, perhaps from Greek *verenike*, from *Berenike*, an ancient city in Libya (modern Bengasi), which is named for Berenike II, queen of Egypt, and is credited as the place where *varnishes* were first used. Figuratively, *varnish* has come to mean "specious gloss, pretense," as in *varnished* truth, recorded in the 1560s. Companion words include *Varnishing Day*, or *vernissage*, the day for touching up or *varnishing* a work of art prior to an exhibition, a practice that J. W. Turner notoriously pursued at the British Museum. Edward Hopper wrote, "I use a retouching *varnish* which is made in France, Libert, and that's all the *varnish* I use … If a picture needs *varnishing* later, I allow a restorer to do that, if there's any restoring necessary."

## VILLAIN

*A person guilty of or capable of a crime or wickedness.* A *villain* is a suspicious outsider breaking the law by trying to become an insider, "the person or thing responsible for specified trouble, harm, or damage." In feudal times, a *villain* was a peasant, from Latin *villa*, a simple house in the country.

For centuries, a serf or farmhand was considered by aristocrats or anyone outside cities a degenerate, sometimes (rather *villainously*) a churl, a boor, a lowborn rustic, a knave or scoundrel. Ever since, *villain* has been used in a pejorative sense. Not until 1822 do we hear of a *villain* as a character whose "evil motives or actions help drive the plot." Shakespeare said, "I like not fair terms and a *villain's* mind." Speaking of plot, Hitchcock told an interviewer, "The more successful the *villain*, the more successful the picture." Actor Kirk Douglas said, "I always hated the whole thing—the blacklist. Actors who couldn't work. I mean, actors who couldn't express themselves. That was a terrible thing. The heads of the studios. They were the *villains*." Companion words include *rogue, scallywag,* and *knave.*

## VOLUME

*A single book or a bound series of printed sheets.* A scroll, a collection. To unscroll this voluminous word and appreciate its poetry, imagine the ancient Library of Alexandria and its estimated 700,000 books, which were really *scrolls*, sheets of papyrus that were "wound into fairly tight rolls about sticks, one stick at either end of the roll." The scroll was unwound from one stick, and as the reading proceeded, wound up on the other, then inserted into slots in a wall, like an old mailroom. That's the first library. Slots and sticks, not stacks and stocks. Fast-forward to the late 14th century: the ancient Greek sense of a long book on a roll had evolved from papyrus to **parchment**, but the idea was stowed away on the ships bound for Rome. A **manuscript** was referred to in Latin as *volumen*, roll, coil, or wreath, which itself derived from—and you've got to love this—*volvere*, to turn around, and *volvo*, the old librarian's term for the rolling and unrolling of the scrolls. Later, the word *evolved* in the early 1500s to mean a single book that was part of a set, and later "bulk, mass, quantity." San Francisco's Gordon Getty, son of oil tycoon Jean Paul Getty, once said, "I was in Paris at an English-language bookstore. I picked up a *volume* of [Emily] Dickinson's poetry. I came back to my hotel, read 2,000 of her poems and immediately began composing in my head. I wrote down the melodies even before I got to a piano." Companion words include *volume*, sound intensity; *voluminous*, from *volumen*, many-coiled; and *vulva*, a rolled opening, an odd but real connection to *rock and roll*, a very old euphemism for having sex, which probably has its roots in Africa.

## VOLUPTUOUS

*Beautiful, desirable, pleasing.* Said of a curvaceous, sexually attractive woman who is characterized by luxury or sensual pleasure. *Voluptuous* is as *voluptuous* does, and what it does is come into English sensuously, from the Old French *voluptueux* and Latin *voluptas*, pleasure, delight. So pleasurable, so pleasing, so delightful was this word that it led to the assumption, by the 15th century, that a voluptuous

woman must be susceptible to addiction to sensual pleasure. "Tamed as it may be," wrote Susan Sontag, "sexuality
remains one of the demonic forces in human consciousness—pushing us at intervals close to **taboo** and dangerous
desires, which range from the impulse to commit sudden
arbitrary violence upon another person to the *voluptuous*
**yearning** for the extinction of one's consciousness. Even
on the level of simple physical sensation and mood, making
**love** surely resembles having an epileptic fit at least as much
as, if not more than, eating a meal or conversing with
someone." Companion words include *voluptuary,* a person
devoted to pleasure, sensuality, and luxury, and *Voluptas*,
Joy or Pleasure, the son of Eros and Psyche

Voluptuous: *Under the El*

# W

## WALRUS

*An enormous, flippered, tusked sea beast.* A large **gregarious** marine mammal (Odobenus rosmarus) found in the Artic Ocean, related to the eared seals, having two large downward-pointing tusks. The 17th-century word derives from the Old Norse *hrossvalr,* horse-whale, which was passed to the Dutch, inverted, as *walvis,* whale, and *ros*, horse, and then into North German as *Walross.* Modern folks more likely know the word from the poem "The Walrus and the Carpenter" by Lewis Carroll: "The time has come to talk of many things: Of shoes and ships—and sealing wax—of cabbages and kings." Who can forget John Lennon's chortling cry, inspired by one of his boyhood heroes, Carroll himself, "I am the *walrus*, GOO GOO GOO JOOB!" In "The White Seal," from Rudyard Kipling's *The Jungle Book,* "the old Sea Vitch" is a "big, **ugly**, bloated, pimpled, fat-necked, long-tusked *walrus* of the North Pacific, who has no manners except when he is asleep." Companion words include *walrus mustache*, imitative of the long whiskers of the *whale-horse*.


## WANTON

**Lewd**, *lubricious, and reckless*. Originally another **rambling** word, as in wandering around **town** without **scruples** or restraint, suggestive of visits to the **bawdy** house. Now used with relish to describe someone's uncorralled desires: *wanton* ways. It has ever been thus, as revealed by its Middle English roots in *wantowen*, rebellious, lacking discipline, from *wan*, badly, and Old English *togen*, trained. *Towen* later yielded such innocent words as *team* and *tow*, but seen together, Madame Wan and Monsieur Towen were considered an unsavory couple. *Wantons*. Sexually immodest, promiscuous, deliberately cruel, as in the war correspondent's **cliché** "*wanton* violence." Thus a *wanton* person is someone untrained in civil behavior, undisciplined in sexual behavior, unsavory in habits. Shakespeare nails it: "As flies to *wanton* boys, are we to the gods: They kill us for their **sport**." Feminist icon Erica Jong updates the Bard: "Back in the days when men were hunters and chest beaters and women spent their whole lives worrying about pregnancy or dying in childbirth, they often had to be taken against their will. Men complained that women were cold, unresponsive, frigid. They wanted their women *wanton*. They wanted their women wild. Now women were finally learning to be *wanton* and wild—and what happened? The men wilted." Companion words include the archaic *word-wanton*, speaking obscenely, and "The *Wanton* Song," about illicit sex with a *wanton* woman, by Led Zeppelin.

## WAVE-STEED

*A boat.* A stunning example of Old English **kenning** that rides across the waves of time to us, revealing the Early English genius for using extraordinary **metaphors** for ordinary things. The term **kenning** itself was born in an Old Norse or medieval Icelandic study on poetics, as an idiomatic use of *kenna við or til*, which translates as "to name after." Early English abounds in kennings, as Melvyn Bragg points out in *The Adventure of English*, such as *ban-hus*, bone-house, for "body"; *gleo-beam*, glee-wood, for "harp"; and *wig-bord*, war-board, for "shield." *Wave-steed* can also be called an example of *metonymy,* a figure of speech that uses an attribute of something as the thing itself, such as "sails" for "ships." Companion words include the Old Norse word *kenna*, which means to know, recognize, perceive, feel, show, or teach, as does the Scottish word *ken*, to know or understand.

## WELTANSCHAUUNG (GERMAN)

*A comprehensive worldview; a personal philosophy of the world that encompasses a wide-world perception.* My son Jack's

favorite word, he told me when he was 8, because of the
way it *sounded* when he said it. Wikipedia defines it as
"the fundamental cognitive orientation of an individual
or society encompassing natural philosophy; fundamental,
existential, and normative postulates; or themes, values,
emotions, and ethics." The term, composed of *Welt*,
world, and *Anschauung*, view or outlook, and is a concept
fundamental to German philosophy and epistemology and
refers to a *wide-world perception*. The German adventurer,
scientist, biologist, philosopher, and memoirist Alexander
Von Humboldt wrote, "*Die gefährlichste Weltanschauung ist
die Weltanschauung derer, die die Welt nie angeschaut haben.*"
("The most dangerous worldview is the worldview of
those who have not viewed the world.")

## WHALE FALL

*The carcass of a fallen whale lying on the ocean floor.* Although
millions of whales must have silently fallen over the
millennia, they weren't discovered or observed until the
invention of deep-sea *robots* and submarines. On the floor
of the deep ocean divers and robots reveal something far
different about the fate of whales than is seen when they die
in shallow water, where they are usually savaged by scav-
engers relatively quickly. At great depths scores of species
such as lobsters, bristle worms, crabs, octopuses, clams,
even sleeper sharks have been photographed and filmed
as they gnaw away for months at the deep-sea cafeteria

offerings of whale carcasses. Synchronistically, a fellow named Matt Greenberg, member of a rock band called Sutro, attended a live radio broadcast of "West Coast Live" for my book *Wordcatcher* in Berkeley, in 2009, and afterward wrote a note to me. During my live interview with Sedge Thompson I had mentioned that new and exciting words are being formed every day and mentioned that I had recently come across *whale fall* in a magazine article. The musician mentioned that my reference was exciting to him because he had recently joined another band and they had just named it *Whale Fall*. "You can imagine my surprise when you brought up this term. We really love the name." Companion words include *ashfall, deadfall* (a Gold Rush term for a bar), *dewfall, icefall,* and *pratfall.*

## WINDOW

*An opening in a wall or roof of a building or vehicle that is fitted with glass to admit light or air and allow one to see out.* During Viking times a *window* was no more than an opening, an unglazed hole in a roof, a *vindauga, window,* from *vind,* wind, and *auga,* eye, a mirror of the time when *windows* were glassless. *Wind-eye* is a **keen kenning**, as *whale road* is for the sea. It evolved into the Old English *eagþyrl,* literally an eye hole, and *eagduru,* an eye door. In Latin it was *fenestra*; most Germanic languages used the term to describe the openings when they were first covered with glass, which was adopted into English *fenester.* A beloved

Window: *Die Kathedrale der Bucher (The Cathedral of Books)*

adage reveals that "Eyes are the *windows* to the soul." Nancy Griffiths says, "Being a good songwriter means paying attention and sticking your hand out the *window* to catch the song on the way to someone else's house!" Companion words and phrases include *window dressing*, first recorded in 1790; *window seat,* attested from 1778; *window-shopping*, from 1922; *window of* **opportunity** (1979), from earlier figurative use in the US space program, launch *window* (1965). To *windle* is to turn in the wind. Throwing a person out a window is known as *defenestration*.


## WORDPECKER

*Someone who plays with words.* A *wordcarrier* is one who speaks for royalty, a term Paul Theroux employs in *The Tao of Travel*. A *wordwrecker* is a person with the habit of **throwing** *ahems, likes,* and *You know what I means* into an otherwise perfectly good **conversation**. Companion words include *wordwatch*, the occupational hazard of dictionary workers; *wordsville*, '50s hipster **slang** for a *library*, and *wordridden*, as Mackay writes, "to be a slave to words without understanding their meaning; to be overawed by a word rather than an argument." A warning to us all!


## WORM

*A slithery little creature that lives underground.* It's surprising how many words it has inspired, including *sinworm*, a vile sinful creature, according to Johnson. Emily Dickinson wrote, "In Winter in my Room / I came upon a *Worm*— / Pink, lank and warm— / But as he was a worm / And worms presume / Not quite with him at home— / Secured him by a string / To something neighboring / And went along ..." Winston Churchill said, "We are all worms. But I believe that I am a glow-worm." An *earworm* is a ditty that gets into your ear, usually a vile sinful commercial jingle, and you can't get it out again. I still can't extricate a muffler commercial from my teen years in Detroit: "Ten Mile at Mack, get your money back …" Companion words include *wormwood*, absinthe; and *wormhole*, a hypothetical "shortcut through spacetime."

## XENOGLOSSIA

*The reputed ability to speak a language never studied.* The **strange** word derives from Greek *xenos*, stranger or foreigner, and *glōssa*, tongue or language. The putative phenomenon is the ability to speak or write in a foreign tongue by means beyond one's control. If someone suddenly began speaking fluent German but had never studied it, never traveled to Germany, never knowingly spent time with Germans, they would be considered *xenoglossic.* Such a case came to light in spring 2011. An American woman from Brooklyn was given novocaine by her dentist and emerged with the ability to speak German with a German accent. Companion words include *polyglossia*, the putative ability to speak in several previously unstudied languages, and *glossolalia*, commonly known as "speaking in tongues," often witnessed in religious observances—generally, the uttering of indecipherable or nonsense words.

## XYSTER

*A bone-scraper or body oil scraper; a strigil or Greek curved skin-scraper.* You've seen this object in any museum of ancient Greek and Roman sculpture. If you've ever gazed upon statues of the **athletes** of old and wondered how the ancients got rid of all that olive oil they lathered on their skin to avoid sunburn—and the grips of fellow wrestlers—then you've seen a *xyster* (pronounced "*zyster*"). In the Roman equivalent of the Greek **gymnasium**, the workout room for young bucks, were buckets of "scrapings," according to legend: a mixture of sweat, olive oil, and blood that was gathered in urns and sold to *sports* fans who believed it could cure sore muscles, and probably much more. Should you think that odd, a piece of chewed bubble gum by Tug McGraw, the great relief pitcher for the New York Mets, sold on eBay for $500, as reported on *Good Morning America*. Companion words include *xyster*, a surgical instrument used to scrape or study bones.

# Y

## YAMAKASI

*An acrobatic group of practitioners of parkour, an urban sport originating in Paris that combines athletics, gymnastics, and street play. Parkour,* originally termed *l'art du déplacement*, was invented by David Belle in France in the 1980s. The nine young men who founded The Yamakasi are Belle, Yann Hnautra, Châu Belle Dinh, Laurent Piemontesi, Sébastien Foucan, Guylain N'Guba-Boyeke, Charles Perrière, Malik Diouf, and Williams Belle. The word *ya makási* originates from the African Congolese Lingala language and can mean "strong body," "strong spirit," or "strong person." It sums up the original and still core aim of the discipline: to be a strong individual, physically, mentally, and ethically. "When engaged in parkour, it is important to utilize all of your senses, especially your eyes," says Stephen Slade. The techniques were first seen by the mass public in the 1996 James Bond film *Casino Royale*, then in the 2001 French film *Yamakasi*. In the 2004 film *Les Fils du Vent* the group used parkour and acrobatics to steal from seven rich people to get enough money to afford heart replacement surgery for a child. The techniques are now being taught in British Royal Marines and the United States Marine Corps. Companion words include *traceur*, a participant in *parkour*.

## YARN

*A long tall story from the long tall ships.* A spinning of story, from the sailor's practice of twisting *yarn* for his ropes and spinning tall tales, which became synonymous with his *yarning*. If you can unravel the **ball** of meaning, you get back to the Old English *gearn*, related to the Dutch *garen*, probably rooted in an older word for "guts," and possibly to the Latin *hariolus*, soothsayer, and Greek *haurspex*, the seer who claimed to read omens in the entrails of sacrificed animals. The common idiom *spin a yarn* is an old sailor's term for telling a story. In "Sea-Fever," the English poet John Masefield wrote, "I must go down to the seas again, to the vagrant gypsy life / To the gull's way and the whale's way, where the wind's like a whetted knife; / And all I ask is a merry *yarn* from a laughing fellow-rover, / And quiet sleep and a sweet dream when the long trick's over." Companion words include *thread*, as in the narrative through line of a story.

## YO-YO (TAGALOG / FILIPINO)

*A wooden toy with a string that is yanked to perform tricks.* One of the few Filipino words commonly used in English, for a children's toy that dates back thousands of years. In the rice-terrace *town* of Bontoc many years ago I saw this piece of graffiti next to a roadside stand where an old Igorot was hand-fashioning *yo-yos*: "Life is like a *yo-yo*; people pull all the strings and then get tied up in knots." The legendary cellist *Yo-Yo* Ma is fond of saying, "After reaching fifty, I began to wonder what the root of life is." Companion words include *see-saw, teeter-totter,* and *dilly-dally.*

# Z

## ZANY

**Crazy**, *loony*, **hip**; a *comic performer*. During the late 16th century in Italy, a clown was called a *zanni*, from *Zanni*, Venetian for Giovanni, which is identical to our English John. A *zanni* was a stock character in old comedies who aped the principal actors. The wild and crazy Jim Carrey reveals the inspiration for his loony brand of humor: "For some reason I did something where I realized I could get a reaction. That was when I broke out of my shell at school, because I really didn't have any friends … and then finally I did this *zany* thing, and all of a sudden I had tons of friends." Companion words include *zany bars*, street **slang** for the drug Xanax.

Zenith: *Empire (for RB Morris)*

## ZENITH

*The peak, the acme, the summit achieved by a celestial or other object.* Technically, the *zenith* is the point directly above an observer; figuratively it is the highest point of **achievement**, on this celestial sphere or any other. According to wordsmiths, it derives from the Old French *cenith,* from the Middle Latin *cenit,* or *senit,* from the Arabic *samt,* the way or road, short for *samt ar-ras,* the way or path overhead. The word fell like a comet from the Arabic astronomers camping out in Spain in the 11th century, and as loanwords always do, it filled in a gap, or a hole in the sky. Nine centuries later, in 1918, two young wireless radio operators in Chicago set up shop in their kitchen and helped turn on the **infant** radio industry, choosing the name "Z-Nith," which happened to be the call letters for their station, later adapted to *Zenith* by its subsidiary, the company that advertised itself as the acme of television making. Fifty years later I still remember the jingle: "*Zenith*: The quality goes in before the name goes on." Go figure how these *zenith* moments of memory work. His Holiness, the Dalai Lama, writes: "Nowadays, the world is becoming increasingly materialistic, and mankind is reaching toward the very *zenith* of external progress, driven by an insatiable desire for power and vast possession. Yet by this striving for perfection in a world where everything is relative, they wander even further away from inward peace and happiness of the mind." Companion words include the *zenith angle,* which names a coordinate in astronomy, the direction between a specific point overhead and the local *zenith*.

## ZEST

*The tangy feel for life.* The tang is in the word for a good reason, since it comes from the peel of a citrus, added to give a drink *piquancy*. From there to here is unclear, though I can just about smell it as I write it, a **synesthetic** response. Coined in the 1670s from the French *zeste*, the peel of an orange or lemon commonly used to flavor a variety of foods, recorded in a **recipe** in 1709; the sense of "zeal or flair or **keen** enjoyment" came in the late 18th century. Philosopher Bertrand Russell opined, "What hunger is in relation to food, *zest* is in relation to life." Fashion designer Christian Dior echoed him: "*Zest* is the secret of all beauty. There is no beauty that is attractive without *zest*." Companion words include *zestimate,* a neologism for an enthusiastic price estimate, and *Zestra*, an arousal massage oil for women.

## ZOOLITE

*A fossilized creature.* A cute little creature of a word, from *zoion*, animal, and *ithos*, stone. I have on my desk as I write a fossilized nautilus shell that I inherited from my father, and a **zesty** memory of him wondering out loud one time, "I wonder what the *real* name for this might be?" The early geologist Georges Cuvier said, "My object will be, first, to show by what connections the history of the *fossil* bones of land animals is linked to the theory of the earth and why they have a particular importance in this respect." Figuratively, Emerson wrote, "Language is *fossilized* poetry." Companion words include *trilobite*, an extinct group of marine arthropods that flourished around 500 million years ago.

Zuithitsu: *Follow the Brush*

## ZUIHITSU (JAPANESE)

*A spontaneous jotting down of one's thoughts.* Literally, in Japanese, it means "Follow the brush," or in some Zen circles, "First thought, best thought." Lance Morrow, in an arresting essay on writing essays, compares the Japanese monk Kenko's thoughtful pieces with those of Montaigne, commonly recognized as the first such exercises in the West. Both attempt to put down on paper the fleeting thoughts, the painted words that come to us when we ask ourselves, as did Montaigne in his château, *"Que sais-je?"* What do I know? Can I put what I know into words? Can I paint my thoughts to give my words some ***color***?

## ZZXJOANW (MAORI)

*A linguistic* **hoax** *name for a Maori drum.* First recorded by Rupert Hughes, in his *The Musical Guide*, in 1903, with the suggestion to pronounce it "shaw," it went uncontested over the years by such stalwart lexicographic sources as *Mrs. Byrne's Dictionary*, until the hoax was revealed in 1996, by Ross Eckler. Thus, one of the most infamous "ghost words" in word history and the last word of this book is no word at all. Companion words, nonetheless, include *dord*, supposedly meaning "density," but a misspelling that went unchallenged in the OED for years.

# AFTERTALE

"A postscript sometimes added when the tale or story is, or ought to be, ended."
—Charles Mackay, *Lost Beauties*

There was a curious review of *The Oxford English Dictionary* in 1928 that described the dilemma in compiling a collection like the present one, which is that there is no end of fascinating words. "Truly our dictionary-makers are toilers at a Sisyphean task," the reviewer commented. "Just as soon as they have got 'Z' neatly caged an enlarged and adipose 'A' has broken loose at the other end of the menagerie."

If not a dilemma, then a champagne worry, as my grandfather used to describe a minor fret. At the risk of inducing an *oculogyric,* or eye-rolling, reaction in my readers, I would like to include a few last "lost and found beauties," to paraphrase Mackay, dab a few more colors onto our painter's palette, in the humble hope of drawing attention to a few more unusual words that are *wishworthy*, worthy of our desire to revive them. But if you love it, it isn't work, which is why I've gone long and far, to bookstores and libraries from San Francisco to Detroit, Paris, and Athens, to find the root stories of many of the most beautiful words in the English language. On my word pilgrimages I often thought about the efforts that Thoreau made to maintain his friendships: "I frequently tramped eight or ten miles through the deepest snow to keep an appointment with a beech-tree, or a yellow birch, or an old acquaintance among the pines."

For our *Whataboutery*, as my friends in Belfast describe whatever hasn't been talked about yet, there is the sonicky Scottish word *sloom,* to sleep deeply and soundly, in lovely contrast to *slumber,* to sleep lightly. Years ago, while canoeing in Algonquin National Park, I learned from a Huron Indian the magnificent word *ondinnonk*, which is loosely defined as a private desire in the soul that is expressed in a dream. A *downcome* provides linguistic balance to *outcome*. *Infonesia* is a useful neologism that might just catch on, considering the modern plague of forgetting where we found so much of our current information. Its kissing cousin is *pseudomnesia*, the memory of things that never happened. The lovely *snow-blossom* is a picturesque option for *snowflake*. The scandal of tomb robbing in Italy has at least unearthed a vivid new word, *tombaroli*, looters by any other name. A *snurl* is a startling word to describe the ruffle of wind over water. *Molendinaceous* is a whirlwind of a word, to describe exactly that, the motion of a windmill. Tilt at that, Don Quixote!

Have you ever reveled in a walk through a strong wind? Well, the Dutch have a word for it, *uitwaaien*, to walk in the wind not for self-improvement but for the sheer fun of it. "The wind-mill doesn't care for the wind that's gone past," says an old Dutch proverb, which is balanced by the poetic notion that it is bracing if not lovely to walk in the wind. *Wanweird* is a ghostly Scottish word for misfortune, unhappy fate. *Icarian* personifies the fatal state of being unprepared for flight, whether in the air, in love, or in business, inspired by the Greek myth of Icarus and his melting wings. *Curple* is a synonym for buttock, in case you ever need one, while *quakebuttock* is the old English word for a coward. At the *butler's* side, but rarely acknowledged, is the *pantler,* the servant who attends to the bread (French *pain*) in the house.

"Let words laugh," wrote Patrick Kavanagh, so let's end with a few laughers. If you have ever wondered where *duds*, clothes, came from, consider the *dudman,* the rag man, the one who sells old clothes and even dresses scarecrows. An *obsimath* is a *polymath-plus*, someone who learns in later life. A romantic alternative to the pallid *pretty* can be heard in the 1940s flick *The Huckster*, in which the dapper Clark Gable describes his **gorgeous** lover as "lusciouser and lusciouser." Speaking of luscious, here's one to make your mouth water: *druplets*, those pulpy little grains on a berry.

Over the last few years travelers have carried back from New Guinea the word *mokita*, which expresses "the truth that everybody knows and nobody speaks," and it hovers as a possible void-filler for business meetings or trials. The poet Samuel Coleridge used *heavenriche* to describe the sky, the place where *nimibification* or cloud-forming occurs. I can scarcely think of a lovelier word to end a book on.

# SOURCES AND RECOMMENDED READING

American Heritage Dictionaries, eds. *Word Histories and Mysteries: From Abracadabra to Zeus*. New York: Houghton Mifflin, 2004.

American Psychiatric Association. *A Psychiatric Glossary*. Washington, DC: American Psychiatric Association, 1964.

Asimov, Isaac. *Words from the Myths*. New York: Signet Books, 1961.

Ayto, John. *Dictionary of Word Origins: The Histories of More Than 8,000 English-Language Words*. New York: Arcade Publishing, 1980.

Barfield, Owen. *The History in English Words*. Foreword by W. H. Auden. Great Barrington, Mass.: Lindisfarne Press, 1985.

Bartlett, John. *Bartlett's Shakespeare Quotations*. New York and Boston: Little, Brown, 2005.

Bartlett, John. *Dictionary of Americanisms*, 1877.

Berlitz, Charles. *Native Tongues: A Book of Captivating Facts on*

*Languages and Their Origins.* New York: Grossett & Dunlap, 1982.

Bierce, Ambrose. *The Devil's Dictionary.* Cleveland and New York: World Publishing, 1941.

Black, Donald Chain. *Spoonerisms, Sycophants and Sops: A Celebration of Fascinating Facts About Words.* New York: Harper & Row, 1988.

Blount, Roy Jr. *Alphabet Juice: The Energies, Gists, and Spirits of Letters, Words, and Combinations Thereof; Their Roots, Bones, Innards, Piths, Pips, and Secret Parts, Tinctures, Tonics, and Essences; With Examples of Their Usage Foul and Savory.* New York: Farrar, Strauss, and Giroux, 2008.

Blount, Thomas. *Glossographia.* 1656.

Bowler, Peter. *The Superior Person's Book of Words.* Boston: David R. Godine, 1977.

Brewer, E. Cobham. *Brewer's Dictionary of Phrase & Fable.* Centenary edition, revised. Edited by Ivor H. Evans. New York: Harper & Row, 1981.

Bryson, Bill. *Made in America: An Informal History of the English Language in the United States.* New York: William Morrow,1994.

Cassidy, Daniel. *How the Irish Invented Slang: The Secret Language at the Crossroads.* Petrolia, Calif.: CounterPunch/AK Press, 2007.

Cawdrey, Robert. *The First English Dictionary: 1604.* John Simpson, ed. Oxford: Bodleian Library, University of Oxford Press, 2007.

Chapman, Robert L. *The Dictionary of American Slang.* New

York: Collins Reference, 1998.

Ciardi, John. *A Browser's Dictionary: A Compendium of Curious Expressions & Intriguing Facts*. New York: Harper & Row, 1980.

Clark, Kenneth. *Looking at Pictures*. New York: Holt, Rinehart, Winston, 1960.

Coleridge, Herbert. *A Dictionary of the First or Oldest Words in the English Language: From the Semi-Saxon Period of AD 1250– 1300: Consisting of an Alphabetical Inventory of Every Word Found in the Printed English Literature of the 13th Century.* London: John Camden Hotten, Piccadilly, 1862.

*Concise Oxford Dictionary of Current English*. H. W. Fowler, ed. Fourth Edition. Oxford at the Clarendon Press, 1956.

Décharné, Max. *Straight from the Fridge, Dad: A Dictionary of Hipster Slang.* New York: Broadway Books, 2001.

Ernst, Margaret S. *More About Words*. New York: Alfred A. Knopf, 1951.

Finlay, Victoria. *Color*. New York: Random House Publishers, 2002.

Florio, John. *A Worlde of Wordes, Or Most copious, and exact Dictionairie in Italian and English*. First published in 1598. Republished in 1611 as *Queen Anne's New Worlde of Wordes*.

Funk, Charles Earle. *Thereby Hangs a Tale: Stories of Curious Word Origins*. New York: Harper & Row Publishers, 1950.

Funk, Charles Earle, and Charles Earle Funk Jr. *Horsefeathers & Other Curious Words*. New York: Harper & Row, 1958.

Funk, Wilfred. *Word Origins and Their Romantic Stories*. New York: Bell Publishing, 1978.

Garrison, Webb. *Why You Say It*. New York and Nashville: Abingdon Press, 1955.

Green, Jonathon. *Chasing the Sun: Dictionary Makers and the Dictionaries They Made*. New York: Henry Holt, 1996.

Grose, Francis, Captain. *Dictionary of the Vulgar Tongue: A Dictionary of Buckish Slang, University Wit, and Pickpocket Eloquence*. Unabridged, from the original 1811 edition. Nu-Vision Publications, 2007.

Halliwell, James Orchard. *Dictionary of Archaic Words*. London: Bracken Books, 1989. Originally published in London, 1850.

Heifetz, Josepha (Mrs. Byrne). *Mrs. Byrne's Dictionary*. Secaucus, N.J.: Citadel Books, 1974.

Hellweg, Paul. *The Insomniac's Dictionary: The Last Word on the Odd Word*. New York: Ballantine Books, 1986.

Hook, J. N. *The Grand Panjandrum: And 1,999 Other Rare, Useful, and Delightful Words and Expressions*. New York: MacMillan Publishing, 1980.

Johnson, Samuel. *A Dictionary of the English Language*. First published in 1755. New edition, edited, compiled by David Crystal. London: Penguin Books, 2002.

Kacirk, Jeffrey. *Altered English: Surprising Meanings of Familiar Words*. Petaluma, Calif.: Pomegranate Books, 2002.

Knowles, Elizabeth. *How to Read a Word*. Oxford: Oxford University Press, 2010.

Lemprière, John. *Lemprière's Classical Dictionary of Proper Names Mentioned in Ancient Authors*. London: Routledge & Kegan Paul, reprinted 1958. First published in 1788.

Levy, Mervyn. *The Pocket Dictionary of Art Terms*. London: Studio Books, 1961.

Macalister, R. A. Stewart. *The Secret Languages of Ireland*. Armagh, Ireland: Craobh RuaBooks, 1937.

Mackay, Charles. *Lost Beauties of the English Language*. London: Bibliophile Books, 1987. Originally published in 1874.

MacNeil, Robert. *The Story of English*. Revised edition. New York: Penguin Books, 1993.

MacNeil, Robert. *Wordstruck*. New York: Viking Press, 1989.

Madrone, Michael. *It's Greek to Me! Brush Up Your Classics*. New York: Harper Collins, 1991.

Manser, Martin H. *Dictionary of Proverbs*. Second edition. New York: Checkmark Books, 2002.

Mencken, H. L. *The American Language*. Volumes 1–4, plus Supplements 1–2. New York: Alfred A. Knopf, 1936, 1945, 1977.

Metcalf, Allan. *The World in So Many Words: A Country-by-Country Tour of Words That Have Shaped Our Language*. New York: Houghton Mifflin Harcourt, 1999.

Moore, Christopher J. *In Other Words: A Language Lover's Guide to the Most Intriguing Words Around the World*. New York: Walker & Company, 2004.

Mugglestone, Lynda. *Lost for Words: The Hidden History of the Oxford English Dictionary*. New Haven and London: Yale University Press, 2005.

Novobatzky, Peter, and Ammon Shea. *Depraved and Insulting English: Words to Offend and Amuse*. New York: Harcourt Brace, 1999.

Ogg, Oscar. *The 26 Letters*. New York: Thomas Y. Crowell Company, 1948.

Olive, David. *A Devil's Dictionary of Business Jargon*. Toronto: Key Porter Books, 2001.

O'Muirithe, Diarmaid. *The Words We Use*. Dublin, Ireland: Four Courts Press, 1999.

*Oxford Concise English Dictionary*. Oxford: Oxford University Press, 19xx.

*Oxford English Dictionary* (OED). Oxford: Oxford University Press, 1989.

*Oxford Dictionary of Quotations*. Oxford: Oxford University Press, 1949.

Patterson, Ian. *A Dictionary of Color*. London: Thorogood Publishers, 2003.

Payack, Paul J. J. *A Million Words and Counting: How Global English Is Rewriting the World*. New York: Citadel Press, 2008.

Pierce, Charles Smith. *From Abacus to Zeus: A Handbook of Art History*. Englewood Cliffs, N.J.: Prentice Hall, Inc., 1968.

Polastron, Lucien X. *Books on Fire: The Destruction of Libraries throughout History*. Rochester, Vt.: Inner Traditions, 2004.

*Random House Dictionary of the English Language: The Unabridged Edition*. Jess Stein, ed. New York: Random House, 1967.

Rawson, Hugh. *A Dictionary of Euphemisms & Other Doubletalk*. New York: Crown Publishers, Inc., 1981.

Reisner, Robert. *Graffiti: Two Thousand Years of Wall Writing*. Chicago: Cowles Book Company, 1971.

Rheingold, Howard. *They Have a Word For It: A Lighthearted*

*Lexicon of Untranslatable Words and Phrases.* Los Angeles: Jeremy P. Tarcher, 1988.

Rosten, Leo. *Hooray for Yiddish: A Book about English.* New York: Galahad Books, 1998.

Salny, Abbie F. *The Mensa Book of Words, Word Games, Puzzles & Oddities.* New York: HarperCollins, 1988.

Shea, Ammon. *Reading the OED: One Man, One Year, 21,430 Pages.* New York: Perigee Books, 2008.

Skeat, Walter W. *Concise Dictionary of English Etymology.* Hertfordshire, UK: Wordsworth Editions, 1993. First published in 1882.

Sheridan, John D. *I Have Been Busy With Words.* Selected and Introduced by Gay Byrne. Dublin: Ireland: The Mercier Press Limited, 1979.

Stevenson, James A. C. *Dictionary of Scots Words & Phrases in Current Use.* London: Athlone Press, 1989.

Taylor, Joseph. *Antiquitates Curiosae: The Etymology of Many Remarkable Old Sayings, Proverbs, and Singular Customs.* Originally published in 1820. Reprinted, San Francisco: Familiar Productions, 1995.

Wentworth, Harold, and Stuart Berg Flexner. *Dictionary of American Slang.* Second Supplemented Edition. New York: Thomas Y. Crowell Company, Inc., 1975.

Winchester, Simon. *The Meaning of Everything: The Story of the Oxford English Dictionary.* New York and Oxford: Oxford University Press, 2004.

~~~

# NOTES ON THE ARTWORK

When I was young, the form of words—the way they looked—intrigued me and I often wondered what it would be like to look at a word and not be able to read or understand it. In essence, I wondered about the indecipherable mystery behind the word. The artworks I have created for *The Painted Word* take that sense of mystery into the world of paint and image.

Each creation began with that wonderful, slippery stuff that never wants to be tamed or pinned down: paint. Specifically, I use oil paint for its historical resonance and also because of its liquid origins in the oil pressed from flax. From this plant comes both linseed oil, which is mixed with dry powdered pigments to create oil paint, and linen, which traditionally has been used as the surface that oils are painted upon. Whenever I unroll a new bolt of linen in my studio a rich fragrance reminiscent of a newly cut field fills the room.

I find that freshly stretched paintings waiting for their first touch of color invite the mystery of life and creation. The word stories written by Phil Cousineau opened up a similar sense of wonder. Like the words, each tube of paint also brought its history into the room. Color names are words steeped in myth and meaning. *Lapis Lazuli* evokes dangerous treks along the Silk Road into Afghanistan that brought this exquisite blue stone into the workshops of Renaissance artists. The pigment was so expensive and so important it was often reserved for coloring the heavens and Mary's garments. A separate clause in the artist's contract would dictate how much the client would pay for the *Lapis Lazuli* in addition to the amount paid for the artist's services. Other colors weren't so dear but were still rich in lore. *Burnt Sienna* is a warm brown earth pigment that was dug up in the fields surrounding Siena, Italy. *Cinnabar*, a brilliant red originally found in minerals veined with mercury, also made its way along the Silk Road from its source in China. I used all three of these colors in many of the paintings in *The Painted Word*.

Gregg Chadwick
Santa Monica, California
February 2012

Chadwick's Flickr page, which is often updated with new paintings and work in progress, is at http://www.flickr.com/photos/greggchadwick.

# ABOUT THE ARTIST

**GREGG CHADWICK** is a Santa Monica–based artist who has exhibited his artworks in galleries and museums both nationally and internationally. Chadwick earned a bachelor of fine art at UCLA and a master of fine art at NYU. He has had notable solo exhibitions at the Manifesta Maastricht Gallery (Maastricht, Netherlands), Space AD 2000 (Tokyo), and the Lisa Coscino Gallery (Pacific Grove), among others. He has participated in a variety of group exhibitions, including at the LOOK Gallery (Los Angeles), the Arena 1 Gallery (Santa Monica), and the Arts Club of Washington (Washington DC). Chadwick is frequently invited to lecture on the arts and social justice; in 2011–2012 he spoke at UCLA, Monterey Peninsula College, the Esalen Institute, and at the World Views forum in Amsterdam.

Gregg's blog, Speed of Life, explores the intersections between the arts and social justice: http://greggchadwick.blogspot.com/.

# ABOUT THE AUTHOR

**PHIL COUSINEAU** was described by mythologist Joseph Campbell as a five-tool threat—a writer, photographer, filmmaker, editor, and teacher. A *tale-teller*, creativity consultant, worldwide lecturer, and wordcatcher, Cousineau has published over thirty books, including *Wordcatcher,* named one of the Best Books of 2010 by NPR; *The Art of Pilgrimage,* which has been translated into six languages; *The Hero's Journey: Joseph Campbell on his Life and Work*; and the Pushcart Prize–nominated *The Oldest Story in the World*. The *quizzacious* Cousineau has also written or co-written eighteen documentary films and contributed to forty-two other books. Currently, he is host and co-writer of *Global Spirit*, on LINK TV and PBS. With his family, Jo and Jack, he is a Telegraph Hill dweller in San Francisco, where he enjoys the *sprezzatura* of North Beach life in its strong *coffee,* sweet *croissants*, rowdy *sandlot* baseball, and the *ol'* comfort of its Irish pubs.

# TO OUR READERS

Viva Editions publishes books that inform, enlighten, and entertain. We do our best to bring you, the reader, quality books that celebrate life, inspire the mind, revive the spirit, and enhance lives all around. Our authors are practical visionaries: people who offer deep wisdom in a hopeful and helpful manner. Viva was launched with an attitude of growth and we want to spread our joy and offer our support and advice where we can to help you live the Viva way: vivaciously!

We're grateful for all our readers and want to keep bringing you books for inspired living. We invite you to write to us with your comments and suggestions, and what you'd like to see more of. You can also sign up for our online newsletter to learn about new titles, author events, and special offers.

Viva Editions
2246 Sixth St.
Berkeley, CA 94710
www.vivaeditions.com
(800) 780-2279
Follow us on Twitter @vivaeditions
Friend/fan us on Facebook